LeGrand Richards

BELOVED APOSTLE

To the readers of this book:

As I near the end of my long life, I realize that next to my love for the Lord and my precious family, comes my love for my many friends.

Through this book it is hoped they will come to know me better.

— LeGrand Richards

LeGrand Richards

BELOVED APOSTLE

Lucile C. Tate

BOOKCRAFT·SALT LAKE CITY, UTAH

Library of Congress Catalog Card Number: 82-70691
ISBN 0-88494-457-3

2 3 4 5 6 7 8 9 10   89 88 87 86 85 84 83 82

Lithographed in the United States of America
PUBLISHERS PRESS
Salt Lake City, Utah

Contents

Foreword

Few men in our generation have done more to advance the work of the Lord than has Elder LeGrand Richards.

To have served so long and so ably in a variety of capacities, and particularly as a General Authority of the Church, and to have done so with vitality and enthusiasm, is a remarkable accomplishment, in many ways unique.

While yet alive he has become almost a legend. His singular qualities as a speaker have made him a favorite with congregations around the world. He is a stranger to written talks, but his audiences unfailingly respond when in a voice ringing with conviction he unhesitatingly recalls scripture, literature, and anecdote to give interest and persuasiveness to his message.

He is a man of remarkable faith in the cause to which he has devoted his life. For him there is no doubt concerning its bright future. Problems may be legion, but LeGrand Richards overlooks them in favor of the affirmative side of things. There is sunlight breaking through every cloud of adversity. His absolute and certain faith that this is God's work and that it will triumph over every enemy shines through all of his words and works.

His example in never permitting physical limitations to restrict his service has given courage to thousands of others who suffer from handicaps. Lame from childhood, and seldom without pain, he has kept up a demanding regimen of travel, speaking, and administrative duties.

Lucile C. Tate has captured in this volume the essence of a man whose life can stand as a beacon for all of us. He has indeed been a special witness of the name of Christ in all the world, an example to every member of the Church, our friend, our associate, and our teacher in this the great work of the Master.

— GORDON B. HINCKLEY

Acknowledgments

When in October 1980 Elder LeGrand Richards assented to have his life story written, he promised to be as cooperative and helpful as possible in the work. Never did anyone keep a promise more perfectly. He made time for weekly interviews during which he exercised his remarkable powers of recall, answered every question, and freely discussed each matter brought to his attention. He made available his journals, personal letters, papers, writings, blessings, and pictures. This book is the result of his generous gift of himself. It could not have been written without it. Nor could it have been written without the added help of family members, friends, and associates who provided stories, experiences, and insights covering the long span of his life.

Beyond this, perceptive friends of the project read and commented upon the chapters as they were written: Elder Boyd K. Packer of the Council of the Twelve (others in the Councils of the First Presidency and the Twelve also read varying portions of the manuscript); Robert K. Thomas, Presidential Fellow, Brigham Young University; and H. George Bickerstaff, Editor in Chief, Bookcraft. My husband, George F. Tate, a nephew of Elder Richards, read the manuscript and helped in various aspects of the research and in proofreading the documentation. The director and staff of the Historical Department of the Church gave competent and courteous assistance. To all of these I express deep appreciation.

It has been an incomparable privilege to "experience" Elder Richards's life at close range and to attempt to capture the essence of it so that his many friends—present and future—may come to know him better.

Child of Promise

1886-1896

*L*eGrand, my son. . . . Thou hast not come here upon earth by chance, but in fulfillment of the decrees of the Almighty to accomplish a great labor in the upbuilding of God's kingdom. . . ."

The speaker was George F. Richards, the thirty-two-year-old Tooele Stake patriarch. The boy on whose head his hands were laid was his eight-year-old son. After this indication of the lad's potential, the patriarch continued in more specific terms:

> Thou shalt be able to fill a useful mission in the gathering of scattered Israel, the establishment of Zion, and the redemption of the dead. . . . Many shall seek thy counsels and be benefitted and blessed thereby. The power of God shall be made manifest through thee and thy ministrations.
>
> Under thy hands the sick shall be healed, the bowed down shall be cheered up and comforted, and many shall receive blessings at thy hand, both spiritual and temporal. . . . friends [shall be raised up] on every hand, whose benediction and blessings shall follow thee through life; and thou shalt be exalted among thy fellows, and if thou shalt live for it, thou shalt preside in the midst of the Lord's people. (Tooele City, Utah, February 12, 1894. *Patriarchal Blessings*, vol. 411, pp. 82-83, LDS Church Archives.)

Such were the promises pronounced in the patriarchal blessing given to the young LeGrand Richards. In retrospect, as all prophetic utterances must eventually be viewed, the father's choice of words is seen as doubly inspired: LeGrand would be exalted not above but *among* his fellows; he would preside not over but *in the midst of* the Lord's people. The wording indicates that George F. Richards "saw" not only the reality of his son's future mission but the congenial, loving, compassionate quality of it as well.

A few years later, LeGrand was on a Tooele dry farm at midday with his father and a cousin, Stephen L Richards, who was visiting from Salt Lake City. The sun beat down from a cloudless sky. No tree or building afforded shade. Even the horses tugged, sweat, and came to a halt. George F. Richards lowered the tines of the hayrake and, with the help of the boys, covered them with newly mown hay and spread more hay on the ground beneath. Hungry and fatigued from the heat and labor of the morning, the three crowded under the improvised canopy and ate their lunch.

Reflecting upon this incident, LeGrand Richards said: "I have since had this thought. There under that hayrake on a dry farm in Tooele were three future apostles: my father, my cousin, and myself, yet a boy." Simple yet remarkable as was the enactment of this little drama, the selection of the participants was not coincidental. It was foreshadowed by and in fulfillment of an earlier promise given to LeGrand's grandmother Nanny Longstroth Richards when she was but a seventeen-year-old girl living in the "City of Joseph" (Nauvoo, Illinois). In a blessing pronounced upon her head on January 27, 1846, the patriarch John Smith (uncle of the Prophet Joseph Smith) declared, "Prophets, seers, and revelators shall proceed forth from thee and thy name shall be had in honorable remembrance in the house of Israel." (*Patriarchal Blessings*, vol. 10, pp. 105-6, LDS Church Archives.)

The promise was expansively fulfilled, for Nanny Longstroth Richards became mother to George F. and grandmother to Stephen L and LeGrand—the three future apostles who ate lunch together under the tines of a hayrake. (She also became grandmother to Stayner Richards, who served as an Assistant to the Twelve.)

In the formative years before LeGrand's 1894 blessing was given, and in the years then still to come, George F. Richards was a powerful and loving influence in the life and development of this child of promise. And in his own right he forged an indivisible patriarchal link between his faithful fathers and

LeGrand. Those fathers were Willard Richards and Franklin D. Richards. Nanny was wife to both.

Nanny Longstroth first became the wife of the apostle Willard Richards, a man who signified his loyalty to the Prophet Joseph Smith in Carthage Jail by offering his own life, if that were possible, in exchange for the other's freedom. After the Prophet's martyrdom, he further demonstrated his devotion to the Church by serving as a counselor to President Brigham Young from December 1847, when the First Presidency was reorganized, until his death at age forty-nine (1854).

After Willard died, his nephew, the apostle Franklin D. Richards, married Nanny Longstroth, fulfilling a promise made to his uncle that he would thus care for her and her three young children and raise up further posterity to Willard. To Franklin D. and Nanny Longstroth Richards was born a daughter, Minerva (1858), and two sons, George F. (1861) and Frederick W. (1866). So it was that these three children were privileged to have two fathers—by birth, Franklin D.; by sealing, Willard Richards. (Letter from Franklin D. Richards to his son, George F., September 5, 1893, soon after the latter became a patriarch.)

Franklin D. Richards was a great father and a faithful servant of the Lord. He had been put to extreme tests and had proven equal to them—the loss of one brother at the Haun's Mill Massacre, of another with the Mormon Battalion at Pueblo, of his son at Mount Pisgah, of his second wife at Winter Quarters, of his little daughter at Cutler's Grove. Long missions, deprivation, persecution, many families to provide for, and many high callings were his lot; yet he could write as a latter-day Job, "Father, I own thy dealings just; thy blessings have been more than my deserts. . . ." (Franklin L. West, *Life of Franklin D. Richards* [Salt Lake City: Deseret News Press, 1924], pp. 71-72.)

Because of his many families, his missions, and his official Church responsibilities, Franklin D. could spend but little time with his individual wives and children, so the care of Nanny and her six children fell largely upon her two eldest sons Stephen L. (Willard's son) and George F. (son of Franklin). (Nanny also raised three of her sister's children after Sarah's death in 1858.)

When Stephen L. left on his mission (1876), George F. became head of the home at fifteen. His half-brother had left him a yoke of oxen, a canyon cart, and log chain, and with these he hauled wood from Farmington Canyon to supply the family's needs and for use as a medium of exchange for grist and molasses and for labor to help improve the house. (*Life of George F. Richards* by his daughters, [Alice] Minerva Richards Tate Robinson, Sarah Richards Cannon, and Mamie Richards Silver [Provo, Utah: J. Grant Stephenson, 1965], p. 4.)

"Want of age is no bar to obtaining the favor of the Lord," George F. wrote. At age fifteen he was ordained to the Melchizedek Priesthood, and he received his temple endowment at that early age. When he was seventeen he performed the ordinance of administering to his sick mother and witnessed the power of the Lord in healing her—a blessing which he felt was given "to teach him that the Priesthood in the boy is as sacred and potent as in the man when the boy lives as he should." (George F. Richards, *Personal Record*, p. 51, LDS Church Archives.)

At age nineteen he attended the University of Deseret, from which he received a certificate of graduation. (GFR *Diary*, vol. 1, p. 2.) He then began work at two dollars a day. This gave him the financial means to marry his Farmington sweetheart, Alice Almira Robinson, on March 9, 1882. Alice's family descended from the Pilgrims John Alden and Priscilla Mullens through one line, and her immediate predecessors were of pioneer stock who had been seasoned by faith and sacrifice. Her grandfathers, Henry William Miller and Joseph Lee Robinson, were early Church leaders and both were faithful friends of Joseph Smith and Brigham Young. Alice's father was Oliver Lee Robinson; her mother, Lucy Miller. (George F.'s distant progenitor, Edward Richards, had a part in America's early history, for by 1634 he was established in Lynn, Massachusetts.)

George F. and Alice had not lived long in Salt Lake City, where he was working, until they were asked to come and live at his mother's home in Farmington because she was ill and needed help. Always solicitous of his mother's needs, George F. took his new bride and went. It was at the Farmington home that Alice gave birth to the first of their fifteen children, a son: George F. Jr. This handsome, dark-haired child was to find a singular place of affection in his father's heart, so that in later years they would say it was "almost as if we grew up as boys together." A daughter, Alice Minerva, was also born (1884) in Nanny Longstroth Richards's home.

George F.'s young married life was one round of clearing, plowing, planting, harvesting, building—all with small material returns. He marked his twenty-third birthday with a lament that he had never been on a foreign mission and that he was four hundred dollars in debt and paying interest on it. His total assets were harness, wagon, six horses, a cow, two calves, and not quite two acres of land.

At the same time (1884), he wrote what became for him a full consecration of his life to the Lord. "While I feel that I am poor, I do not wish to let that stand between me and my duties as a Latter-day Saint. That which I have is upon the altar and subject to the direction of those in authority, as is also my time and life if necessary." (GFR *Diary*, vol. 1, p. 65.)

He labored on. At year's end he fasted, settled his account with the Lord, and freshened his resolves for the year ahead. (This became a sacred ritual for all his years to come, and when his children were old enough to comprehend he made them part of the accounting. LeGrand would later tell of helping to figure pigs, chickens, eggs, garden produce, milk, and the growth of calves, plus the extra "thrown in for good measure.")

By the time LeGrand was born on February 6, 1886, his father had prospered. He had purchased a 160-acre farm in Box Elder County (Plymouth), where he lived with his little family in a nine-by-twelve-foot shack during the summer, returning to Farmington for the cold winter months. There they stayed with George F.'s sister Minerva and her husband, B. F. Knowlton. This home was LeGrand's birthplace. (GFR *Diary*, vol. 1, pp. 99, 102.)

The next eighteen months would prove to be the most disruptive and mobile period in the family's life. It was February 25,

1886, when George F. returned to Plymouth, leaving his family in Farmington until the weather warmed. For the next month it snowed and rained, and he worked in mud and slush. He moved the shack and improved it, dug a well and put a frame over it. When the weather finally broke he again made the seventy-five-mile trip to Farmington and brought his family and their meager furnishings home. He put in thirty-three acres of barley and then began hauling material to make an adobe house.

In the evenings when the day's work was done, the older children were asleep, and baby LeGrand nestled and rocked in his mother's arms, George F. read by light of a coal oil lamp. He read literature, philosophy, and a practical book on etiquette. He made long lists of gospel questions, then searched the scriptures for answers. (GFR *Diary*, vol. 1, pp. 81-86.) These formed the basis for many gospel discussions when the children were older and worked with him in the fields, sat at table in the evenings, or traveled with him to some assignment.

In May, Alice's father, Oliver Lee Robinson, came to help build an adobe house for them. The next day George F. left Alice and the children to visit with her father for a few days while he joined his parents and other relatives at the Logan Temple to do work for their dead. While there, they received word that Joel Grover, husband of Willard and Nanny's daughter Aseneth, had died in Nephi. Nanny and Franklin D. Richards left immediately for Salt Lake City, from which point she continued on to Nephi. George F. returned to Plymouth and worked with Oliver Lee on the house. With two men on the job, it took form rapidly.

Alice and the children watched the progress of the house with lively interest and looked forward to the day they could move in. LeGrand, now less than four months old, was by nature of a pleasant disposition but was suffering from some baby ailment that made him fussy. After several attempts to get the washing done, and with no carriage or play pen to keep him off the floor, Alice finally tied LeGrand to her back, papoose-fashion, and carried him about as she rubbed the clothes, ironed, cooked, or scrubbed. In this position he was comforted and content.

By August the snug two-room adobe house was complete, with a kitchen lean-to attached. It seemed luxurious. The family hated to leave it even to take Grandfather home again. Not long after they arrived in Farmington, young George F. Jr. took desperately ill with cholera. Then Oliver Lee came down with the same malady, and within two days he died, on August 18, 1886.

When the funeral was over, George F. took Alice and the children back to Plymouth, where the heavy work of harvesting and battening down for winter was immediately upon him. This was no sooner accomplished than an urgent plea for help came from Nanny and Aseneth in Nephi. Never one to shirk a family responsibility, George F. packed the wagon and left on October 26, traveling with his little family the 175 cold miles to Nephi. The children were bundled almost to the eyes. LeGrand at nine months was interested in everything he saw, and he enjoyed the warmth and nearness of his mother as they joggled along the rough roads.

For Alice, who was expecting her fourth child, the journey was difficult. They arrived at the Grovers' on November 4. It was April 5, 1887, when Alice's son Joel was born, and May before Alice could travel again. This time they made the journey home in four days, George F. being anxious to get his own crops in after having left Aseneth's affairs in good order.

Summer passed, and the harvest was gathered once more. Before the snow began to fall, the couple took up the rugs, shook them free of dust, and put them down again over fresh, sweet-smelling straw. On the twenty-third of December (1887) they shopped at the Deweyville store, eighteen miles away, for "Christmas goods." On Christmas Eve the stockings of four little children—George F. Jr., Minerva, LeGrand, and Joel—were hung up to await Santa's visit.

From our modern vantage point, the two little rooms and lean-to kitchen seem quite inadequate for a family of six, but George F.'s account of their first Christmas by themselves speaks of warm hospitality. Two families came for Christmas dinner with them. Then on New Year's Day he wrote, "Stayed in house all day with the children and Mama. Made molasses candy. . . ." (GFR *Diary*, vol. 1, p. 111.)

Shortly before LeGrand's second birthday on February 6, 1888, his father had an offer to take over the operation of the ranch of his uncle, Abraham F. Doremus, in Tooele, Utah. The terms were agreeable and the family moved there knowing that it would yield long-term benefits for them all.

The children considered the Doremus house immense, with endless places to explore—such as porch, lean-to, attic, and dirt cellar. There were sheds, a barn, haystacks, and a large fenced corral. There were orchards at the north and a lucerne patch between house and street. It is from the Doremus Ranch that LeGrand brings his earliest recollections. He remembers when his mother took him out of dresses and put him into boys' pants at age three and a half.

LeGrand also remembers the birth of his second sister, Sarah, on July 13, 1889. The four children were sent to play in the apricot orchard, where people were picking and drying the ripe fruit on shares, the drying racks being furnished by the ranch. As they watched the pickers, played among the trees, and ate fruit from the ground, LeGrand heard his mother's moans and cries and afterwards his father's call to come in and see the new sister, all sleepy and content in her mother's arms.

Although the Doremus Ranch home seemed a mansion to the children after the small adobe house in Plymouth, conditions there were primitive compared to present standards. There was no indoor plumbing, and water had to be carried for table, bath, and laundry use. Washings were put out by hand at first, then by a hand-turned washer when these became available. Weekly baths were taken in a big washtub by the stove, with only a quilt hung to give a measure of privacy. Fruit was bottled in the hundreds of quarts for the large and still growing family, and this on the wood-burning stove. Hard work was the order of life, and even the small children had their share in it. Each was taught to do the tasks which were commensurate with his age and level of

LeGrand at the age of three.

understanding. He was then encouraged to take hold and perform his work unfailingly.

Before LeGrand was old enough to do a man's work with his father, Alice requested that "Grandy" help her with the washing. He recalls how she would sometimes stand and rub the clothes on a washboard with big tears rolling down her cheeks from weariness or discomfort when a new baby was on the way. He was able to lighten her work by fetching water, wringing, and hanging the clean things on the line. When George F. purchased one of the first hand-turned washers in Tooele, LeGrand did the turning until Joel was old enough to take over.

But the parents were wise about the children's need for recreation; in fact, George F. and Alice themselves enjoyed breaking the routine of hard work to have a good time. Games, simple refreshments, songs, and stories made up their usual home fun, and work or play was enhanced by the parents' outward show of love and affection for each family member. LeGrand recalls how his mother would draw him near and stroke his hair as she read stories from the *Juvenile Instructor* about early Church leaders

and missionaries whose converts gave up home, family, posses-
sions, and their very lives for the gospel. And he remembers too
the thrill he felt while, safe and comfortable at his mother's side,
he dreamed of faithful men and the good they do.

In January (1890) George F. was ordained a high priest and
set apart as second counselor in the Tooele Stake presidency. He
was twenty-nine. From then on the children knew their father as
a churchman of note, traveling in all kinds of weather to speak
and serve wherever he was assigned. Even so, he kept close contact with his family and made sure that home evenings, games,
and outings broke the round of work and responsibility.

Of special significance in LeGrand's early life were three
events. First, the Salt Lake Temple became ready for dedication
after forty years of labor and sacrifice. The family eagerly awaited
the occasion, especially when the children were told they could
attend; for the parents took every opportunity to include them
in special meetings and conferences so they could become acquainted with Church leaders and experience their influence.

Now as the days drew near, Alice prepared the children. She
told them of the leaders who would be there along with their
grandfather, Franklin D. Richards. She said that on such a
sacred occasion angels might be present. George F. attended the
"first service" on Thursday, April 6, 1893, "during which time a
hurricane raged, blowing down houses, trees, and fences." (Newspapers for that day confirm his report.) On April 7 he took
Alice, her sister Estella, and the two older children George F. Jr.
and Minerva, to the "fourth meeting," after which they returned
to Tooele. (GFR *Diary*, vol. 3, p. 115.)

Special sessions for unbaptized children were held two weeks
later, and on Saturday, April 22, George F. reports that "Alice
took the four small children, LeGrand, Joel, Sarah, and Amy
[Amy would die November 10, 1894] to Salt Lake with the
Sunday School to see and attend the Temple dedication. I took
them to the depot." (GFR *Diary*, vol. 3, p. 119.)

After the session in the assembly room of the temple,
LeGrand, now seven, was taken to greet his grandfather, Franklin D. Richards, as he came down from the stand. This is "the

The Doremus Ranch home.

first and only time" LeGrand remembers meeting him, although the apostle had been in George F.'s home when this grandson was yet very small. LeGrand was impressed to see President Wilford Woodruff when he dedicated the temple, and he remembers exactly how he looked. With typical candor he adds, "And I looked around for angels, but I didn't see any."[1]

The second outstanding event was LeGrand's baptism in Coleman's Pond, Tooele, on June 11, 1894, by Moroni England. He was confirmed the same day by his father. (*Tooele LDS Ward Records*, bk. 7716A, p. 5, LDS Church Archives.)

The third event, which was of the greatest significance, actually preceded the second. It was occasioned when, on July 23, 1893, George F. Richards was called to be patriarch of Tooele Stake. By the authority of his calling he gave their patriarchal blessings to certain of his family members along with the many

---

[1]Throughout this book, wherever material is quoted without a source reference, it has come from an interview the author had either with Elder LeGrand Richards or with the individual named at that point in the text.

to other members of the stake. With a twinkle of humor, LeGrand says, "Father practiced on us four older children." Far from practicing, however, his father gave to George F. Jr., Alice Minerva, and Joel abundant blessings of promise and potential; and upon his second son, LeGrand, he pronounced blessings previously quoted.

In a later blessing (1905), his father prophetically warned LeGrand that "as the Lord designs your salvation and your eternal glory so does the adversary design your destruction." Looking back from the time of that pronouncement, it seems both significant and remarkable that this boy, LeGrand, survived so many accidents and illnesses, any one of which might have maimed or killed him.

On one occasion when LeGrand's father was chopping wood for the stove, his small son drew near him from the rear. The back swing of the ax caught LeGrand on the head and sent him sprawling upon the ground stunned and bleeding. The first recourse at such a time was a priesthood blessing, which was followed by medical aid. As a result, each child came to feel that if Father blessed him he would be all right. It was so with LeGrand and he survived.

Shortly after this accident, LeGrand was standing in the wagon, to which a team was attached, when he was suddenly thrown out by the horses' unexpected motion backward. As he hit the ground, the wagon wheel passed over his head. Before he could be pulled away, a quick forward movement of the team caused the wheel to pass over his head a second time. His frightened father gathered the crying boy up into his arms and blessed him. Again he recovered.

At age eight, LeGrand contracted some type of hip-bone disease. For nine months he wore a plaster cast on his leg from shoe-top to hip and around his waist, during which time he used crutches and missed a year of school. Later that year, and during the time that his parents were attending their dying child Amy in Salt Lake City, LeGrand and his brothers were playing in a neighbor's yard when a vicious ram charged the boys. The others made their getaway, but his cast made LeGrand's escape impossible. The animal came at him time and again as he braced against the fence and tried to ward off its attack with his hands. One of the neighbor boys mustered the courage to drive off the enraged animal with LeGrand's crutches. It was the plaster cast around his waist that is thought to have saved LeGrand's life.

Still on crutches at age nine, he was hit by another misfortune. He tells about it.

> We sold a lot of hay to different people in the community. The Bowen boys came for a big load one day and I was the only one at the Ranch, so . . . I loaded the hay for them, and they asked me to drive the team away from the stack so they could scrape up the loose hay. I got the lines mixed and pulled the team toward the stack instead of away from it, which tipped the load over, and I fell underneath. The wheel ran over my arm and broke it. I felt around to find my crutches and then managed to crawl out from under the load. My arm was bent at an awful angle, but I wouldn't let the doctor set it until my father returned from the Basin Pasture to give me a blessing. (*Blue Book*, p. 26, and interview.)

George F. Jr., who turned twelve that day, was with his father when he returned from the pasture. George had been given a diary for his birthday. Included in his first entry is an account of LeGrand's accident. He wrote: "Both bones were broken above the wrist. We found Dr. F. M. Davis prepared to set the bones. LeGrand suffered. . . ." (GFR Jr. *Diary*, vol. 1, April 23, 1895, LDS Church Archives.)

Once when LeGrand was sleigh riding with companions, he was hit in the eye with a water-hardened snowball. The area from his nose to his temple turned a livid blue, black, and purple. The same year he was stricken with a severe case of scarlet fever and his temperature ran dangerously high for many days.

Finally, at age nineteen, when ready to leave for his mission, LeGrand was again on crutches, this time with a painfully enlarged knee in a cast. He was advised to stay home and take care of himself. Instead he asked for his father to give him a priesthood blessing, and he then left as scheduled with neither cast nor crutch. (On two handwritten pages [*Blue Book*, p. 20j.],

LeGrand's father, George F., chronicled some of these accidents and illnesses.)

From all accidents and maladies except one, LeGrand was spared permanent disability. The exception was the hip trouble, which resulted in one leg remaining an inch and a half shorter than the other, causing him to limp and to have almost constant discomfort and pain. So used to his limp did his friends and family become that they scarcely noticed it.

One daughter, when questioned about it, said, "Why, Daddy didn't limp." Of her remark, he said, "Then why did I have my left shoe built up an inch to minimize it?" He says his limp could be likened to the iron fence in this story he tells:

> While attending a conference some years ago, I stood looking at the stake tabernacle grounds with a member of the stake presidency during the interval between the morning and afternoon sessions. There was an iron fence around the grounds with dagger-shaped pickets. One was bent this way and another that, each at a different angle all the way in front and around the corner.
>
> The man to whom I was speaking was a blacksmith. I said, "President, how long would it take you to straighten those pickets?" He looked at the fence and then at me. "I surely owe you an apology," he said. "I come here at least three times a week every week of the world, and this is the first time I've noticed that the pickets were bent."

After his heart attack in 1942, LeGrand Richards found walking more difficult and felt more secure when using a cane. In late years his leg has stiffened, and he vigorously exercises it at night to keep it as limber as possible. When he preaches, the listeners are so caught up in what he says that even many on the stand do not notice that he rests the afflicted leg by placing the toe of one foot upon that of the other and stands that way during his entire speech.

This malady has never slowed him down, nor has it brought forth complaints. (Perhaps that is why his limp went unnoticed until recent years.) It did not prevent him from dancing, leg-wrestling, or doing heavy manual labor, nor has it kept him from full performance during his entire ministry. But it has been with him for life—"a thorn in the flesh" which reminds us of Paul's words:

> And lest I should be exalted above measure through the abundance of the revelations, there was given to me a thorn in the flesh, the messenger of Satan to buffet me. . . . For this thing I besought the Lord thrice, that it might depart from me. And he said unto me, My grace is sufficient for thee: for my strength is made perfect in weakness. . . . (2 Corinthians 12:7-9.)

The Lord's grace has been sufficient also for LeGrand Richards, making it possible for him to live above his infirmity during the nearly ninety years which stretch back from the present to the boyhood era when the difficulty first appeared.

The Lessons of Youth

1897-1902

From the open windows of the Tooele Ward meetinghouse on a warm summer Sunday could be heard the strains of the familiar hymn, "Ere you left your room this morning, did you think to pray?" Seated with the deacons, young LeGrand Richards raised his lusty voice with the congregation. When he came to the words, "Prayer will change the night to day," he stopped singing. The message of the song penetrated his mind and drove away the melody. He recalls:

> We always had our family prayers morning and night. My mother had taught me to say my secret prayers at night but had not taught me to offer them in the morning. I was so impressed with that hymn that I started having my secret prayers in the morning too. I recall working on the farm and reciting to myself often, "Prayer will change the night to day." The fact that prayer would do just that was marvelous to me.

Perhaps no characteristic of his youth is so pronounced as LeGrand's receptiveness to correct teaching. Like a hungry plant taking in essential nutrients, he accepted each good suggestion, useful piece of information, or valuable lesson to which he was exposed. He tried it out promptly, then made it his own so that it was ready for immediate recall or use. As a result, and after over eighty years of constant application, the ideas, principles, and skills he learned are still an integral part of him.

His Primary teacher, Sister Gillespie, taught her boys the courtesy of tipping their hats when they passed a lady on the street. LeGrand's first opportunity to follow her instruction soon came when he met Mrs. Dodds, county treasurer and a non-

Mormon, in town. "LeGrand," she said, "you're the first man in this city who has ever tipped his hat to me since I've been here."

Without a doubt George F. Richards was LeGrand's greatest teacher, and all his children bear witness to his influence upon them individually. LeGrand's stories of lessons learned from "Father" have enlivened his talks and writings during his entire adult life. They teach the principles of Sabbath observance, tithing, honesty, virtue, and the Word of Wisdom as no amount of moralizing could ever do, and they are made relevant and new with each telling because they are taken from real life and are part of the teller's first-hand experience.

George F. Richards was no ivory-tower theorist but a practical parent who knew the temptations and evils that existed and to which each child would be exposed. As the fifteen children came along, each one lively and spirited, they were subject to the normal misdemeanors of the growing child. Tempers flared, teasings occurred, and there was an occasional breach of honesty or a challenge to the observance of the Sabbath or the Word of Wisdom. In such cases correction was needed, and it was given lovingly and promptly and with lasting effect.

Undergirt with his early commitment to the Lord, George F. was guided by his own carefully written priorities, which included "raising, providing for, and properly teaching our children," as well as "conquer thyself." (GFR *Diary*, "Three Grand Divisions of Labor for the Saints," vol. 1, p. 277.) George F. functioned as a patriarch on the premise that his children were choice spirits from the Father; that they were innocent of wrongdoing until taught correct principles; that he and his wife were responsible for that instruction (both as examples and as effective teachers); that children learn best if taught with love and understanding; and that if they err, they must be corrected and encouraged to do better. Discipline, though firm, was fair and kind, and it was usually followed with an affectionate kiss or embrace. Beyond this, George F. was unfailingly consistent of word and action in both lessons taught and correction given.

Two stories will illustrate. The experiences occurred twenty-five years apart and under totally different circumstances. One concerns the next-to-eldest son, LeGrand; the other, Ray, the youngest of the fifteen children. The subject of each story is observance of the Word of Wisdom. LeGrand tells the first about himself.

> Brother Ebeneezer Beesley, former director of the Tabernacle Choir, came to Tooele and organized a martial band. My brother George played a flute and I played the snare drum. When we were having a band practice one evening, Brother Beesley said that Brother Meiklejohn was celebrating his eightieth birthday, and he suggested that we go and serenade him. [When we did so] we were each served a small glass of wine. [This was a time when many faithful foreign-born Saints still clung to their hot drinks or home-made wine for festive occasions.] I drank my small glass, not knowing it was wrong, and the other boys did, and also my brother. It made me tipsy and they had to hold my drum for me while I played. My brother was afraid to take me home, so he kept me rolling around for some time in the new-mown hay adjoining our home. The next day Brother Beesley came and apologized to my father, who just advised me that if I would drink but milk and water I would never get in trouble. (*Blue Book*, p. 27.)

That he never forgot this lesson is borne out by an oft-told experience of his youth. When at a dance at Saltair, he was invited by a young lady friend to join her party at dinner. She and LeGrand held hands and "went hopscotching down to the table." He stopped when he saw a bottle of beer at each place. "What's the matter," she asked, "are you too good to drink a little beer?" He did some quick thinking. "I guess I am," he said, "and I thought you were too." He then went up the stairs faster than he had come down.

Ray's story is about Mr. Klink, a non-Mormon who lived near the Richards home in Salt Lake City. He was a homey sort who of an evening would sit before the fire and read the newspaper while he smoked his pipe. Ray sometimes visited him, and he was so impressed with the man's obvious contentment that he approached his father, now a member of the Quorum of the Twelve, and innocently asked the question:

"Father, why don't you sit by the fire and smoke a pipe like Mr. Klink?"

"My son," George F. responded, "I'm glad you asked me that."

He then explained about the effects of tobacco upon the health, adding, "Now, anything you see your mother or me do, you are free to do, and if there are other things you meet with which you do not fully understand, ask me and I will tell you." He then put his arms about his son, kissed him, and assured him of his love. As a result of that lesson, tobacco never tempted Ray.

When LeGrand was ten years old (1896), George F. gave up the Doremus Ranch to open a lumber and implement business near the center of town, where he also built a large brick home. LeGrand remembers helping to haul lime and brick for that project. It took two wagons and six horses to bring the bricks from the railroad station to the building site. On May 29, 1897, George F. wrote in his diary, "Finished moving today, occupying basement, kitchen, bathroom, and upstairs bedrooms."

At age eleven LeGrand was now old enough to do a man's work, and because of his great love for his father he enjoyed working with him and profited from his daily instruction and the gospel discussions that were often part of their conversation. He helped hoe weeds from a forty-acre corn patch, plowed the land, ran his father's twelve-foot header, and hauled hay, lumber, adobe, lime, and wood. Whatever the task that needed doing, winter made it more difficult. LeGrand tells of going into the canyons with his father to get wood, of frozen gloves, tipped-over loads of cedar stumps, and near-runaways. "It was so cold," he recalls, "that Father would try to smile but couldn't because his face was frozen stiff." (*Blue Book*, p. 26.)

Another winter experience gives a word picture of the difficulties and of family cooperation in the midst of them. LeGrand is narrator:

My brother George and Max Gordon were bringing two loads of lumber from Salt Lake, and I was sent with an extra team to

Aged thirteen.

help them up the hill. I stayed with the Yeates family in E. T. [Lake Point] until we heard the lumber clapping as they came along near midnight. We hitched one of my fresh horses onto each wagon. It had been snowing for some time. We hadn't gone far until Father arrived on our riding horse. Mother had gotten to worrying about her sons, so Father let George take the saddle horse and go home, since he had been riding longer in the storm. Father and I stayed with one load of lumber; Max, with the other. By the time we reached home, we couldn't stand to remain in the house. Our hands and faces were frostbitten, so we took a tub of cold water onto the porch until we thawed ourselves out. (*Blue Book*, p. 26.)

Even with the lumber and implement business, farming still supplied much of the family income and continued to provide work for George F.'s growing sons. Particularly during harvest time, it was necessary to hire outside help. George F. was careful to see that these men were of good character so that their influence upon his boys would be acceptable. Once, a man using bad language and telling dirty stories was summarily dismissed from his employ.

His father's watchcare over his boys so impressed LeGrand that he took responsibility to safeguard his own mind by controlling what he allowed to enter it. "I walked away from the old Co-op corner, where we used to play our first games," he says, "and I resolved that no friend of mine would ever be able to accuse me of befouling his mind with dirty stories like I had heard there." And he has repeated many times the classic statement, "I can go back to the town where I was raised as a boy and can tell parents how to raise their children, and I don't need to worry about old women my age sitting down in the back saying, 'Yes, but you should have known him when we knew him as a boy.' "

In the matter of honesty and integrity too George F. served as an impressive example to his boys. LeGrand tells of an experience which he never forgot:

> We used to take our wheat to the grist mill and then draw on it until our credit was gone. A new miller came into Tooele to operate the mill. I went there one day to get grist. We had no credit, so he wouldn't give it to me. I asked him to check with the owner of the mill.
>
> I went back within a few days with a load of wheat and got our grist, and when I asked, "Did you check with the owner of the mill?" he answered yes.
>
> "And what did he say?"
>
> "He said, 'The next time one of those sons of George F. Richards's comes to this mill, if he wants the mill, get out and give it to him.' "
>
> It is wonderful to have a father so honored.

Because of his father's example and his own willing spirit, service came naturally to LeGrand. As deacons quorum president, he served in that office as faithfully as his father served in the stake presidency. In his *Blue Book* (p. 27), he wrote the following: "We had to sweep our meetinghouse each Saturday; chop wood for our two big stoves, carry it in to the wood box, and then go early Sunday morning and dust and make the fires to warm the building. We had to clean the chimneys of our coal oil lamps and fill them. We also had to take care of our meetinghouse grounds."

Tooele meetinghouse.

It is instructive to note LeGrand's use of the word *our* as he tells how he filled his assignment. This willingness and full participation in Church service became a lifelong attitude. It bears out the truth of a statement by his daughter Nona R. Dyer: "The Lord cannot make an able man willing, but he can make a willing man able."

LeGrand's other Aaronic Priesthood assignments were carried out with the same commitment. As a teacher in his ward, he was assigned to home teach with the mail carrier. They knelt in prayer before going to the homes. After greeting the people, each had a turn to present a prepared message which they gave while standing before family members. Before leaving, they asked, "I guess you have family prayer. Would you like us to pray with you before we go?" In accepting their offer, one widow said, "You are the first home teachers who have offered to pray with us since my children and I came to Zion."

During the time LeGrand was a priest he did not have opportunity to baptize anyone, but he considered blessing the sacrament such a privilege that he would not perform that ordinance until he had memorized the prayers letter-perfect.

The family's life was not all labor and Church activity. As in earlier years, time was allowed for recreation, which now included skating, sleighing, programs, outings, parties, and dancing. LeGrand tells of the dances above the store owned by Peter (christened Pierre Appolinaire) Droubay. He and his friends danced with the identical Bryan twins. "One would wear a posy, then she would let the other wear it for a while so that we boys never could tell which one was which."

Concerning the dances and parties, LeGrand remembers an incident which shows him to be not just a blind follower of counsel and instruction but a thinking, strong-willed, responsible young man. He and Joel went to a party from which their father expected them to return by ten-thirty. They were late in returning and their father was asleep. They wakened him, and LeGrand said, "Father, I don't want to go to any more parties unless you can trust us to leave at the appropriate time." LeGrand had a fine social sense which forbade him to embarrass a host or cause inconvenience. He notes also that sometimes parents are so restrictive that they breed rebellion or deny normal friendships. He tells of one woman he knew who had three lovely daughters. So strict was she that boy friends stopped coming to see the girls, none of whom married.

As much as was consistent with his parental responsibility, George F. tried to understand his children's viewpoint. Where it seemed wise, he gave them their choice. One story of LeGrand's demonstrates both the father's understanding and his firm direction.

> When we were boys, the greatest sport the young people could have on Sunday was to go buggy riding in the afternoon. Father would never let us boys do that, so my younger brother and I went to him one day and decided that we would have it out. Father explained that his children had to set an example to others, yet he did not like to deprive us of the enjoyment we should have. He offered to let us leave one of the teams at home any day during the week, quit our work at noon and come home, and have a fresh

team so we could buggy ride. Of course, we thought it would be ridiculous for us to be the only boys out buggy riding during the week when the other boys did it on Sunday, but it taught us a lesson. Father was willing to sacrifice a day's work of the team and a half day's work of his boys in order that we might have the enjoyment we desired, but he taught us that it was not appropriate on the Sabbath. (LeGrand Richards, *Just to Illustrate* [Bookcraft, 1961], pp. 12-13, and interview.)

Another incident LeGrand remembers shows how George F. allowed himself to be influenced by his sons' combined sense of fairness.

The men used to bring "wild" horses in off the range, put them in the stray-pound, and then auction them off. My brother George had a buckskin riding horse. Joel and I had none. George set his mind upon a little bay mare in the pound, and Father agreed with him to let Lone Gowens go and bid on it for George. Joel and I didn't think it was fair. I had a little temper in those days, so I went to Mother and said, "Those two horses will never live on our place as sure as I'm alive."

That night she told Father what I'd said. He felt bad that Joel and I had feelings about the matter, but he could understand our point of view. The next morning he called off the bid and offered to give Joel and me an old roan horse that he had traded for. (The horse had "a head nearly as big as his body," but Father let us get him shod so he'd be in fit shape to ride, which we did.)

Some time later, Father decided to sell this horse, and he was going to keep the money. Joel and I thought it was our own horse and if it had to be sold we ought to have the money, so with our parents' permission we held a family court. Mother agreed to be the judge and she was all for her boys. She ruled that the proceeds from the sale of the horse should be divided equally between Father, Joel, and me. Father agreed to the terms; Mother was pleased; and we boys felt that justice had been done.

Concerning his temper and the lesson he learned, LeGrand tells how his older brother teased him about a girl that he had no interest in at all. (He does not think that parents should allow one child to tease another.) George F. Jr. says of himself that at the time he was "permitted to be a little bit obstreperous with the other boys." (Oral History Program, *George F. Richards Jr.* by William Hartley, p. 23, LDS Church Archives.) When this brother left for school in Salt Lake, LeGrand was glad to see him go and said so emphatically. "Father, observing my temper, said, 'LeGrand, I don't blame you, because I had a temper when I was young, but I think you should correct it.' I then thought to my-self, 'If Father could break his temper, so could I.' " From then on, LeGrand worked hard to master it.

He came to understand that a temper, unleashed, is a dan-gerous animal, but controlled, it is a safe mount upon which to ride. So firmly did he take hold of the lesson that he came to feel that even petulance and irascibility are inexcusable. Says he, "An irritable man or woman is about the most objectionable creature there is. They should get down on their knees and ask the Lord to give them strength to overcome it as much as they would the habit of liquor or tobacco. Harsh words cut deeply. It takes a long while for such wounds to heal, if ever they do."

LeGrand graduated from Tooele District School (eighth grade) in 1901. The Richards boys had missed weeks of lessons in spring and fall for seedtime and harvest. In addition, LeGrand had missed the year his hip trouble began, so his brother Joel caught up with him. He states that Joel learned more rapidly than he. "We both got good grades, but I had to work twice as hard." Perhaps the added effort he expended increased his powers of retention, one of his distinguishing characteristics throughout life.

LeGrand's desire for further education was intense, but there were some moments of disappointment when it appeared that no cash was available for that purpose. His father suggested, as an alternative, that he return to the district school for a year and learn whatever he could. "I could not do that, Father," he said. "I would rather stay home and work on the farm." Seeing his disappointment, George F. "hustled around and got the money." So it was that LeGrand left to join his brother George in Salt Lake.

When the brothers, boarding together, became reacquainted as young men, they learned to appreciate each other and became the best of friends. Each would have done anything for the other. George F. Jr. compared them to "David and Jonathan."

George F. Richards's Tooele home, scene of LeGrand's early teenage years.

Salt Lake Business College (top floor of Templeton Building) when LeGrand attended.

(*GFR Jr.*, William Hartley, p. 23.) LeGrand often thought that they were like Joseph Smith and his older brother Hyrum. Their friendship remained close throughout their adult life.

The importance of LeGrand's year and few months at Salt Lake Business College (1902-1903) can scarcely be overemphasized. The school advertised to "educate for a useful life *now*," and for LeGrand it did just that. He came with an eager spirit, and superior teachers were there to give him what he needed. J. Reuben Clark, Jr., taught him mathematics and English, the latter so effectively that in all of LeGrand's writings and sermons, folksy and people-oriented as they are, his language is not only grammatically correct but clear, precise, and uniquely his own. Ada Bitner (who would become the mother of Gordon B. Hinckley), taught him typing and shorthand—skills he still uses to excellent advantage. While he claims his penmanship is less perfect than that of his brother George, his handwriting is easy to read and his signature is distinctively clear and graceful.

From Matthew Miller he learned bookkeeping. The college used the mind-stretching, competitive "cabinet" system, which taught in an outstandingly practical way the rudiments of many different businesses—jobbing, grocery, hay and grain, furniture, dry goods, lumber, banking, and corporations. These LeGrand mastered to the degree that upon completion of school he was able always to find good employment, invest, or successfully enter into business on his own. In his education there were no tentative theories, controversial philosophies, or academic frills— only the unadorned basics; but what he learned, he retained and built upon. Though he had less education than his brothers, he was able at various times to help them in business partnerships with him or in ventures of their own. With only this same basic training, seasoned by practical experience, he would become Presiding Bishop of the Church with all of its temporal affairs under his jurisdiction (subject to the direction and approval of the First Presidency), a position he held for fourteen years.

While LeGrand and George F. Jr. were attending business college in Salt Lake, their father came and visited whenever he had business in the city. He often stayed overnight with them, discussing their school affairs and their future prospects. He never left without reaffirming his love for and trust in them. He would say, "I never thought I could let a boy of mine go and live in the city, but I would trust you two to go anywhere I would go myself." Their hearts swelled with love and pride at his words. LeGrand later said, "They put rods of steel in our spines, and we couldn't do anything that would disappoint him."

George F. Jr. left school for Tooele in December 1902 to marry his childhood sweetheart, Edith May Dunn. LeGrand stayed on in Salt Lake, where his brother Joel later joined him. The lessons he had learned at home, coupled with those he was now learning at school, laid such a solid base upon which to build the structure of his life that there would be no need in later years to shore up, remodel, or redo it as his character took on the mature outlines of wholeness. There were many lessons yet to master, many skills yet to acquire. Winds would blow and shake the framework, and shadows would sometimes cover it, but it would endure upon the base which had been so carefully set in place.

Chapter 3

Preparing for a Mission

1900-1905

W hen I heard Elders Alex Bevan and John E. Isgreen bear their testimonies [1900] and tell of traveling without purse or scrip while on their missions in the Eastern States, I don't know if they said something unusual or not," LeGrand Richards relates. "If they didn't, then the Lord certainly did something unusual to me, because when I went home I felt as if I could walk into any mission field in the world if I had a call." He continues, "I went into the bedroom, got down on my knees, and asked God to help me live worthy to be a missionary when I was old enough to go."

Thus into the mind and heart of this clean, responsible, thinking young man—a fertile seedbed for the missionary spirit to take root—came the distinct inner "call" to declare the restoration of the gospel. The incident happened while he still lived in Tooele, antedating his official mission call by four years.

LeGrand was again touched by the Spirit when he read George Q. Cannon's *Life of the Prophet Joseph Smith* (Deseret Book Company, 1958, but originally published in 1888). "It so impressed me," he says, "that I found myself wishing I had lived in the days of the Prophet so I might have been one of his helpers and have stood by his side."

Determined to prepare himself for the coming of his mission call, he carried with him a pocket-sized book, *A Practical Reference*, by Louis A. Kelsch (Chicago, Illinois: Northern States Mission 1897). It was a compilation of scriptural texts arranged by subject. He does not remember where he obtained it, but it became his guide as he studied the scriptures and memorized the referenced passages, a practice that has been lifelong. By this means he helped to make the various parts of the gospel clear to him and he began to see them as they related to a logical and intelligible whole.

His study also familiarized him with the prophets so that in a special sense they became his friends. "We can't all have the most learned companions," he later wrote, "but we can have the daily association of the great men of God by becoming acquainted with their lives and labors and teachings, as they have been recorded and handed down to us. . . . (*Black Book*, p. 27.) "From them," he states, "I tried to pattern my life and prepare myself to declare the restoration of the gospel." When he left for school in Salt Lake he took the little Kelsch volume and his scriptures with him and continued to study and memorize at every free moment and on Sundays.

Upon completion of his fifteen months of schooling at Salt Lake Business College, LeGrand worked for a few weeks for Rosenbaum Brothers in the absence of their secretary. After that he was employed by the Consolidated Wagon and Machine Company, where he remained for the next two years (1903-1904). During that time he saved his money, determined to earn the total amount needed for the mission which was now his most urgent goal.

During the summer, LeGrand occasionally went to Tooele to satisfy his home-hunger and to visit with family and friends. He sometimes made the nearly forty-mile trip on a bicycle. He tells that he and Joel had a commercially designed contraption which made it possible to pedal along the railroad tracks. A wheel attachment on the bike fit the track at the side where the rider was seated. A support bar reached from the top of the bicycle, forming a triangle with the axle to the other track, where a matching wheel-fitting was located. By this mechanical means a fairly smooth but very long ride was assured. To build up his endurance for the journey, LeGrand exercised his legs by pedaling many times around the perimeter dirt road at Liberty Park.

In December 1903 LeGrand and Joel planned to go home for Christmas, never having been away from their family for the holidays. LeGrand tells the following story about that trip:

LeGrand (nearest camera) as bookkeeper for Consolidated Wagon and Machine Company.

It snowed about a foot the night before we were to go home by train. We took our grips down to the depot, where Joel waited while I went up to about Eighth East [867 First Avenue] to get Grandmother, Nanny Longstroth Richards, who was going to Tooele with us.

The streetcars were tied up and delayed because of the snow, and by the time I arrived at Grandmother's she had become anxious and had left for the station. When I got back to Main Street, I ran the remaining way to the Union Pacific Depot and arrived just in time to wave goodbye to the train carrying Joel and Grandmother.

With no other way to reach home, I went to the Farrington Livery Stables, rented a saddle horse, and started out in that snow for the long, cold ride so that I could be home with my loved ones.

When I reached the Point of the Mountain, about halfway home, I was mighty glad to see George with team and buggy to pick me up. He had no knowledge that I was coming, but he had said, "I know LeGrand; he'll be here." We tied the horse to the side and I rode with him in the buggy. When we arrived at our home, I got cleaned up and went to a dance that night. The next day I had a glorious Christmas with the folks.

The brothers returned to Salt Lake, where Joel resumed his studies and LeGrand went back to work. During this period, the latter came under the tutelage of James E. Talmage, who taught a class on the Articles of Faith. LeGrand was greatly moved by the spiritual power of his teaching. It was from here that he was called to attend the missionary class taught at the LDS University by Benjamin Goddard. LeGrand found it both stimulating and instructive.

When LeGrand's mission call finally came, it was to the Southern States Mission. His bishop, Oscar F. Hunter (Eighth Ward, Liberty Stake), however, was impressed that the young man's place was in Europe. (At that time, a bishop could suggest areas to which his missionaries might be sent.) When the matter came to the attention of Brother George Reynolds in the office of the First Presidency, he was perfectly willing to change the call. He asked LeGrand if he would like to go to Germany. The young man replied, "I want to go where I can preach the gospel, and I understand that the missionaries are being put in prison in Germany." Brother Reynolds said, "We will send you to Holland. They have religious freedom there."

But in this good man's opinion there was a problem. LeGrand was on crutches with a painful "floating kneecap," and his leg was in a plaster cast. Brother Reynolds said, "It looks to me as if you had better go home and take care of yourself."

In saying this, he had not taken into account the faith of this eager young man, who had already challenged his employer and triumphed over one obstacle put in his way. So reluctant had the company officials been to have LeGrand leave, that one had interceded with the Presidency of the Church to have his mission deferred by some months. When he found out about this, LeGrand took a dim view of the proceedings. He had earned all the money needed for his mission and could hardly wait to be on the way, so he persuaded the Church authorities to reactivate his call. Determined to let nothing else interfere, he now said to Brother Reynolds, "You book me, and I will be ready to go." With that, he left for Tooele and asked his father to bless him so he could go on his mission as scheduled.

Benjamin Goddard's missionary training class (LeGrand at extreme left of top row).

And bless him his father did. Not only did George F. promise that he would have strength and vitality and not be overtaken with sickness, but he blessed him that the "spirit of this mission [would] rest mightily" upon him and that his greatest desire would be to warn both the wicked and the honest in heart and to teach them the "principle of eternal life in plainness unto understanding." He stated that LeGrand would desire their salvation and would testify of the "divine mission of the Prophet Joseph and the restoration of the Church."

Again he saw his son as a "leader among men," but counseled him to be submissive in spirit, to control passions, and to be humble and childlike, yet "powerful under influence of the Spirit of God." He promised that as years and experience were added, LeGrand would increase in faith, knowledge, and power for good. If he were cautious and awake to temptation, he would not be overcome by the power of the adversary, who had (as before mentioned) "designed his destruction." (*Patriarchal Blessings*, April 2, 1905, bk. 411, p. 357, LDS Church Archives.)

On the same day that he blessed LeGrand, George F. or-

dained his son an elder. Now, in full confidence, LeGrand prepared to leave. Three days later (April 5, 1905) he received his
endowment at the Salt Lake Temple. Shortly afterwards he had
his leg cast removed, discarded his crutches, and reported that he
was "almost well."

On April 15 he was set apart for his mission by President B.
H. Roberts of the First Council of the Seventy, assisted by
George Reynolds and George F. Richards. In his missionary
blessing to the young elder, President Roberts reiterated many of
the promises formerly conferred through his father. He further
stated that this was but the commencement of LeGrand's
ministry; that he should have "mighty intelligence in His work";
and that he would be given a "love of the people so they shall be
dear to your heart, and by this token you may know His spirit is
resting upon you." Another gift would be "light, intelligence,
and every qualification needed to equip you for this great work
of the latter days." (*Missionary Blessing*, LGR papers.)

President Anthon H. Lund of the First Presidency counseled
the departing missionaries in LeGrand's group to remember two
things: First, if they were called upon to speak and found themselves with nothing to say, they should bear their testimonies
"that Jesus is the Christ and Joseph Smith is his servant, and He
will give you something to say." Second, "The people will love
you, but don't be lifted up in the pride of your hearts and think
that it is because you are better than other people. They will love
you because of what you bring to them." As was his way, Le-
Grand tucked away this counsel in the file of his memory to
recall when experience would bring it back again.

Before his departure, LeGrand's brother George (now a
regular diary-keeper) gave him a journal to record the days of his
mission. As a beginning entry in it, George had summarized the
important events in LeGrand's life to date. The gift pleased the
younger brother, and he expressed his appreciation by never
missing a day's entry for the next three years.

LeGrand left Salt Lake City for his mission to Holland on
Monday, April 17, 1905, in company with four of President
Joseph F. Smith's sons, one of whom was his cousin Willard. As

he bade his family good-bye, he said, "This is the happiest day of my life!" He had dreamed of it, prepared in every way for it, and now that it was an actuality his heart was filled with joy.

Once aboard the train, LeGrand learned that the Smith boys were riding Pullman, while he was booked for a chaircar. President German E. Ellsworth of the Northern States Mission, who was leaving at the same time for Chicago, caught the situation in a moment and said, "You are my boy, you come with me," and they occupied the same Pullman berth for the two nights en route to Chicago. This was the beginning of a lifelong friendship between the two men. President Ellsworth's kindness to the younger man speaks for itself, but it also partially demonstrates the fulfillment of LeGrand's promise received as a child, that the Lord would raise up "friends on every hand whose benediction and blessings" should follow him through life.

LeGrand proved himself an able observer and journal-keeper, not only describing what he saw but indicating his thoughts and feelings as well. For a young man who had never traveled beyond Utah the sights were wondrous. He described the temple site in Independence, Missouri, and wrote of the stirring Church history events which took place in that area as if he had been part of them. He wrote about the great "hot house" in Chicago's Lincoln Park, where plants and flowers gave him "an idea of what the Garden of Eden might have been," and of Queenstown, Ireland, where "the sun arose out of the eastern water like a great ball of fire" and seemed to fill his soul with joy. (LGR *Journal*, vol. 1, pp. 5, 12.)

In Liverpool, where the European Mission was headquartered, he wrote about the apostle Heber J. Grant, president of that mission, and of the valuable instructions he gave the new missionaries. (LGR *Journal*, vol. 1, p. 13.) "He told us how to cure homesickness, and he wanted us to put it down in our books," Elder Richards wrote. "He says, 'Work, work, work, and you won't get homesick!' He advised us never to baptize without consent of husband or parents. He taught us the correct way of confirming members in the Church and instructed, 'that in administering to the Saints, we should pray for the healing power of

God, and not that the oil should penetrate their systems.' He told us, 'to keep ourselves clean and pure,' and 'never to go any-place where we would be ashamed to take our mother, sister, or sweetheart.' "

Taking down the president's advice and realizing he was actually in the mission field, Elder Richards found that the spirit of his mission "rested mightily" upon him, as his father had prayed that it would. He wrote, "I felt as though I could leap for joy!"

Chapter 4

Holland

1905-1908

I had no difficulty in becoming accustomed to their money, but saw at once that I had a job on my hands to learn their language." So wrote Elder Richards upon his arrival in Rotterdam. (LGR *Journal*, vol. 1, p. 15.) He and his companions, Stephen D. Markham and Melvin H. Welker, "felt like strangers" in that city of dog-carts, wooden shoes, and speech that sounded like "one long unbroken word." Yet he felt confident that if the dogs, whose barks sounded familiar, could understand Dutch, so in time could he.

There was no one to meet them at the boat that Sunday, May 7, 1905, but fortunately a *dienstman* (baggageman) recognized them as missionaries and helped them find Boezemsingel 116, the mission home. They found no one there either. Elder Richards then got a young man, Bote Dokter, to take them to the branch meeting, where Mission President Jacob H. Trayner finally welcomed them.

For the few days the president kept them in the city they studied, visited, and observed the quaintly dressed citizens. Elder Richards was sure that if he could get to the people with printed tracts and smiles he could begin to proselyte at once; study and practice would do the rest. Then came the day. On May 10, President Trayner called the elders in and gave out their assignments. Elder Markham would labor in Rotterdam, Elder Welker in Groningen; and Elder Richards would serve as mission secretary. His mind wrestled with the prospects of office routine and confinement. A disappointed yet submissive spirit is reflected in his journal entry that day. "I had felt as though I would prefer to get out and do tracting, and labor among the people, but then I realized that the office work had to be done as well as the other . . . so I told him that I would help him all I could." (LGR *Journal*, vol. I, pp. 15-16.)

Reinforcing to his own resolve was a dream which he felt was given to help him in his disappointment:

> In the dream I was keeping books for Father in his lumber and implement business, and I said I was tired of it and wanted to do ordinary work. He agreed to let me seek other employment. I came to Salt Lake and worked with a railroad maintenance crew pushing one of their little carts along the track in company with three other men. One said, "What have you been doing?" "Keeping books," I answered. "What did you earn?" he asked. I told him. "You will never earn that on this job," he said. "Anybody can push these carts, but not everyone can keep books."

Not only did the dream comfort Elder Richards, but he came to appreciate his assignment because it taught him the inner workings of a mission and prepared him for his later call as a mission president.

There was a great need for his help. President Trayner of the Netherlands-Belgium Mission was new to his call, having served under the former president, Willard T. Cannon, until just three weeks before Elder Richards arrived. With five districts and thirty-nine elders under his jurisdiction, his schedule of travel was heavy, and the office work was in arrears. He had prayed for a good man for secretary and he now felt that his prayers had been answered. The president was single, so a Sister d'Hulst took care of the mission home. (It was this Moe [mother] d'Hulst who worried that the new secretary would wear his teeth away from brushing them so often.)

Elder Richards soon began to help with emigrations for German, Belgian, and Dutch Saints bound for the United States. He says: "I'd go down to the hotel, and I'd have a note book where I'd list the money I got from each one to pay for his transportation. I would change their money and give them back what they had coming to them—enough English coin for their crossing and debarkation from England, and the rest in American currency." He learned both Dutch and German words enough to count their baskets, trunks, and boxes and to give instructions. Because he was a member of the Church and represented the mission president, the Saints trusted him as their friend. (In contrast with present Church policy of encouraging the Saints to stay in their own lands and taking the blessings of temples, conferences, and instruction to them, the Church in 1905 was still encouraging as many as could afford it to immigrate to Utah. [The final policy change was announced in 1921. See James B. Allen and Glen M. Leonard, *The Story of the Latter-day Saints,* Salt Lake City, Utah: Deseret Book Co., 1976, p. 497.])

Another change in general policy and practice was a minor one, but it affected Elder Richards. Near the turn of the century, Church and civil authorities as well as the majority of other men wore beards, and a former mission president, Francis M. Lyman (1901-04), had suggested that beards would give the missionaries a look of greater maturity. Elder Richards complied with the suggestion, since his duties required him to work with banks and emigration officials. (One woman judged the bearded nineteen-year-old to be thirty-nine.)

As with emigrations, so with other aspects of his work; Elder Richards felt the urgent need to learn the language and often felt hampered because of his lack. He pushed to get the office work current so he could study Dutch. Beyond that, the spirit of his mission "rested mightily upon him." He wrote, "I was so anxious to preach the gospel that I found myself arising before 5:00 A.M. to study Dutch and get my office work done so I could go out tracting in the afternoon." (*Blue Book*, p. 40.) Day after day he recorded that he distributed tracts—50, 92, 110 tracts a day. His return calls to gather them yielded many gospel conversations, halting and incomplete as they no doubt were at first on his part. The kind of effort he was expending as a "part-time" missionary is clear from the fact that, in comparison, an average of only 197 tracts per missionary had been given out for the whole month of January 1905. (*Netherlands Mission Historical Record,* LDS Archives.)

For what this diligent effort cost him in discomfort and pain we have only one clue—a journal entry in which he mentions his hip trouble. "This evening when I went to bed about 1:00 A.M., it was impossible to get to sleep for quite a while as my leg bothered me again, and I couldn't get in a position so it was

As a nineteen-year-old missionary in Holland.

comfortable.... After thus being troubled ... I asked the Lord to cause the pain to cease so that I could sleep, and it left me immediately.... The praise be to the Lord, who is all powerful." (LGR *Journal*, vol. I, p. 50.)

Elder Richards had another challenge which was with him from the time he arrived in Holland (1905) until he left in 1908 to return home. It was fleas. Neither President Trayner nor Imke Kooyman (editor of the mission paper, *De Ster*, who also lived at the mission home) was afflicted in this way; but, said Elder Richards, "Fleas seem to have a way of choosing whom they want to bother." He would get up several times a night to fight them off, shake his clothing out the window, bathe with Peneroil and vinegar, but nothing helped. With wry humor, he relates: "When I took care of emigrants, I did their figuring with one hand and fought fleas with the other. When I preached, I used one arm for that and fought fleas with the other."

This constant "fight" afforded him a further tough exercise in endurance in order to rise above another difficult problem and focus upon his priority—a mission. There is no indication that he grumbled about it; in fact, he counseled himself: "Be habitually cheerful. Don't be ever plaintively whining and discontentedly murmuring, and this both for your own sake and those about you. Let your face and general demeanor be like sunshine and not like a cloudy day, east wind, or a damp blanket." (*Green Book*, p. 8.)

Elder Richards' most pressing need was to master the Dutch language. His method of study was a combination of dictionary use, practice, and common sense. He explains: "The mission office was right across from the cattle market, and I would go along those lanes where the animals walked ... and I preached to the trees. When I couldn't get the word I wanted, I'd have a little notebook in my pocket in which to write it down and then go back and look it up." This method of learning was in line with his observation that little children learn to talk by finding words for everything they see.

His self-tutelage was effective, for after seven weeks in the field he blessed the sacrament, prayed, consecrated oil, and bap-

tized "four souls in the Maas River," including Arie Sandman
(whom he later helped to emigrate). Of the baptism he wrote: "It
was after ten o'clock at night and it had been raining quite hard,
but as soon as we got about ready, it cleared off. . . . It made me
shake like a leaf to go in the water, as it was quite cold, but I had
already asked the Lord several times to help me as it was my first
trial and I had to do it in Dutch. . . . The moment I raised my
hand to perform the baptism, I felt just as steady as I ever have
and I was able to say the words nicely. . . ." (LGR *Journal*, vol. I,
p. 24.)

Although he did well with memorized prayers, ordinances,
and blessings, he was still struggling to gain facility in conversation and preaching. Nevertheless he did well when President
Heber J. Grant called upon him to speak at the combined mission conference held in Rotterdam, February 1906 (after President Trayner had assured him he would not be called upon
because he was taking the president's talk down in shorthand).
Elder Richards bore testimony with such freedom and power
that nonmembers in attendance later remembered him for it and
one joined the Church.

President Grant too was impressed with the young elder.
After the meeting, he dictated fifteen letters to Elder Richards
and then asked how he would like to go to Liverpool with him.
In that situation he no doubt could have worked out arrangements for proselyting similar to those he had made in his current
position. The young elder admitted that he would be thrilled
with the prospects of ending his grueling study of Dutch and his
fight with the fleas, and felt it would be an honor to serve under
President Grant. The president said he would think it over until
morning.

When the two men met again, the president said, "I have
decided that if I took you, it would be because I have the authority and would like to, but President Trayner needs you as
much as I do, and I think you should remain." His words came
as a great disappointment, but in so deciding the president
proved himself a great friend. He kept the young elder on course,
never forgot him, and played an important role in his later
ministry.

Missionaries with European Mission President Heber J. Grant at Delftshaven, Holland (Elder Richards with arm on the President's knee).

Just a month after the conference, Elder Richards spoke in church for twenty-seven minutes. On March 11, 1906, he wrote, "I never felt more like speaking in my life. I was so full of the Spirit, I felt that should the floor slide from under me, I could still stand there and testify to the things of God." It was a significant breakthrough. Increasingly he became master of the language, and he experienced great freedom of expression as he taught the Bible-reading Dutch. His new-found facility coupled with their knowledge of the scriptures made religious discussion both challenging and profitable.

As he labored to obtain in Dutch the doctrinal knowledge he had in English, his comprehension expanded; and as he met questions and explained Church doctrine, his studies made him a keen scripturalist. He added to his store of gospel knowledge by deep study of such subjects as the Holy Ghost, the Gathering of Israel, and the Apostasy. Scripturally, he could prove the Apostasy to a people who accepted the Bible as the word of God, and with the "falling away" clearly shown, he could establish both the need and the promise of a restoration. These two themes were and are central to Elder Richards's preaching. With his own firm conviction and a command of the language with which to share the gospel, he could now teach and preach and be the Lord's instrument in conversions.

Many impressive conversion stories are contained in Elder Richards's journal and his *Blue Book*. The one that follows comes from the period in which he labored as mission secretary. It serves as an early example of his ability to boldly challenge without giving offense, to retain the lead, to explain the gospel in plain terms, and to bear testimony unto conversion—skills for which Elder Richards later became noted.

He lent his own money for fifteen-year-old Arie Sandman to immigrate to America. (It was arranged that when the lad found work there he would repay it, which he later did.) The boy's uncle, Marinus de Rijke, and his wife, a Sandman, allowed missionaries in their home only if they did not discuss religion. When Arie told his uncle of the emigration loan, the older man said, "I would like to meet this man Richards." He came to the boat to bid his nephew farewell, and Arie introduced the two men to each other.

Mr. de Rijke was somewhat pompous and proud, wore a stovepipe hat, carried a walking stick, and smoked a big cigar. At first Elder Richards paid him little attention, but after seeing Arie off, he asked, "Mr. de Rijke, have you ever attended a Mormon meeting?"

"No!" was the emphatic answer.

"Well," Elder Richards said, "the Mormons are cutting enough of a figure in the world that from an educational standpoint it wouldn't hurt you to know a little about them."

He then added, "A man of your learning and experience couldn't be misled."

"Well, I will come," de Rijke said.

The next Sunday he and his wife were at the sacrament meeting. After the meeting, Elder Richards asked him how he had liked the service. He said, "*Tamelijk,*" which means fairly well. Elder Richards then suggested, "I would like to come to your home next week, and you take your Bible and I will take mine, and I will show you things in your Bible you have never read before."

Marinus asked his wife, "What do you say?"

"Oh, let them come," she answered.

The appointment was kept, and they had a "wonderful evening." As the missionaries took their leave, Elder Richards said, "Now, when your minister hears we've been here, he will tell you we are the most wicked people in the world. I suggest you invite him to your home, at any hour of the day or night that meets his convenience, and then invite us also, and you decide which one has the truth." He continued with a paraphrase of John 10:11-13: "He will refuse to come because 'the hireling fleeth when the wolves come, because he is an hireling, but the good shepherd giveth his life for the flock.' You will determine whether he is a hireling."

Mr. de Rijke was the foreman in a distillery, and when the employees left each day he would say to them, "I have had the Mormon missionaries in my home, and my minister will not meet them. If any of you know a minister who is not afraid of Mormons, I would like to get hold of him—I don't care what church he belongs to." Some fine discussions resulted, and after one of them Mr. de Rijke said, "Mr. Richards, I would give everything I own if I could prove you wrong." The young elder laid his little Bible before the man and said, "That is all I ask you to do, and then I will never ask the privilege of coming in your home again."

The man replied, "That is what I have been trying to do, and I have failed."

"I want to thank you for bearing your testimony that you have found the truth," Elder Richards said. "Now what are you going to do about it?"

Shortly after this, Mr. de Rijke and his wife were baptized and immigrated to Utah. Although childless in Holland, they had two children in Utah. The son, Harry, became the "best worker with the Aaronic Priesthood" that Elder Richards ever knew in the Church. The daughter, Nellie, filled three missions. (*Blue Book*, pp. 42-43.)

As capable as this conversion story shows him to be, Elder Richards readily admits that he learned part of the technique from Alex Nibley, who later became the mission president. While Elder Richards yet could not speak Dutch very well but could understand it, he and Elder Nibley made their first visit to the Herman Schilperoort family. Elder Nibley explained to the man what brought them to Holland, and the man spoke up and said, "Well, what about polygamy?"—a "red-hot" subject at that time.

Elder Nibley replied: "Now, that is a good question, and if you hadn't asked, we would have told you all about it in due course. But if you were going to build a house, you wouldn't try to put the roof on before you got the foundation in, would you?" He added, "Write in your little memorandum book, *polygamy*, so we will not overlook it, and we'll talk about that later."

When the coffee and cookies were served, the missionaries "did justice to the cookies, but refused the coffee." Schilperoort said, "That isn't against your religion, is it?" Elder Nibley said,

"Yes, we are taught not to drink coffee." The man responded, "I would never join your church, then. I couldn't live without my coffee."

"Now write that in your book," Elder Nibley said.

Of the experience, Elder Richards comments: "It was worth a lot to me in my future missionary work. How my companion could make polygamy and coffee so interesting on our first visit that we could get back into that home and then convince them that the Lord had restored his Church and kingdom upon the earth—it was a great lesson to me." When Elder Nibley finally said to the man, "Get out your memo book," all his questions had been answered, the missionary had been in command all the way, and the family joined the Church. (*Blue Book*, pp. 40-41.)

Although his diligent labors preserved him from homesickness, Elder Richards notes in his journal the letters he received from home and something of their contents. Because of the impact it had upon him, the one received from his father on April 9, 1906, is notable. From it he quotes:

> Last night, I dreamed of seeing the Savior and embracing him. The feelings I cannot describe, but I think it was a touch of heaven. I never expect anything better hereafter. The love of man for woman cannot compare with it. May we be faithful and make every sacrifice necessary . . . to live in his presence forever. (LGR *Journal*, vol. I, p. 52.)

To this excerpt, Elder Richards adds that which is reminiscent of his father's early commitment to the Lord, and it bound him even more firmly to follow in his father's path. "I resolve that, with the help of the Lord, I will try as nearly as my knowledge goes to serve God and assist in every way possible, that I might obtain the blessings about which my father speaks." (LGR *Journal*, vol. I, p. 53.)

Two days later, when President Grant and his wife arrived at the Rotterdam railroad station, Elder Richards handed him a telegram that had come to the mission home. It read that three vacancies in the Quorum of the Twelve—Taylor, Cowley, and Merrill—had been filled by Richards, Whitney, and McKay. "I

wonder who this man Richards is," said the president. He then
mentioned two of Elder Richards's uncles, Franklin S. and
Charles C., along with his father, George F., and decided that it
must be the latter. Elder Richards felt that because of his father's
dream it must surely be he, and so it proved to be. Of his father's
call Elder Richards wrote, "I do feel to thank the Lord, and hope
and pray that I may remain true, virtuous, and industrious in
the Lord's work, that my joy may be united with his." (LGR
Journal, vol. I, p. 53.) To mark the occasion, President Grant and
his wife took Elder Richards sightseeing in a hired carriage.

Concurrently with his new resolve, Elder Richards received
an increase in responsibilities. He now handled all emigrations,
and in the mission president's absence he assigned new missionaries to their fields of labor. President Trayner went home on
April 23, 1906, and Alexander Nibley succeeded him (1906-07).
The new president also traveled much on mission business, and
while he was in Liege, Belgium, an emergency arose. Elder
Welker, who had arrived in Holland with Elder Richards, came
down with smallpox in Groningen. All the missionaries fasted
for him, and the mission secretary continued his fast until noon
of the next day. That night, Elder Welker died.

Alone at the mission office, Elder Richards asked President
John P. Lillywhite of the Rotterdam Branch to accompany him
to Groningen. They tried to have the burial deferred until it
could be done properly, but because of the danger of contagion
they were unable to do so, and the missionary was buried
"fourth class" in a stacked grave. The elders from Rotterdam and
two from Groningen (including Abraham J. Gold, who had
nursed the sick elder until he entered the hospital) carried him to
his grave. Because there was no marker, they carved the date of
his death along with his initials and theirs upon the crude box.

Under the circumstances many would have thought all had
been done that could be, but Elder Richards did not feel
content. He obtained permission from the mayor to have the
elder's body taken up, put in a good casket, and buried "first
class," a thing the mayor said had never been done in his time
for a case of death by smallpox. The elders then returned to
Rotterdam.

Two weeks later Elder Gold died of the same disease. "It is a terrible thing to think of," Elder Richards said, as he left again for Groningen. He arranged for the dead elder to be buried by the side of his companion, Elder Welker. When that sad work was done, he wrote letters to the parents of the young men telling of their work and testimonies and giving words of comfort. (LGR *Journal*, vol. I, pp. 56-60.) He never forgot these elders who gave their lives in service to the Lord. On his second mission five years later he raised money through the returned missionaries from Holland for a large stone marker and for a wrought iron fence to place around the graves, and when he returned to Holland in 1959 and 1980 he visited there to pay his respects to them.

Already an effective missionary with a command of the language, and having proven himself a capable administrator, Elder Richards was called on September 18, 1906, to preside over the Rotterdam Branch, where he served for seven months. He worked diligently to reactivate members who had fallen away. Nearly six hundred Saints were listed on the books, but attendance was low. If a member was absent from church, he would call at the home, ask if there was illness or need, and let the person know he had been missed. There seemed to be no limit to his diligence. During one three-and-a-half-month period he made 223 such home visits.

As he worked with his people, he grew in tenderness and love. His journal shows that time and again he gave money to the poor. He later told his mother that he used more of his means for them than for himself. When children were ill, he watched at their bedsides so the parents could rest. (LGR *Journal*, vol. I, p. 91.) When Brother de Waal was sick and not able to eat, Elder Richards "bought five pounds of Germade . . . and made some mush, toasted bread, and left him eating nicely." (Vol. I, p. 93.) He and the elders administered, blessed, and comforted wherever there was need. He sensed the fulfillment of the words of Elder B. H. Roberts in his setting apart blessing—that his love for the Dutch people, and their dearness to his heart, would be the "token" by which he would know that "the Spirit of the Lord was resting upon him."

While the branch business took the major portion of his time, he continued to proselyte, and for the period he served in Rotterdam as mission secretary and then as branch president, conversions resulting from his own contacts numbered forty. In the ensuing years their descendants have multiplied by the hundreds. In the Abraham Seiverts family alone there were 154 direct descendants in the Church in 1970. Thirty-five of these had filled full-time missions and four had been stake missionaries. One of the forty-three family units had kept two Indian children in their home, and one of these was then in the mission field. (*Blue Book*, p. 45.)

On April 11, 1907, Elder Richards was sent to preside over the Amsterdam Conference (district president). There he initiated an administrative approach to the work which he has used in each local leadership position he has held. The technique (which will be demonstrated more fully in later chapters) consisted of calling in his priesthood leaders, taking inventory of all members —active and inactive alike—and then putting everyone to work in some capacity or other.

In all administrative positions in the Church, there are negative aspects of the work. Elder Richards dealt with family quarrels, crying women, and contention, including "such a terrible condition of babbling in one branch" that it took two and a half hours to bring it under control. (LGR *Journal*, vol. I, p. 186.) Solving these problems gave him experience and wisdom, but far outweighing them were the great spiritual times that brought him joy. Preaching with freedom, sparring with ministers ("Talk about your fun!" he says of these), convincing a stranger that the gospel is true—these were the activities he loved. Of the ordinances he performed—blessing little children, baptizing and confirming new converts, administering to the sick—he writes, "What a joy above words to express is the great privilege of officiating in the name of God the Father and His Son!" (LGR *Journal*, vol. I, p. 202.)

This deep sense of gratitude became a keynote in his life. He recalls that while serving in Amsterdam he "used to go over to the little chapel, and kneel down back of the pulpit and thank the Lord for the privilege of being in the mission field, and for the opportunity . . . to bear witness of the gospel. It seemed such a part of me that my heart would just bubble over." The joy with which he began his mission, and which he labored so faithfully to retain, now found permanent lodging within him, and he knew from this time on that, for him, the Lord's work would take precedence over everything else in his life. It seems that this same joy gave to his spirit its singular and appealing quality of radiance.

He continued to study the scriptures. He drew a great lesson from Luke 10:5-7, wherein the Savior's words read: "And into whatsoever house ye enter, first say, Peace be to this house. And if the son of peace be there, your peace shall rest upon it. . . . Go not from house to house." Elder Richards explains his application of this scripture as follows:

> I figured that if I were in a home one night, and the peace of heaven rested there, it was my responsibility to bring the family into the Church. If I didn't, it was because the devil was a better salesman than I. Now, I visited a home in Amsterdam, and on our first evening, tears rolled down the lady's cheeks because of what we said. Upon leaving, I said, "If your minister learns we've been here, he will tell you we are the wickedest people on earth, and if you believe him, you will not want us to return."
>
> That is just what happened. A daughter from that home met one of the Saints on the street and said, "When Mr. Richards comes to see us on Tuesday, Mother and Father will not be home." So we made another appointment for Tuesday, and called at their place on Monday. I put on all the smiles I could and said, "Pardon us, but something came up for Tuesday and we couldn't come. We knew you spend each evening at home, so we didn't think it would make any difference if we came Monday or Tuesday." We were in, and we brought that whole family into the Church.

A month after Elder Richards had begun his work in Amsterdam, Sylvester Q. Cannon succeeded Alexander Nibley as president of the mission, and toward the close of Elder Richards's mission he traveled with President Cannon to Liege for a conference. After the meetings, the elders left for Brussels and there

attended the opera with President Cannon, who had with him a
book from which he explained what was happening. (In his journals, at various points in his mission Elder Richards notes visits
to operas, museums, galleries, and such places of historical interest as Waterloo and Delftshaven.) He came to know and love
President Cannon and his wife and family. (In fact, so greatly did
the elder admire the president's qualities of refinement, optimism,
and pleasantness that he hoped sometime to find and marry a
girl who had the same excellent nature in feminine counterpart.)

Elder Richards was released from his mission in January,
1908. As he prepared to leave, he poignantly expressed the two-
way love that existed between him and the Saints. His journal
entry is dated January 5, 1908:

> In the evening meeting I spoke first to give my farewell. As I
> walked into the pulpit and viewed the faces of the brothers and
> sisters all sitting with awe to see what was to be said, a feeling
> came over me that I had never had before. To think how I had
> preached them the word of the Lord with all the power the Lord
> had given me. . . . I had learned to love them, and they in turn
> placed me far above what I really am. . . . I never in my life felt
> happier than under the influence of the Spirit present this evening.
> (LGR *Journal*, vol. II, pp. 149-50.)

Elder Richards now knew fully what President Anthon H.
Lund had meant when he said, "The people will love you because of what you bring to them." Before leaving Amsterdam, he
visited his friends for a final good-bye. He went to the home of
one little woman. She was so short that she had to look way up
to him. He had been the first missionary in that home and had
brought the whole family into the Church. When he went to
leave, tears rolled down her cheeks and she said, "Elder Richards,
it was hard to see my daughter leave for Zion a few months ago,
but it is much harder to see you go."

He went to bid another convert good-bye, a man who stood
erect in the uniform of his country. This friend got down on his
knees and took the elder's hand in his, hugged and kissed it, and
bathed it with his tears of gratitude for the gospel the missionary
had brought. Elder Richards said upon leaving him, "I wept all

the way from Amsterdam to Rotterdam, thinking that I might never see those friends of mine again. It was much harder to leave them than it was my own family when I left on my mission."

In Rotterdam he visited thirty or so of his families for a last good-bye, then left Holland on the Batavier ship bound for England. When he arrived in Liverpool he no longer wore his beard. He attended a Sunday meeting, and President Charles W. Penrose, now president of the European Mission, called upon him to speak and include a few words in Dutch. He wrote that he felt like "a prisoner turned loose." English was now his foreign tongue. After the meeting, the president appointed Brigham A. Seare as president of the company, with Elders Richards and Sloan as counselors. They sailed January 23, 1908, in the S.S. *Canada* of the Dominion Line. There were twenty-six in their company, including an old friend, Stanley F. Kimball.

It proved to be a rough crossing. As they neared the American shore a terrible storm arose. Gigantic waves rolled about, and everything not attached to the deck was thrown around. A sister returning from Scandinavia said, "Brother Richards, you don't seem a bit worried." He answered, "Well, I don't know what's going to happen to you and the rest of the passengers, but I feel just as much at ease as if I were sitting in my mother's parlor. I had a promise that if I filled an honorable mission I'd return home in safety, and I have had the assurance that my mission was acceptable to the Lord, so I am going home." (*Blue Book*, p. 49, and interview.)

His father met him in Chicago (where his brother George was studying dentistry), and after visiting there they traveled home together. They shared a Pullman on the train. LeGrand recorded: "Of course we had prayer, and Father took the lead. He prayed that the Lord would help me find a companion my equal, so we could become parents of some of the choice spirits of heaven." (*Blue Book*, p. 50.) They arrived in Salt Lake on February 12, 1908, six days after his twenty-second birthday. Of his homecoming, he wrote: "It was snowing in fine style. . . . Joel was there to meet us. He had grown so; he is two inches taller

*Elder George F. Richards with his family at time of LeGrand's
return from Holland (LeGrand stands behind his father).*

than I am. We then took the [street]car to Third [Avenue]. I got
off the car first; all were looking from the window. Little Nina
ran out to meet me, and oh how strange it did seem to see so
many little sisters, and so grown up! I could hardly believe my
eyes." (LGR *Journal*, vol. III, p. 23.)

One day soon after, as he sat at dinner and saw what his
mother had put before him, he wept. She said, "What's the
matter, son? Aren't you happy to be home?" LeGrand answered,
"Yes, Mother, but I'm looking at what you're feeding me, and
I'm thinking what those poor Dutch friends of mine have to live
on, and I can't help but weep."

LeGrand not only thought of them and wept for them but
continued to serve them. On February 25, two weeks after his
arrival home, he and his mother did the temple work for fifteen relatives of his Dutch friends in Holland, people who had
died without a knowledge of the gospel. During the ensuing years
he lent money for many to immigrate to Utah, prepared and
signed their bonds, and then helped them to find work and to

make the difficult transition from old to new country after they arrived.

Both his Eighth Ward in Salt Lake and Tooele Ward held homecoming services for him. The latter took place on March 15, 1908, where his parents, his brother Joel, and his sister Nina were present. He spoke with complete freedom as he told of his experiences in Holland. He voiced his deep gratitude for the privilege of serving there. He expressed his great desire never to lose the Spirit he then felt, and he hoped the Lord would send him on a mission often enough so that the Spirit could always remain with him.

Miss Ina Jane Ashton, a former teacher at the Tooele District School, had become acquainted with the Richards family through one of her pupils, Mamie Richards. She was in attendance at the homecoming and was much impressed. In the evening she was among the young people who gathered for a fireside at the home of John W. Tate, where LeGrand and Joel stayed that night. Both she and LeGrand say that it was "love at first sight" when they met.

It was a month later when LeGrand and Joel went to Saltair, and there LeGrand danced with "Miss Ashton." Looking back he recalls, "She was so sweet to me, and those little piercing brown eyes of hers did something to me, and she seemed to respond." When Ina suggested he come to see her and she would bake him a pie, he lost little time in doing so. He recorded in his journal, "I had a talk with Ina that I don't think I shall forget. It has been a happy day for me."

There followed many talks, meetings, canyon and beach parties, and dances. LeGrand says, "We had a very happy courtship."

Chapter 5

The Partnership

1908-1913

When LeGrand Richards proposed to Ina Jane Ashton she ran from him, for his words were not what she had wanted or expected to hear—"There will always be one that will come ahead of you." When he caught her, he had some explaining to do. "Ina," he said, "I had such a wonderful experience in the mission field, I almost feel that I walked and talked with the Lord. My duty to him and his Church will have to come first. If you want second place, it is yours." After his explanation, she wanted that place.

With true understanding she accepted his commitment to the Lord, and with total sincerity she gave her promise to him. Although in later years she would tell her children that he belonged to the Church and they belonged to her, yet they were sweethearts in the finest sense of the word. In this dainty and adorable girl LeGrand had "met his equal," as his father had prayed that he would.

Ina was a "little bundle of sweetness" (standing a mere five-foot-three), with soft black-brown eyes and an abundance of dark brown hair—a perfect complement to LeGrand's bigness and strength. His eyes were blue, his hair rich and dark, and he stood just under six feet tall. Totally feminine, Ina liked pretty things—flowers, jewelry, clothes—and took pride in "always looking nice." Her disposition was cheerful and optimistic, her nature sensitive and refined. She would not laugh at the crude or unseemly, and she tended to block out the negative and the bad. Of a firm, no-nonsense turn of mind, she had a streak of "darling spunk"—high spirits that held no rancor or bite. It was probably this spunk that sent her running from LeGrand when he proposed. She was a creative cook and had already reached his "heart" with her even-then-famous lemon pies. She loved babies, little children, and big families.

Of her inner character, it is said that she was spiritual and capable of deep devotion. In the patriarchal blessing she had recently received (April 19, 1908), she was told, "The Lord is pleased with thine integrity. . . . thou shalt secure unto thyself the companion of thy choice, and the time is not far distant when thou shalt be called to labor among those upon whom much responsibility rests, therefore, thou shalt reflect often upon the past, present, and future, that you may realize your position, and comprehend the blessings promised unto the faithful." Perhaps it was these last words that inspired her life's motto: "Keep the commandments; it pays good dividends."

The temperament and character which Ina Jane Ashton brought to the future marriage partnership on that warm summer evening of August 9, 1908 (and which would grow and mature in their future lives together) were traits and qualities which had been nurtured in the climate of a great home and fostered by parents of high principle and intrinsic goodness. She was born on September 14, 1886, and was raised in a two-family home environment; her mother Cora Lindsay was the second wife of Edward T. Ashton, prominent contractor-builder and bishop of the Fifteenth Ward.

Cora had come to Salt Lake with her convert family from Bridgewater (near Morgantown), North Carolina, when only seventeen, bringing with her memories of gracious Southern living and its disruption when the Civil War claimed husbands, sons, and sweethearts for the conflict. (Her own father served as an officer throughout the war.) Soon after their arrival in Salt Lake, Cora was asked to help Effie, first wife of Edward T. Ashton, when her first child was born, and it was Effie who suggested and approved (after a full day of prayer and soul-searching) the pretty Southern girl as Edward's second wife. Effie Morris bore him five children; Cora, twelve, of whom Ina was the second. The two wives were mutually loving and helpful to each other and came to be best of friends, a fact which contributed

greatly to the harmony and happiness of the two families. They
also learned about sharing and sacrifice when Edward served a
mission in Wales. His letters from there were treasured by the
wives and children alike. Ina remembered them throughout life,
although she was still a small child while he was gone.

Edward's mission to Wales was especially significant because
the Ashtons were of Welsh descent. They had a great love for
music and met often in the evenings to sing. They were a handsome group and were quick of wit and full of fun. Children loved
to visit there, where grandfather Ashton "carved beautiful white
horses from their mashed potatoes," where cakes were baking in
the oven of the black coal range which dominated the big sunny
kitchen, and where children must not dance about or tussle lest
"the cake should fall." They liked to "lower notes on strings
down the long, dark clothes-chute to the basement or venture
down it themselves." (Recounted by Edward's granddaughter,
Mercedes R. Kiepe.) It was a happy home which, with its harmonious and fun-loving atmosphere, played an important part in
developing cheerful, optimistic attitudes in all the children while
allowing for high spirits and individual expression and growth.

Ina enjoyed books, sometimes to the exclusion of household
chores. She said, "We used to go to the public library and bring
home three or four books. Then we'd go into the corn field
where we were hidden, so our parents couldn't see us to call or
bother us" (As told to Gerry Avant, *Church News*, Sept. 28,
1974). She read Alcott, Kipling and Stevenson as a youngster
and the focus of her reading continued in the field of literature
in later life. The English writers were her favorites—Shakespeare,
Browning, Ruskin, Carlyle. She also collected quotations and
poems from many sources and copied them in a small black
book. These reflect her desire to be uplifted, motivated, and
inspired.

After elementary school she attended LDS University
(actually high school with a teacher's normal course added). She
graduated with a teacher's certificate and was interviewed for a
position out at the Tooele District School. The superintendent
queried her: "What would you do if the children became irri-

LeGrand and his sweetheart, Ina Jane Ashton, about the time of their marriage.

table, or upset, or needed disciplining?" With no hesitation she answered, "I'd throw open the windows and let them exercise." She was hired. Several grades were included in her class, and some of the boys were bigger than she, but she kept them in line and successfully completed the year.

While in Tooele she became acquainted with the George F. Richards family, whose daughter Mamie (as previously mentioned) was in her class. Mamie's recollections of Ina as a teacher are that she was skilled and appealing. She also remembers the Hiawatha costume Ina made for her.

Although the superintendent wanted Ina back for a second year, she did not return. She had been receiving attentions from a non-LDS doctor in the area, and her father therefore thought it best for her to come back to Salt Lake City. This she did. She then worked for him at the Ashton Improvement Company, her father's expanding contractor business which later furnished the exterior stone for the Utah State Capitol (1915), the Church Administration Building (1917), and other important structures. (*Deseret News*, February 20, 1923, p. B-1.)

During this time LeGrand had been serving his mission in Holland, returning to Salt Lake on February 12, 1908. Shortly after that, Ina and he met and began courting. When Ina accepted LeGrand's proposal it was a time of great joy for him. That night he recorded his entry in shorthand (ordinary words would not suffice). "I asked Ina to be mine," he transcribes, "and she gave me the kind of an answer that has made me the happiest man in the world ever since. It seems too good to be true." (LGR *Journal*, vol. III, p. 23, and interview.)

It was some time before LeGrand gave Ina a diamond. He wanted it to be just right, it must be carefully selected, and money must be earned to pay cash for it. (He worked temporarily in the Church Tithing Office but soon found steady employment keeping books for Pratt and McBeth Brokerage at sixty dollars a month.) He tells that one of his brothers went to Park Davis Jewelers to see what he had chosen and then said, "Oh, you wouldn't pay that much for an engagement ring!" LeGrand responded, "If I don't have much in the way of house or furniture when I get married, I can add to that, but I'll never be able to add to Ina's engagement ring because I'll only get engaged once." So he paid a lot more for the diamond than his brother thought he should. LeGrand presented the ring to Ina in her parent's home at 138 South Seventh West, and, he says, "She ran to show her mother what she got."

The couple spent the next month talking over plans, looking at lots, apartments, and houses. Hardly able to contain the happiness of sharing their many dreams, LeGrand wrote, "These are times never to be forgotten. How strange it does seem, but oh, how sweet!" (LGR *Journal*, vol. III, p. 56.)

It was shortly after the above entry was made that LeGrand discontinued the daily recording of events in his First Mission journals—vols. I, II, and III. For the five-year interval before he left for his next mission, he wrote a careful summary of business and investment activities, family happenings, labors with his beloved Dutch people in Utah, and his Church assignments and calls. (Vol. III, end part.) His meeting attendance was regular, he was a faithful ward (home) teacher, he occasionally had speaking engagements, and he continued to meet with his father's prayer circle at the temple, to which he had been an invited member since his return from Holland—a privilege which he valued very highly. George F. Jr. was also a member at various times.[1]

Another experience that meant a great deal to LeGrand was when his father took him to visit his mother (LeGrand's grandmother), Nanny Longstroth Richards, who, as Willard Richards's wife, had known the Prophet Joseph Smith very well. From her lips LeGrand heard the impressive story: "I was in the meeting following the martyrdom of the Prophet, when Sidney Rigdon spoke and claimed that he should take the Prophet's place as head of the Church." She said that "when Brigham Young

---

[1] "It was not uncommon, at the beginning of the century, for some of the apostles to preside over prayer groups that met regularly in the temple. The George F. Richards prayer circle had earlier been presided over by President John Taylor. Meetings took place once a week. Naturally those who belonged to the same prayer circle came to feel a close relationship." (Leonard J. Arrington and Davis Bitton, "Apostle's Life a Link to Pioneer Times," *Church News*, April 19, 1980, p. 13.)

spoke, he sounded like the Prophet Joseph and looked like him, so we all knew whom the Lord wanted to lead his people."

On August 16, 1908, LeGrand was sustained as superintendent of the Twenty-seventh Ward Sunday School, succeeding William T. Atkin. He served in that position until he left Salt Lake.

He continued to work for Pratt and McBeth until the first week of April 1909. His wages had increased from $60.00 to $110.00 a month, with another raise promised. He recorded that he made several investments in mining stock and "made considerable gain at first, but had about the same experience as most men who follow that kind of business, and [I] finally quit the [stock investment] game for all time to come. . . . This makes me about even on all my investments in stock up to date, having made quite a little on Consolidated Wagon and Mach[ine] Co. stock before I left on my first mission." (LGR *Journal*, vol. III, pp. 57-58.)

That same April he left Salt Lake for Portland, Oregon, to accept a position as assistant secretary of Portland Cement Company, with Aman Moore as manager and Alex Nibley (his former mission president) as secretary. There he prepared to have Ina join him. The following month he returned to Salt Lake, and on Wednesday, May 19, 1909, he and Ina were married. His father records the event in his journal. He had attended a meeting with the First Presidency and two others of the Twelve in the upper room of the temple. "I went downstairs at the conclusion of our meeting, 2:00 P.M., and solemnized the marriage of my Son LeGrand to and with Sister Ina Jane Ashton in the presence of about fifteen of the relatives. I there bid them good-bye as I would not be able to attend the reception, and they would be leaving for Portland, Oregon, before my return." (GFR *Diary*, vol. 12, p. 109.) George F. left that night for conference assignments in the Uintah Basin. The newly married couple, along with other family members, remained in the temple to do sealings for "our dead, the Longstroths."

The couple were entertained at a family dinner in the Ashton home that evening and left for Portland the next day. With the journey by train and some beautiful walks among the flowering shrubs and trees in the Portland area, their honeymoon was to become a sweet memory to them. Ina carried among her things a plaque which they hung in each of their homes until it was lost in a later move. Its message has been given before each marriage ceremony LeGrand has performed. The words are neatly copied in Ina's *Black Book* (p. 77).

> Whoe'er thou art that entereth here,
>   Forget the struggling world
> And every trembling fear.
>
> Take from thy heart each evil thought,
>   And all that selfishness
> Within thy life has wrought.
>
> For once inside this place thou'lt find
>   No barter, servant's fear,
> Nor master's voice unkind.
>
> Here all are kin of God above—
>   Thou, too, dear heart; and here
> The rule of life is love.
>   (Max Ehrmann.)

Again LeGrand came to the notice of a Church leader. He tells that when he first went to Portland, he met Melvin J. Ballard and his wife, Martha. They were on the same train, and were going to Portland for President Ballard to succeed Nephi Pratt as president of the Northwestern States Mission. The mission secretary was Hemming Mortensen. "I audited the mission books, balanced the accounts, and set up a new bookkeeping system for him," LeGrand says. "Monthly thereafter I helped get out the mission financial reports." As in Holland, his secretarial skills made possible some valuable service to a mission office. It is not surprising that shortly afterwards, when President Ballard reorganized the presidency of the Portland Branch, he appointed LeGrand, whom he had come to rely on, as the president. Alex Nibley was called to be first counselor, and Lehi Pratt, second.

Martha Ballard and Ina became good friends, and when the Richardses' first baby, Mercedes, was born on President Ballard's birthday, Martha was there to help Ina. Elder M. Russell Ballard remembers the story and further recalls that his own father, son of Melvin J., was LeGrand's home teaching companion in Portland, an opportunity he greatly valued.

The cement company engaged a bonding firm to float a bond issue for them. LeGrand gave up his secretarial position to sell bonds on a straight commission basis in a two-county territory. He and Alex Nibley were the two top salesmen in the venture until the company stopped construction of the plant to core-drill lime-rock deposits, fearing that there wouldn't be sufficient rock to justify building the plant. As a result, some of the orders LeGrand had taken were cancelled. Disappointed, he accepted stock in settlement of bond commissions due him. He afterwards regretted not holding on to the stock, since the company became very prosperous.

LeGrand was not only successful in selling bonds but was ever alert for opportunities to "sell" Mormonism. In the course of his work he received letters of introduction from some of the prominent bankers in Portland, so he had no difficulty in contacting other important business and professional men. One day he called on a doctor in Oregon City who had been city mayor and president of the Chamber of Commerce. He was just ready to call on some of his patients, and he invited LeGrand to go along in his rubber-tired buggy pulled by a fine team of horses.

As they rode along, LeGrand told of a company directors' meeting that had just been held at which Mr. Charles W. Nibley from Salt Lake City had been present. "Who is this man Nibley —is he a Mormon?" the doctor asked. "Yes," LeGrand replied, "He is the Presiding Bishop of the Mormon Church."

The doctor made some very derogatory statements about the Mormons, then started on the Mormon missionaries. LeGrand let him finish and then said, "Doctor, have you ever met a Mormon?"

"No," he replied.

"Have you ever read a Mormon book written by a Mormon?"

"No."

"Now, Doctor, I want to tell you something," LeGrand said. "You are sitting right here at the side of a Mormon missionary." The man's face colored. "You need not feel embarrassed," LeGrand went on. "I qualified you. You have never met a Mormon — you have never read a book written by a Mormon. Now, I would like to tell you what the Mormons really are."

When the two men returned to Oregon City, the doctor tossed the lines to LeGrand, asked him to drive his team to the livery stable, and said, "If that is Mormonism, I could be a good Mormon — don't ever come to Oregon City without calling on me." (*Blue Book*, p. 52.)

When baby Mercedes was old enough to make the journey, Ina took her to Salt Lake to show her off to the families and to visit with her folks. It was a lonely LeGrand who remained in Portland and wrote letters to them every day, then anxiously awaited Ina's answers. In one, dated April 13, 1910, he wrote: "I met the postman at 7:30, but no letter, so I patiently waited for his next trip, and you should have seen the change in [my] expression. Oh, Ina . . . I do love you both so very, very much." He received a letter from his father and wrote of its contents, "Father says he thinks [Mercedes] is so sweet, but so little and dainty that he can hardly think she is for this world. I didn't like him to say that, but her Daddy certainly believes she is going to remain with us. . . ." Always solicitous of Ina's comfort and health, he adds, "I have made up my mind, Ina Dear, that as soon as we get straight with the world, I am going to have a girl [help you], and my Darling is going to have her time with Papa and . . . Mercedes." (April 17, 1910.)

Although he desired to provide help for Ina, there were few times in their lives, except for mission home experiences, when paid help was available; but in lieu of such help, LeGrand provided loving service himself. Of this he says matter-of-factly:

> While the children were babies, I don't think my wife ever got up at night unless they were sick. I figured that if she took care of the kiddies in the day (and it is a wrestle to keep them happy), and I just had book work to do, that I could afford to spell her off at

*Ina with the couple's first
child, Mercedes.*

night. So, if a baby cried, I'd be out of bed in a hurry; if it was a
bottle they needed, I'd get it; or I'd change their pants. As long as
they weren't sick, I relieved her of the responsibility of caring for
them at night.

Though he claims not to have helped the children when sick, the
record is to the contrary, for each child tells of his gentle care in
times of illness—how he tucked and soothed them; how he
rubbed aching legs; and how he blessed them. His love for them
all has been deep, sure, and ever-present.

Some time after Ina returned, Orson Romney called on LeGrand and offered him $125.00 a month to return to Salt Lake and work for his father's firm. The couple discussed where they wanted to raise their children and they decided that for that purpose Salt Lake City, with their families and friends and with the Saints all around them, was preferable to any other locale. Accordingly they returned to Salt Lake in October 1910.

LeGrand began work with the George Romney Lumber Company and also kept books and made collections for several other firms on the side. His transportation from the apartment on Fourth Avenue to work and for calls consisted of a bicycle. While the couple lived there, a second daughter, Effie Norinne, was born on August 18, 1911, a time partly remembered because it was the very day Grandfather George F. shaved off his beard. ("Now Papa can smile," his daughter Edna said.) LeGrand's diligence and hard work made it possible for him to pool funds with his brother George and build a duplex on S Street, his family occupying the lower floor, and George's the upper. They moved in on Ina's birthday, September 14, 1912, and on December 31 their third daughter, Marian Louise, was born.

During that year LeGrand was stricken with the dread disease smallpox. He was quarantined and ran extremely high temperatures. His father was very concerned and recorded LeGrand's progress day by day. Elder James E. Talmage of the Council of the Twelve kept in close touch also, and he instructed Ina in shading the light from LeGrand's face to avoid pitting from the illness. LeGrand finally recovered, and he carries only one small pit mark, on his forehead.

While working at the Lumber Company, he had a number of very successful investment experiences. He was approached by various businessmen with a view to obtaining his services or to begin new companies. Most of these he turned down, but he decided to join with his friend and former employer E. H. McBeth and his present company's yard foreman, Alma Brown, to begin a lumber company of their own. They later admitted a Mr. Dailey "who has lots of money," so they could potentially increase and enlarge their operation and also "handle a coal business if desired." LeGrand recorded: "The four of us together purchased an acre and a quarter of ground situated on the east side of 11th East near 12th South. [He evidently transposed the figures in 21, because the actual address was 1969 South.] We paid $3500.00, $300.00 down and $25.00 per month with 6 percent int[erest] on the deferred payments." (LGR *Journal*, vol. III, p. 66.) Mr. McBeth had agreed to furnish fifty thousand dollars cash, and they would pay him interest on his investment and divide profits. There was a railroad spur right in front of the property, and there was irrigation water on the place—an ideal location. The prospects for a solid and lucrative business with highly compatible associates were excellent.

At that point, in late August 1913, LeGrand was called as president of the Netherlands Mission.

Business plans were set aside, and with the approval of the other partners LeGrand took over the property and held it until his return from Europe. He sold his share in the S Street duplex to his brother Joel and wife Georgina; then, for the balance LeGrand owed on the duplex, sold Joel's note to the George Romney Lumber Company at 10 percent discount, "receiving $1,000.00 cash, which enabled me to straighten up all my affairs before leaving for my mission." (LGR *Journal*, vol. III, p. 65.) He was receiving rent from a home on Tenth Avenue which he had purchased by trade of a quarter-section of land near Tooele that his father had given him. (George and Joel received a like amount from George F. at the same time.)

LeGrand had been ordained a seventy on his birthday the year before (February 6, 1912). Now he was released from his positions as ward clerk and parents class teacher, having held the dual jobs for the year before his present mission call. He and Ina then made final preparations to leave for Holland with their three little girls on November 13, 1913. He wrote: "President Joseph F. Smith asked me to go for two or three years, while President Lyman said if I was a good President, they might keep me a long time." (LGR *Journal*, vol. IV, p. 1.) He and Ina were set apart for the mission by his father, George F. Richards. The

Dutch people of Ogden and Salt Lake entertained them and presented them with money gifts. In their combined opinion, Elder Richards was the only possible choice for the position to which he had been called, an expression of confidence which pleased him very much.

The family traveled by train to Chicago in company with Elder Grant M. Romney, who was going to Holland with them. There they visited a missionary, Lutzen Buma, one of LeGrand's Dutch converts. At Niagara, Elder Romney, Ina, and little Mercedes, "went down under the Falls on the Canadian side," while LeGrand tended Norinne and baby Marian. Part of his enjoyment on the journey was in his showing the new places to Ina. On the train from Toronto to Montreal they found that there were only upper berths left on the Pullman cars; sporty male travelers were everywhere; and the children were tired and cross. "We were about to despair," he wrote, but "at this point, the gentleman having [one of] the lower [berths] . . . proffered to let us have his . . . we couldn't help but feel that the Lord was helping us out of our trouble." (LGR *Journal*, vol. IV, pp. 3-4.)

They sailed from Montreal on November 18. The water was rough, and alternately, for the entire voyage, each member of the family was sick and "helping the fishes." LeGrand fared best and gave invaluable help with the children. All were greatly relieved to see land along the western coast of Wales, where the hills were green and beautiful—a sight of great interest to Ina because of her Welsh descent. Three hours later they landed in Liverpool, where they spent the night at the Lord Nelson Hotel. They reported as a family at Durham House, the Mission headquarters, the next morning for their instructions.

One item discussed with President Hyrum M. Smith concerned the release of Acting President Hair of the Netherlands Mission. LeGrand was told that he could release him as soon as he himself was acquainted with mission affairs, but he was sensitive to the situation and suggested that, inasmuch as Brother Hair had been appointed temporary president by the head of the European Mission, he would likely feel better about it if he were released by that same authority. President Smith agreed and said he would await word from President Richards and take care of the matter at the proper time. (LGR *Journal*, vol. IV, pp. 6-7.)

After their mission briefing, LeGrand and Ina took the children by train to Hull, England, wired President Hair the estimated time of their arrival, and set sail for Rotterdam.

Chapter 6

Netherlands Mission President

1913-1916

On his arrival in Rotterdam on Friday, November 28, 1913, the new mission president wrote:

> Soon after we awakened this morning we saw land and were soon sailing up the River Maas. . . . I noticed many changes since I was here before . . . new districts which have been built up, factories, docks, etc. As we neared the dock we saw about a dozen elders waiting, and I waved the first greeting. . . . As we came closer I learned that I had known President [Thomas C.] Hair in Salt Lake. . . . I also picked Elder West out, the secretary of the mission, although I had not met him. . . . The boys had a carriage there for myself and family and a *dienstman* for all the baggage. We had a pretty ride coming to headquarters and Ina was much delighted with the appearance of her new hometown. We found things pleasant at *Crooswijkschesingel* 7b, the mission headquarters, although almost destitute of the little touches that would make it appear that a woman had ever lived there. (LGR *Journal*, vol. IV, pp. 7-9.)

The mission home was no longer near the cattle market, as on President Richards's first time in Holland, but was in a "nice area of town." In front of the building was a beautiful canal with grass leading down to it and fenced off. To the delight of the children, who stayed out in the cold air to watch, a few straggling ducks and geese waddled about near the icy water.

While Presidents Richards and Hair turned to mission business, Ina followed the non-Mormon girl who cared for the home and together they went from room to room. Ina's homemaking instincts were quickened and she made mental note of all the things she'd like to change—a carpet here, crisp curtains there, homey touches everywhere. And the kitchen! It needed a scour-

ing and color. And how was one to bake pies when the stove
had no oven? She looked in the cupboards for such basics as
baking powder and spice. There were none.

At this juncture she sensed the girl's disapproval of her
presence in the kitchen. The girl even stated her terms for stay-
ing on: she must have full responsibility for the kitchen and for
all food preparation—terms with which Ina, the born cook,
could not agree. So it happened that one of President Richards's
first official acts was to hire a replacement in the home. He engaged Cathrine Witteveen from The Hague, a young woman of
excellent qualities. She came to the new mission family as one of
them. Her work and Ina's meshed harmoniously, and later when
Ina wished to travel with her husband, she could leave with confidence that home and children were safe and lovingly cared for.

President Richards searched the stores until he found baking
powder and spices for Ina's kitchen. Later, as time would allow,
he helped her to shop for "a nice green carpet," material for curtains, and other homey things.

What Cathrine was to Ina, the mission secretary, Richard B.
West, was to President Richards—a treasure. The children loved
him and called him "Daddy-Brother-West." He was thoughtful
and good to Ina. Capable in the office, he also traveled with the
president and studied and memorized with him in the early
mornings. Of the latter experience he wrote, "He had me up
before the coo-coo (mission clock) had finished its sixth squak
[sic]." (RBW *Diary*, p. 39.) Elder West did not share his president's ability with the language, and he would be so wrought up
if required to speak that his insides churned and he became ill.
He wrote, "I had considerable difficulty to talk, but Brother
Richards made up abundantly for my failures—in other words, I
built the skeleton and he put the flesh on it." (RBW *Diary*, p.
125.)

Within a week after their arrival in Rotterdam the family was
settled into a workable routine. On December 3, President
Richards arranged for Berand Teimersma to continue editing the
mission paper, *De Ster* (published since 1896). December 5 was St.
Nicholas Day for the children, separate from the religious holiday

of Christmas. St. Nick came with his helper, Black Peter, and in wooden shoes placed by the fireplace left candies and toys for good girls and boys and coal for the naughty ones. Mercedes recalls the experience. "I'm sure I deserved *Swarte Pete's* coal in my wooden shoe, and was told so, but there were toys and the letter M in real Dutch chocolate. Even a child can tell that an M has more chocolate than an N, for which I teased Norinne."

From December 6 to 15, Presidents Richards and Hair toured the mission, which no longer included Belgium as formerly. In 1913 there were four mission districts, all in Holland—Rotterdam, Amsterdam, Groningen, and Arnhem. It was to these areas that the two men now went in order to meet the missionaries and the Saints and to assess needs of those under President Richards's jurisdiction. They moved rapidly for an all-over view of people and conditions. President Richards was gratified that his facility with the language had not deserted him. He could converse with the people easily and could preach sermons which instructed and encouraged them. He was quick to praise elders who worked hard to learn the language, as he had done. Of Elder Steve Love, who had been in the field only six weeks, he said he "spoke for eight minutes and hardly made a mistake. . . . I never saw such a whirlwind with the language before." (LGR *Journal*, vol. IV, p. 106.)

Although many of the Saints he had known during his first mission had emigrated, he found former acquaintances who remembered him. One such family was that of Jacob Bloem, who asked if President Richards could remember what he had told them on his first stay in Holland. "No," he answered. Jacob said, "You told us to pay our tithing and the Lord would bless us." He then told how he had had many salary advances during the years ever since. "Well, you have had your tithing back again," the president told him, to which Jacob heartily agreed.

When the two presidents returned to Rotterdam, they found Ina's brother Henry there on his way home from the Belgian Mission. President Richards showed him about the city, took him to Amsterdam to purchase a diamond, and after his visit with the family, saw him off for America.

By then Christmas was upon them—the family's first in Holland. Interspersed with his home visits to many families— Tellekamp, Kramer, Van Santen, Grootepass, Wiegel, Romijn— President Richards consulted with President Hair, met and assigned new missionaries, attended meetings, and worked on his correspondence. Still he found time to help Ina. She loved to switch furniture around for variety, "so you were never sure which place you were in." It was December 22 when they "commenced changing things around in the mission home. Moved Ina and babies down stairs so we could have the house below and the office above. This was quite a job cleaning out old closets and destroying accumulated rubbish." It was a strategic move, for it effected a general housecleaning as well, and everything was fresh for Christmas. This penchant for moving furniture about was not merely a whim with Ina but a basic need for change and improvement in her surroundings. The attention she gave to the mission home helped to secure it against President Richards's old enemy—fleas—so that he and his family remained virtually free from that misery.

When the family arose on December 24, they found that President Hair and Elder West had left for a short holiday trip to Berlin, leaving their gifts for the family to enjoy while they were gone—a clock and vases for the mantel, dolls for Mercedes and Norinne, and a ball for Marian. After addressing cards to his fifty or so missionaries, President Richards found two home-hungry ones at his door. Although surprised to see them, he took them along to buy the candy, nuts, and tree, and after Ina's delicious dinner they helped him to trim the tree. The children hung their stockings and went to bed.

Of that Christmas, President Richards wrote: "Christmas in a foreign land, yet bright and happy with thoughts of the day, and the pleasure of our little ones." The candles on the tree were lighted, and "Marian nearly took a fit of joy." There was a sad moment too, when tissue paper caught fire on a candle and scorched the "pretty little silk waist I'd bought for Ina." In the evening all the elders from Rotterdam, along with the two from Breda, joined the family for "old-time sherbet," the sharing of family letters, and Christmas fun.

President Hair and Elder West returned from Berlin and again the two leaders traveled into the districts to further the work of the mission. Plans were made to transfer some elders and to release others. Upon their return to Rotterdam, President Richards learned that Elder Hugh R. Woolley had come to Rotterdam very ill. With Ina and Elder West he "went over to the conference office and found him just steaming from the fever." They immediately moved him to the mission home, made a bed for him in the president's office, called the doctor, and then fed him "more food than he [had] eaten for a week."

For the next three weeks (during which time President Hair left for home), they tenderly cared for him, the president often sitting on the bed, and holding him so he could breathe. This he was doing on the morning of February 7, 1914, when the sick elder asked Brother West also to sit by him. Wrote President Richards, "We held him in our arms until he died. We felt awfully bad about his death. We had done all we could."

As with the missionary deaths on his former mission, the president took charge of every sensitive detail. In order to send Elder Woolley's body home, it was necessary to have it embalmed, a practice not then common in Holland. While this was being done, President Richards and Elder West selected a fine casket and secured the necessary papers. They dressed the body in a "beautiful temple suit that I brought over with me." (LGR *Journal*, vol. IV, p. 49.) A cablegram, letters, and cards were sent to President Hyrum M. Smith of the European Mission and the parents.

Elder Woolley's cousin Franklin R. Smith, who had nearly completed his mission in Holland, was called to accompany the elder's body home. The Richards family and the missionaries bade him good-bye on February 13 and sent him with not only money from the elders with which to buy flowers for the funeral but also a prepared "Tribute to the Life and Memory of Elder Hugh R. Woolley" from President and Sister Richards to his folks.

The sickness and death of Elder Woolley left a deep impression upon the mission secretary, who wrote: "I don't think [it] will leave me so long as I have power to remember." The "strain

President of Netherlands Mission, 1913 (seated, third from left).

Graves and monument for Elders Welker and Gold at Groningen (President Richards immediately left of monument).

on nerves, loss of sleep, and close confinement has simply worn me out." (RBW *Diary*, p. 11.)

During the next months a hard and consistent routine was rarely broken. In Rotterdam, President Richards added a second Sabbath meeting to the one being held in addition to Sunday School, and he was gratified that the change actually improved attendance. When he was present he took names of strangers and made follow-up visits. He supervised the publication of tracts and missionary helps such as Parley P. Pratt's *The Voice of Warning*—and even Kelsch's *A Practical Reference*, which had been so helpful in his mission preparation. He obtained permission to purchase property in Amsterdam for a chapel and with an architect considered plans for its erection. Almost every weekend found him traveling to the districts to supervise the missionaries and their work. If he found them hesitant, discouraged, or just lazy, he'd say, "You come along with me," and off they would go tracting, with him in the lead. A powerfully motivated man, he could not abide wasted time that might yield proselyting results. (He could not understand one missionary who let his work go in order to sit and play the piano.)

He counseled his elders to work with people of the middle class; if the branches could have such members, he suggested, the poor would reach up to them, and the more moneyed social class would be more apt to come to their level. It was an approach which he later used in the Southern States Mission. He also counseled the missionaries concerning morality and relationships with women. When he occasionally found local girls trying to get the attention of his elders by pretending to faint, he sent the local brethren to pick them up—an effective method of keeping them on their feet.

Some of the president's trips delayed him past the weekend, and then he missed his family. After one such trip, he wrote: "I had been away just one week and long enough to make me mighty glad that Ina and the babies were in Rotterdam instead of Utah." (LGR *Journal*, vol. IV, p. 19.)

While the president directed the affairs of the mission and worked with Elder West, Ina and the children were fitting nicely

into their new surroundings. From the speech of their playmates
and Cathrine, the children took to the language as naturally as
the ducklings to the canals. "*Kome Kijke Moekje*," (Come look,
Mommy) they said to Ina with every new thing that came into
view from the big living-room window. In winter it had been
boys and girls skating to school with book-bags strapped to their
backs. Now, in spring, it was a boat on the canal, a cart laden
with red balls of Edam cheese jogging over the red brick street,
or children rolling large hoops or tossing wooden spindles from
sticks held in their hands. Mercedes remembers the custard cart
with its tinkling bell, the apothecary, the bakery shop where a
ground-level window let the children peek wide-eyed at the baker
and his big table of decorated cakes and tarts, and the "heavenly
aromas" that drifted out to lure them inside.

Because the children dropped their English and took to
Dutch so rapidly, Ina had to work hard to keep up in order to
understand them. She was diligent in her studies and did well.
President Richards was proud that within months of their arrival,
when she traveled to a conference with him, she could "understand and talk quite a lot."

On May 19, 1915, Elder West wrote about the fifth wedding
anniversary of the President and Ina. He was twenty-eight and
she still twenty-seven. For the occasion, Elders West and Clark
had pooled resources and sent two dozen white roses. "I had
written a little piece to go with them. When I returned to the
house, the roses had just been delivered, and I found Brother
and Sister Richards on the couch, one holding the roses and the
other reading the letter, and both crying like children." (RBW
Diary, pp. 61-62.)

In mid-July 1914, all presidents of missions in Europe came
with their respective missionaries for a conference in Rotterdam.
European Mission President Hyrum M. Smith, whom Elder West
characterized as "a man of such pleasing address and humble
manners as to peculiarly fit him for the calling of special witness
of the Lord," was the presiding officer. The conference proceedings lasted several days and included short trips, sports events for
the elders, testimony meetings and general sessions. Elder West

WERELDOORLOG.

Twintig oorlogsverklaringen.

De verschillende oorlogen in den huidigen wereldkamp begonnen:

1. Oostenrijk tegen Servië 28 Juli 1914.
2. Duitschland tegen Rusland 3 Aug.
3. Duitschland tegen Frankrijk 4 Aug.
4. Engeland tegen Duitschland 5 Aug.
5. Duitschland tegen België 5 Aug.
6. Oostenrijk tegen Rusland 7 Aug.
7. Servië tegen Duitschland 7 Aug.
8. Montenegro tegen Oostenrijk 8 Aug.
9. Montenegro tegen Duitschland 12 Aug.
10. Engeland tegen Oostenrijk 13 Aug.
11. Frankrijk tegen Oostenrijk 13 Aug.
12. Duitschland tegen Japan 19 Aug.
13. Oostenrijk tegen Japan 22 Aug.
14. Oostenrijk tegen België 28 Aug.
15. Rusland tegen Turkije 30 October.
16. Engeland tegen Turkije 2 November.
17. Frankrijk tegen Turkije 2 November.
18. Servië tegen Turkije 2 November.
19. Italië tegen Oostenrijk 23 Mei 1915.

Daar Italië zich ook in oorlog beschouwt met Duitschland, kan men aan dit lijstje gevoeglijk de 20ste oorlogsverklaring toevoegen.

reported that in one of the meetings, Presidents Smith, Christiansen (of the Scandinavian Mission), and Richards talked with such force and effect that a very fine, well-to-do man and his wife expressed a strong desire to join the Church. President Richards too expressed his feelings about the conference. "I certainly feel that my soul has been fed. To me, it has been a genuine feast of fat things. Many of the elders said this was the best meeting they ever attended."

It was only days after this "feast of fat things" that war was declared between Austria-Hungary and Serbia (July 28, 1914), and the whole pattern of existence in Europe abruptly changed.

The small cut from the evening paper, *Rotterdamsche Courant*, shows the rapidity with which country after country was drawn into the war. Its heading, *Wereldoorlog* (World War), is followed by the *Twintig oorlogsverklaringen* (Twenty declarations of war), fourteen of which came within a month.

With Austria-Hungary at her neck, Serbia called upon her ally, Russia, for help. Russia ordered general mobilization. Germany declared war on Russia, and a few days later on France, hoping to bargain for England's neutrality. Germany moved for a rapid victory over France by advancing toward Belgium, where she demanded undisputed passage across that country. The Belgian army resisted. With the aid of their howitzers, the Germans penetrated between the ring-forts of Liege and took the city.

Between the journals of President Richards and the diary of Elder West, there is a day-by-day account of events as they affected life in Holland and the mission. The fifteen brief excerpts which follow represent only a fraction of the entries which, in addition to noting war developments, carry a running account of mission business, but they give a sense of immediacy to what was happening around them.

Richards: *Friday 31, 1914 [July].*
    Germany has ordered mobilization with the view of stopping Russia, and that so implicates the other nations that France, Belgium, Holland and Switzerland have also ordered to mobilize.

Saturday, August 1, 1914.
    All horses were called in today for use of the government. Wagons were left in the yards. . . . The police were hardly able to manage the thousands who swarmed the Savings Banks for their money, and it was impossible to change paper money any place. Prices of everything took a big jump. I cashed money orders, checks, and drafts. . . . Tried to sell some French money, but could not. All exchanges are closed and the only money that will be accepted is gold and silver. . . .

Sunday, August 2, 1914.
    There is a great stir in town today. The Germans took immediate possession of Luxembourg, which has been guaranteed freedom by all nations, and then started the march through Belgium.

Wednesday, August 5, 1914.

England declared war on Germany yesterday, which now makes Austria, Hungary and Germany against Serbia, Russia, France, Belgium and England. Holland thus far is remaining neutral. This has every evidence of the commencement of the greatest war the world has ever known. When one stops to think of 20,000,000 or 25,000,000 men arrayed in battle against each other with the present implements of destruction, the end is a terrible thing to contemplate.

Saturday, August 8, 1914.

The fighting around Liege has been terrible. . . . Went to Dordrecht this afternoon. The train was so full, I had to ride in a box car, and there were also women and children there.

Tuesday, August 11, 1914.

Trains are busy today [taking] soldiers to Southern border. A big battle between the Germans, Belgians, French and English is expected tomorrow. Holland is marshalling in all her volunteers.

West: *Saturday, August 22, 1914.*

The Germans during the week have steadily gained territory in Belgium and are now in possession of the city of Brussels, the main force of the Belgian army having retreated to Antwerp where the King and Queen and the royal family is, and which is strongly fortified.

Richards: (Communication between the United States and Germany was cut off, so we were receiving cablegrams, sometimes two or three a day, instructing us to try and locate certain missionaries and students from Germany. Most all passed through Rotterdam, and we were able to help them on their way home.) *Blue Book,* p. 55.

Richards: *Thursday, September 3, 1914.*

. . . received a letter from President [Hyrum] Smith this morning confirming his telegram of the 29th to order all elders of the Swiss and German and French Missions released, also those from here who are near the end of missions. Mails are delayed between England and here, everything now passing through the hands of "Censor."

West: *Saturday, September 12, 1914.*

The elders of the German Mission have been coming in every day this week. The largest number of any one day left here for London today, the number being thirty-two. . . . [This, of course, put a heavy strain upon those at the mission home who tried to calm, encourage, and feed them. Ina's ability to stretch whatever there was proved a valuable asset during those precarious days.]

Richards: *Friday, September 25, 1914.*

Left office at 10:30 to post some letters and found boy at door with telegram. I began to tremble when I received it. It read as follows: "Send all your missionaries to Liverpool for Oct. 7th. Retain few capable men. Letter following. Hyrum Smith."

I felt very much grieved to receive this word . . . but was glad the Brethren had granted my request that in case the elders should have to leave, that I be allowed to remain and to keep two men for each conference so that the Saints would not feel deserted.

West: *Friday, October 2, 1914.*

The bombardment of Antwerp began today. The office has been a perfect hive for elders. Today, I have done nothing . . . but settle accounts and give the boys enough money to take them to Liverpool. . . . This evening we held a three-hour Priesthood meeting at which all elders were in attendance. . . . [President Richards counseled them to be diligent upon their return home, to serve in smaller jobs as faithfully as if they were bishops or stake presidents, and that then eventually the greater assignments would come.] After the meeting, Sister R. served each of the elders with a piece of lemon pie.

Saturday, October 3, 1914.

The boat carrying thirty-seven of our Holland missionaries. . . . should have left . . . at 4:30 this afternoon, but did not sail until about 7:00 P.M. A large crowd of Saints remained. . . . and as it left the dock, both those on the boat and those [below] joined in *Zingen wij voor scheiding* (Sing We Now at Parting), which made the scene even more pathetic.

Richards: *Wednesday, October 7, 1914.*

Today the people of Antwerp were given until 10:00 P.M. to leave the city, after which there would be no opportunity.

West: *Friday, October 9, 1914.*

Antwerp fell today into hands of the Germans. . . . Refugees are coming into Holland from all sides. . . . During the seige, over 500,000 refugees from Antwerp and its surrounding cities have sought refuge in Holland. Thousands line the roads and byways near the Holland border, being for the most part women and children, without food and with no place of shelter, and whether it rains or not, there are not accommodations to supply the multitude. . . . Here in Rotterdam, trainload after trainload of these poor unfortunates . . . have been coming.

Richards: [Same day, as he watched at the train station.]

One big train was sent right through to Amsterdam . . . [another] to Scheidam, and more to other places. . . . The good Dutch people had bread and cheese to send with them. . . . Mothers with little children and no one to look after them . . . I suppose the men were in the service—young and old together. All were crying. . . . It was heart-rending. . . . ("These poor people were placed in schools and factories all over Holland, and for weeks pictures would appear in newspapers or magazines, trying to locate their parents, husbands, wives . . . and we could hear the cannon roaring.") (Parenthetical quote comes from interview.)

From that day on, for the duration of the war, Holland "hosted" the refugees. The Dutch families, non-Mormon and Mormon alike, generously shared their homes, bedding, and food. Sister Klopmeijer, a "typical *Zeelandsche vrouw* in her quaint Zeeland dress," had nine refugees under her roof. Sister Janse of Middelburg, whom President Richards and Elder West visited, had three, yet she hastened to prepare *aardopelen en jeu*, soup, and a side dish of cabbage for the two, and then insisted they stay with her because all other places in the area were more crowded than hers. She borrowed bedding for herself and husband, then they gave their own bed to the two brethren. Of it Elder West gratefully wrote, "The hole-in-the-wall bed in which we slept was free from fleas, and clean, [though] very short." Thus they traveled to carry on the mission work, finding whatever accommodations they could.

In Rotterdam, Ina's twenty-eighth birthday had been swallowed up in the tumultuous days, but her husband remembered it. He came in from Groningen at 2:00 P.M. on September 14, gave Ina a beautiful cameo brooch, took care of Brother Larkin who was sick at the mission office, sent off another party of elders from Germany, then took Ina and Elder West to a "moving picture show." When they returned, a letter from Hyrum M. Smith awaited with suggested procedures if all elders should have

President and Sister Richards.

to leave. The president spent most of the night working out the details. This was a rather typical day. His attention to such special occasions as Ina's birthday was also typical. The children, parents, and their respective families at home in Utah were remembered with cards and gifts.

As it happened, not all elders were required to leave, but the mission, formerly staffed with fifty missionaries, now was left to carry on the work with only eight in the districts, Elder West in the office, and the president. The immediate challenge was to staff all branches with local priesthood bearers and to train the district men to help the president supervise their work. Despite the difficulties, President Richards's intimate acquaintance with the people, his hard work, and his capable leadership made possible a productive period for the Netherlands Mission during the war.

"I spent nearly every Sunday in a different branch," he wrote. "I kept constantly in touch with the few missionaries in the four districts, and in that way I was able to help direct the work with the Saints in an effort to train them in leadership." (*Blue Book*, p. 56.)

As new branch presidents were called, some demonstrated obvious ability to preside and lead effectively. Elder West, who traveled both with the president and alone, tells of President Aukema in Groningen. He refers to him as "a man of sterling character in the gospel, and in the short time he has presided over the branch, seems to have won the love and support of the Saints." (RBW *Diary*, pp. 133-34.) President Richards too was confident. "I [am] overjoyed with the success we have had in the various branches since the departure of the missionaries. It certainly is an evidence again that it is the work of God . . . and that the Lord did inspire us in the appointments of local men." (LGR *Journal*, vol. IV, p. 237.)

In the four districts he met the local brethren at prearranged meetings and conferences. In a sense, they were like children waiting to be taught. At Amsterdam one opposed tithing, thought it was only for the rich. One held that the Word of Wisdom was only wisdom and not a commandment. In a similar situation at Groningen, the president instructed the branch leaders about keeping their books and about caring for the poor and the sick. He talked about loyalty to the priesthood, and, pouring out his heart and soul under the influence of the Spirit, he bore his testimony. "I thank the Lord that every drop of blood in my body is loyal to the priesthood he has set among men."

Frequently he and the elders were faced with the doctrine of predestination. Old ideas and traditions were hard to replace with the gospel of free agency. A prevalent saying among the Dutch was, *Voor dat ik begone to leven, was alles in uwe bock gschrwen.* (Before I began to live, everything was written in Your book.) The president asked one brother, "If you were to break the window, was that written in the book?" "Yes," the man said. As President Richards labored to teach the new to replace the old, he wrote, "I have learned the full meaning of the parable of 'putting new wine in old bottles.' " For those "who have been steeped in the false doctrines and traditions of the Christian world, it is a hard thing to get the pure gospel of Jesus Christ running smoothly through their souls so that it does not create friction by rubbing up against the old. They are the . . . old bottles and old wine of which Jesus speaks." (*Black Book*, pp. 57-58.)

It was one thing to teach the brethren; it was another to enlighten the sisters. One was disgruntled and "couldn't stand the Word of Wisdom or to hear the local brethren talk when they are learning how." Another, of a little higher class socially, came up to the president after a meeting and gave him an "awful dressing down" because he sat through the service and let a local brother occupy all the time when she had brought a friend along to hear him speak. "Well, sister," he told her, "you don't seem to understand a certain basic thing about Mormonism. There are no preachers in the Church who haven't practiced on somebody, and I don't know that you are better than anyone else that this man shouldn't practice on you." He continued, "Where would I be today if these Dutch people hadn't let me practice on them? Now, someday this man may be one of our best preachers." (The statement proved prophetic, for the man became a popular preacher among the Dutch people and later filled two missions for the Church.)

While the president's schedule took him to the various branches nearly every Sunday, he returned to Rotterdam during the week and visited his investigators "almost every evening." Elder West often accompanied him, sometimes Ina or one of the children. At one point he recorded that he had ten families to teach; at another, he could hardly find time to make the rounds to those who wished to see him. Some names of contacts he had brought from Dutch friends in Utah, many he got from strangers who attended the meetings, and others came from tracting when he could. Occasionally Ina tracted with him. She had memorized a little introduction, "*Als het u bliefth, Vrouw, iets om te lezew, het kost u niets.*" (If you please, Lady, here is something to read. It doesn't cost you anything.) She would take one side of the street, the president the other, and if her approach evoked a question, he would be nearby to answer it. From their contacts and those of the elders came some choice converts.

President Richards felt that the conversion of the Teunis Vujk family alone would have been worth his whole mission. It came about as follows: Only one of the family was a member. He taught in Sunday School, and after one of the meetings the president asked him, "Brother Vujk, do you have a family?"

"Yes," he answered, "I have Father, Mother, four sisters, and a brother."

"Can't you get them into the Church?" the president asked.

"No," he answered.

"Can't the missionaries get them in?"

"No, they've tried, and my uncle, a local elder, has tried and he can't get them either."

President Richards then said, "You go home and ask if I can have an evening with them, and then if they don't want me to return, I won't bother them further." The family agreed that he could come, then that he could keep coming. He continued every week until they were all baptized.

The Sas family joined the Church; and Jan Neerings, whom the president had taught during his first mission, finally overcame the influence that had held her back. Elder West wrote of her baptism, "She appeared to be filled with joy." Both he and the president were also joyous that evening when Pieter van der Werff, his wife, daughter, and eight others were baptized. They gratefully noted that the harvest had "reached proportions beyond our expectations."

As the work went steadily forward in the mission, the time for Ina's baby came. At 2:30 A.M. on December 8, 1914, President Richards sent Elder West for the nurse, and when they returned the doctor was there. The sleepy elder went back to bed until about 5:30 and then "awoke to find a fine baby girl had been born." He added that the child was "just as plump as can be, and the mother is getting along nicely." (RBW *Diary*, p. 145.)

For Ina, the baby's birth was associated with a remarkable experience, which she related to her husband and which he recorded that night. Just before the child was born, she had seen

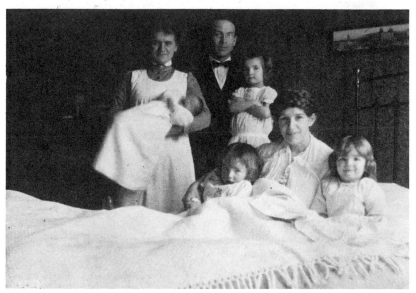

Fourth daughter, Jane, born in Rotterdam 1914.

The four little "Dutchies" — Mercedes, Norinne, Marian, Jane.

with her natural eyes a being in white. The president wrote, "I can't imagine how anyone could be more worthy of the presence of Holy Angels than Ina, and especially at the birth of this Little One, where everything pertaining thereunto has been so sweet and sacred." (LGR *Journal*, vol. IV, pp. 250-51.)

He remained with his family throughout that day and thoughtfully wrote a letter to Ina's mother expressing his love and gratitude for her daughter, his darling wife. A week later when he blessed the baby and gave her the name Jane, he felt a singular spiritual impression which "was different than with any other of the children."

While the war spread its deadly destruction not far from them, there is no indication in either the president's journals or the West diary that they felt personal fear. They were on the Lord's errand, were safe in his care, and felt his peace with them. Ina's ability to create a haven for her family within the home contributed appreciably to their spiritual as well as physical well-being. So it was that Christmas that year was a warm and grateful one. With little Jane nestled in her mother's arms, their thoughts turned naturally to another mother and Child.

Elder West left for home immediately after New Year's Day, and from then until the end of his mission President Richards performed the duties of mission secretary in addition to his own heavy work load. On three separate occasions his eyes suffered severe strain, and he had to turn from the books until the eyes could tolerate close work again.

As in the contrast between the warmth and peace of Christmas and the catastrophies of war (such as the May 1915 sinking of the *Lusitania* by German submarine), the forces of good and evil were apparent in the personal experiences of President Richards. One day he was preaching with such intensity and power that he "felt almost carried away in the Spirit." The next, he was challenged by a spirit which possessed a "nice little woman who was so kind to us." When he asked why she had not joined the Church as her daughter had, she stiffened and said in a sneering voice, "Who are you?" "I am a servant of God," the president answered.

Three times the question was put to him; three times the same answer was given. Then she mocked, "So you are a servant of God, then I have nothing to do here." With Elders Clark and Murray who were with him, President Richards laid hands upon the woman's head and rebuked the evil one. The woman fell limp and they placed her on the bed. The president wrote, "I advised her to be obedient unto the gospel, that she might be able to put herself beyond the power of Satan to trouble her in this manner." (Letter to his parents, June 30, 1915, *Black Book*, pp. 39-40.)

Whether external or self-imposed, challenges came often to President Richards. Although the Presiding Bishopric had approved a chapel for Amsterdam and had sent money for a down payment on the land, when the War came no more building was permitted in Holland. The president was authorized to use the down payment, as well as those funds gathered by the Saints in America, for the relief of the Belgian poor. He tried to get permission from the German Governor General of Belgium to enter that country in order to find and help Church members there. His request was denied in a letter from the German general himself. Accordingly, the only means of reaching the Belgian Saints was through *De Ster* lists and through Dutch friends of the members there.

In spite of the havoc the German militarists had precipitated in the world, neither the Dutch Saints nor the president felt animosity toward the German people. In fact, as a result of his experiences with German emigrants he had a keen desire to learn their language, which had many similarities to the Dutch he knew so well. As a result he somehow made time for a German tutor to come to the office for an hour each week for eight months and teach him. According to the man, his pupil proved more than apt.

Even though he had struggled so hard to gain facility with Dutch on his first mission, he seems to have had particular linguistic skill. When he visited the *Burgemuster* (mayor) of Rotterdam to request permission to hold street meetings, the mayor was amazed that his speech was accent-free, and he said, "Well, I never heard an American talk Dutch like you do."

Whether in conversation or preaching, the president was blessed with unusual freedom of expression accompanied by spiritual intensity and power. At one point he wrote, ". . . since I have considerable freedom in speaking. . . . I have been wondering if I couldn't develop some ability in writing." (LGR *Journal*, vol. IV, p. 240.) He lost no time in trying to put down some of his deepest thoughts and ideas in a small black book separate from his journals. While his writings do not have the sweep and flow of his voiced expression, they are very important for their thought content and for their monitoring and recording of significant spiritual development during his second mission. In them he faced such basic questions as the purpose of life, what constitutes true knowledge and success, and the price of total commitment to the Lord.

In *True Knowledge and True Success* he sees the gospel as "a pearl of great price, for it teaches us first of all the object of man's being." True knowledge and success, he indicates, "come from following the Savior who said, 'I came forth from the Father, and am come into the world: again, I leave the world, and go to the Father,' and later, 'I have finished the work which thou gavest me to do.' " (John 16:28; 17:4.)

President Richards's comment on this epitomizes his longtime desire and his efforts to realize it. "These words of the Savior have always made a great impression. I cannot picture a greater heaven and joy and satisfaction than to be able to stand there in the presence of a loving Father, and be able to say: 'I have finished the work which Thou gavest me to do.' " (*Black Book*, pp. 45-48.) To him, this was the ultimate success.

Achieving that objective and the accompanying reward has its price. In *The Cost of Becoming a Disciple of Christ*, he deeply considered the Savior's words in Luke 14:33—"Whosoever he be of you that forsaketh not all he hath, *he cannot be my disciple.*" (Italics are his.) He then detailed the price that must be paid: repentance unto purification; preaching the gospel; persecution (sometimes from the closest of friends); building the kingdom; redeeming the dead; building temples and meetinghouses; paying proper tithes and offerings. "When we have considered all these things well," he adds, "then we can ask ourselves . . . whether we

have material enough to complete what we undertake to build."
(*Black Book*, pp. 15-20.)

On his first mission a fervent desire for faithfulness was born
within him and he made a sincere commitment to a life of service. Now, in his maturity, he not only reckoned the cost of such
a life but determined that he was willing to pay the price and
would always feel it a joy and privilege to do so. As he labored
with the Saints and elders in Holland and "enjoyed such a fine
spirit," he wrote one Sunday that he "could gladly devote [his]
whole life to such a service." (LGR *Journal*, vol. V, p. 235.)

Having grown somewhat accustomed to the civil uncer-
tainties in wartime, yet feeling an urgent need to keep the work
of the mission moving along, President Richards requested four
replacements for the district elders whose missions would soon
terminate. It was October 21, 1915, when the first two of them
arrived—Elders Rulon J. Sperry and Gerrit van den Berg. From
then until the following July, mission affairs were cared for
against a background of violent events, changing conditions, and
multiple personal challenges, interspersed with moments of satisfaction and joy.

One of those moments of joy had been Ina's twenty-ninth
birthday, of which he wrote. She "was never prettier, and not
half so sweet. I love her more than I have ever done before. I
gave her a little marble statue which I have been saving for
three-and-a-half months" since "she fell in love with it in the
window." (LGR *Journal*, vol. V, p. 152.)

In January 1916 high winds broke dikes, and Rotterdam was
under water from "Hoogstraat to the river," with more water
flooding the streets. A few days later, fierce winds threatened
more dikes and blew the ship *Rijndam* into a mine, killing many
of the crew.

Again the president had severe eye trouble and nausea. "Of
late," he wrote, "I can hardly stand to use my eyes for reading or
writing. I have discovered that my eyes and stomach are con-
nected." Within weeks a painful rash appeared on his face and,
unrelatedly, a finger infection required lancing to the bone. As if
to encourage him in his distress, he had a dream in which he was

preaching to a large congregation. His father and mother were present, and "the look of pride and joy on their faces" gave him the sweet feeling of what it might be like to "meet the reward of a faithful life." (LGR *Journal*, vol. VI, pp. 40-41.)

Ina also had her physical challenge. She was pregnant with her fifth child, and her beloved Cathrine was no longer with them. (They had lent her money to immigrate to Utah, where she married John Kest, also from Holland.) The four little girls looked to her for their daily needs, and in addition she supported the president in all of his work, even when it so often took him away from them.

It seemed that Holland might be drawn into the conflict when on May 31, 1916, the great Battle of Jutland was fought in the sea north of them. The deadly roar of the cannon could again be heard, and the slaughter went on. Approximately six thousand British and about twenty-five hundred German seamen lost their lives.

Within days of that battle, two communications reached the president. His father, George F., had been called as European Mission President, and would leave Salt Lake in August. The second piece of news reached him in Amsterdam, where he was attending meetings. The telegram read, "Honorably released. John Butterworth your successor. Hyrum Smith." He admits that it would have been hard to express his feelings at that time.

For the next few weeks, in addition to visiting the branches for a last good-bye, President Richards worked with John Butterworth to effect a smooth turnover of mission affairs. He helped Ina clean and prepare the mission home for its new occupants. He also had to personally appear before the U.S. Legation minister, Henry Van Dyke, at The Hague to obtain an emergency passport so he could get his family out of Holland. There was a tight moment of uncertainty, but when President Richards sent the picture of his family to the minister via his secretary, he was admitted immediately. With the picture in his hand, Mr. Van Dyke said, "I wish there were a thousand such families as this to send back to America." The president received the needed passport.

On June 20, 1916, with many friends to see them off, the Richards family sailed on the *Nieuw Amsterdam* up the River Maas and into the mined waters of the North Sea. Their voyage up the Norwegian coast, on to Kirkwall, Scotland, to Falmouth, England, and thence to New York was relatively uneventful, as was the overland rail journey to Utah. LeGrand's parents met them in Price, Utah, on July 10 for a joyous reunion. At Provo, other family members boarded the train to visit for the last miles of the journey home.

In the general hubbub at the station, three-year-old Marian stumbled and "let out a regular tirade of Dutch," to the delight and amusement of the families. After dinner at the Ashtons and a night in George F.'s home, LeGrand and Ina were taken by his brother George to see their place on Tenth Avenue. To their great surprise and delight, the folks "had the place clean, [their] furniture in, curtains washed and hung, and food in the cupboard. Ina was so happy, she just sat down and cried."

Two days later, George F. took Ina and LeGrand to see President Joseph F. Smith, uncle of LeGrand, at his office, which was then located in a connecting room between the Beehive House and the Lion House. His counselors, John R. Winder and Anthon H. Lund, were present. Of the experience, LeGrand wrote, "President Smith took me in his arms and hugged and kissed me, saying, 'LeGrand, we love you,' until I surely felt that for such a welcome from the prophet of the Lord it was worth going on my mission." (LGR *Journal*, vol. VI, p. 74.)

Chapter 7

Businessman

1916-1919

Claude Richards, part-owner of Kimball-Richards Realty Company, faced his cousin LeGrand and said, "If I were out of the real estate business I wouldn't be going into it. I'd be going into the automobile business."

"But I don't have any money to finance an automobile business," said LeGrand.

Claude continued, "Do you know how many real estate companies have quit while you've been gone? About twelve."

"Then it looks like there'll be plenty of room for me," LeGrand responded.

The decision made, his determination to proceed in that direction was firm. One thing was certain: he needed at once to earn a living for his growing family. He had been offered a bookkeeping job by Merrill Nibley, manager of Utah-Idaho Sugar Company. He appreciated the offer but declined it because it had no growth potential. His former mission secretary, Richard B. West—energetic, clever in business, and doing well in the Merchants National Bank organization—had suggested the bonding business, but it did not appeal.

LeGrand had a finely tuned business sense, was highly motivated, and had gained much skill with people while handling emergencies, solving problems, and directing the affairs of the Netherlands Mission. He knew he would no longer be content working for anyone other than himself. Further, his former work with Romney Lumber Company and the building trade, coupled with his experience in subcontracting a speculation home for them and the S Street duplex for himself, had resulted in a keen interest in real estate. Whether it was inspiration or determination he wasn't sure. Certainly he had no encouragement from any quarter. The lack of it may have been because the business was just emerging from its "crude beginnings" and real estate men still joked about "carrying their six-shooters in self-defense."

It was of these early times that F. Orin Woodbury, a brother-in-law of LeGrand's, wrote: "Being in real estate clothed the participant with an aura of mediocrity, if not disrespect. No state licensing laws existed. The Real Estate Board's code of ethics was ignored too frequently by members, and not respected at all by non-members." (Letter to author, December 29, 1980. Orin Woodbury later joined LeGrand's company and went on to build a distinguished career in real estate and investment.)

With every negative comment concerning the business, LeGrand's affirmative feelings for it strengthened. On Monday, July 31, 1916, he borrowed five hundred dollars from the Merchants National Bank. He rented office space from Ina's father at 1 South West Temple for $7.50 a month plus his share of fuel in winter. He wrote of opening his business on August 5 as follows: "Moved furniture from George's [dental] office to mine. . . . Opened my books, and found I had a Present Worth of $3,521.88." (LGR *Journal*, vol. VI, p. 78.)

In addition to the equity in his home and the property on Eleventh East, part of his present worth was in the motorcycle his father purchased from George F. Jr. and gave to LeGrand. The gift was to balance, in part, favors and help he had extended to the other sons during LeGrand's absence. Being LeGrand's only means of transportation other than the streetcars, the vehicle was both needed and appreciated.

The day after LeGrand moved into his office, he went to the station to say good-bye to his father, who was leaving to preside over the European Mission. LeGrand's mother was remaining in Salt Lake to care for their young children still at home, but it was hoped she could join George F. later. (LeGrand's brother George F. Jr. and his wife, Edith, and two children were leaving with President George F. Richards for a dual purpose—George to fill a mission in England and Edith to manage domestic affairs at Durham House, the mission home in Liverpool.)

It was a touching scene at the station which George F. Richards described in his diary that night. "The parting of my loved ones caused tears to flow copiously on both sides." (GFR *Diary*, vol. 19, p. 164.) What the long separation meant to this faithful couple, he had expressed when he received the call from the First Presidency and made it known to his family on June 10. "It broke up my wife's feelings and the children cried with her. . . . My true feelings are that I would naturally shrink from such responsibility and having to leave home and loved ones for such a time as this mission will mean, but having put my hand to the plow, there is for me no turning back." (GFR *Diary*, vol. 19, pp. 119-20.)

LeGrand Richards Realty Company officially opened for business on August 11, when LeGrand mailed out announcements to that effect and placed an ad in the newspaper. Shortly after that his old friend and employer, E. H. McBeth (with whom he had earlier planned to establish a lumber company), came from Pocatello with a proposition. He had purchased an implement and hardware business in that city, and he now offered LeGrand half interest if he would come and manage it. E. H. said he would pay him salary to live on and let his surplus earnings pay for his half of the business. LeGrand thanked him for the generous offer but declined. His commitments were already made, he said.

From the beginning the business prospered, and LeGrand made better than wages. He was able to purchase a new stove and other items for Ina before her baby arrived. On October 28, 1916, their first son, LeGrand Ashton, was born. Of him his father wrote, "We surely are grateful for our boy, and love him to death already." (LGR *Journal*, vol. VI, p. 80.)

Although he negotiated his first sales traveling by motorcycle, it wasn't long before LeGrand sold it to obtain a down payment for a new Ford. The car he wanted was not immediately available in Salt Lake, but his brother-in-law Orson Rega Card, who lived about eighty-five miles to the north in Logan, located one there and offered to bring it down for LeGrand. When Rega took delivery on it, the agent asked if he had ever driven an automobile. "No," Rega answered, "but I know how to operate my wife's sewing machine."

*Ina with the children
and the family's first car.*

After receiving a few instructions and cautions, Rega and his wife, Lucena, started for Salt Lake by way of Sardine Canyon. What with starting, stopping, pushing, blocking, and hand-turning of stuck wheels, the trip up and down grades took them a full day and until 2:30 A.M. the next day, while an anxious LeGrand waited for a glimpse of his first auto. One of the first uses to which he put the new car was to drive his Dutch friends Cathrine Witteveen and John Kest to the Salt Lake Temple to be married.

The establishment of his real estate business, in fact, gave him the means, the location, and the control of his own time so he could help his Dutch friends in the area. He had been elected president of the Netherlands Mission Association in April 1912, a position he held until April 1914, five months after he arrived in Holland as mission president. (LGR *Journal*, vol. III, p. 75.)

After his return to Salt Lake City, he attended their Church meetings and preached in Dutch. He visited with the Dutch people in their homes and at his office. Since the office was downtown, they could easily find him there.

Each day two or three came in, confident of an enthusiastic greeting in their own language and of help with their multiple problems. During the next fourteen years that he remained in Salt Lake he was their anchor, mentor, and friend.

The list of Dutch Saints he helped to immigrate is long. Frequently, telegrams would come that someone's relative was detained in Hoboken, New Jersey, and he in turn would wire Utah Senator Reed Smoot in Washington, D.C. The senator would then have the person released and sent on his way west.

During the fourteen years, there was seldom a time when LeGrand did not have several thousand dollars out in loans to the Dutch people. As his own family needs increased, he worked out a system whereby, if a Dutch Saint needed five hundred dollars to emigrate, LeGrand would have him get four other brethren to sign for a hundred dollars apiece. Usually they would do this when it was known that he himself was signing and the bank would lend the money. He never accepted anything for making out emigration bonds, nor for any other service to the Dutch.

Not only did he help them to come to Utah, but he often assisted them after they arrived. He lent Brother Oeds de Waal money to buy a wagon and horse to peddle vegetables, and when he died and left his wife with five children, LeGrand came to help. She lived in a ward where many poor people needed assistance, so her bishop could only give her twenty-five dollars a month for all her expenses. (This was before the present Church Welfare system.) When LeGrand talked with him and confirmed that that indeed was all the bishop could arrange for, he interceded for the widow through the Presiding Bishop and secured the help she needed.

When John Kest's father was accidently electrocuted while working for the power company, LeGrand served as administrator for the estate. With the help of his cousin Stephen L Richards, an attorney, LeGrand negotiated a settlement with the company which made it possible for John Kest to bring his mother and the other children over from Holland. Of his benefactor, John Kest wrote: "Friend to the unfortunate, loyal, devoted, outspoken, with a rare sense of humor, a humanitarian and outstanding Christian. I can never thank him enough for the help he gave me and my family during [the period of] my father's untimely death." He continued, "I thank him for his concern about my personal welfare, and his kindness to the young lady who cared for his children in the Dutch Mission office from December 1913 to May 1915, and who . . . is my wife today." (John Kest *History*, courtesy of his daughter, Norma K. Ericksson.)

LeGrand heard that a couple of his faithful Saints from Holland were about to get a divorce. As soon as possible he went down to the west side and visited them. "The man couldn't speak English," he wrote. "He was timid and backward and didn't know how to look and ask for work, so I said: 'You come with me,' and I took him up town and didn't let him return home until I had found work for him." (*Blue Book*, p. 63.) As it had with many others for whom he found jobs, employment solved this couple's problem.

He found the Dutch to be honest and responsible in paying their debts, but even in the face of possible default LeGrand's attitude tended to be lenient and uncritical. He and one of his better-to-do Dutch friends helped another Hollander to set up a little store business. The prosperous friend heard that the store-keeper was trying to sell and "skip the country," and he vowed it would be the last one to whom he would ever lend money. "Well, you feel differently about it than I do," LeGrand told him. "I went to Holland to help them, now if I can do that here and still be working and taking care of my family, it'll be a little easier than going on a mission."

In retrospect he wrote, "When I returned from my first mission, my strongest desire was that I should not lose the spirit I then had." In no other activity of his life was the spirit of his mission more evident than in his continuing work with the Dutch. In his setting-apart blessing to the young missionary Elder B. H. Roberts had promised he would be given a love for the Dutch people, and they would be dear to his heart; and by that token he might know that the Spirit of the Lord was resting upon him and would guide and direct him in his labors. The blessing did not terminate with either mission release, but it has remained with him throughout his life. All the old Dutch friends except Cathrine Kest (eighty-eight in 1981) are gone, but their children and grandchildren seek him out to speak at funerals and to perform marriages.

Closely associated with his and Ina's memories of their mission together was the little Holland-born daughter, Jane, whose birth and blessing still held spiritual overtones for them. LeGrand had been in business a little over a year when suddenly Jane became ill. Ina's teen-age sister, Minnie, was helping her in the house that morning while the girls played in the sandpile. Marian, age five at the time, remembers that Jane stumbled, bumped her hand, and cried as children do in play, an incident which later haunted her thoughts, although it had no apparent association with her sickness. Jane simply did not feel well that afternoon, and when her father came from work in the evening she was worse. Ina was expecting their sixth baby, and thinking to spare her strength, LeGrand took over Jane's care. He described the experience:

> She complained of a stomach ache, so I slept with her, and during the night she had a convulsion. I called Dr. S. H. Allen, my neighbor and associate in the Seventies Quorum. He pronounced her condition critical, so we rushed her to the LDS Hospital, and with his approval, I called Dr. Gill Richards, my cousin. . . . At 9:00 A.M. the next morning she passed away. (*Blue Book*, p. 29.)

It was November 6, 1917. Jane was not yet three.

Ina's family rallied round. LeGrand's father, a dependable source of comfort, was in Europe. His mother and the younger girls were in quarantine with Ray, who had scarlet fever. One of his sisters remembers that LeGrand carried the little casket to the front porch window at 1010 Third Avenue so they could look upon the lovely child.

At her funeral, great friends—Bishop David R. Lyon, Hyrum G. Smith, the Patriarch to the Church, Elders Stephen L Richards and Hyrum M. Smith of the Council of the Twelve—

spoke words of love and peace. LeGrand had once copied the words, ". . . And you shall shortly know that lengthened breath is not the sweetest gift God sends his friend. . . . Be sure a wiser hand than yours or mine pours out this portion for our lips to drink. . . ." (*Self-Control in Adversity*, May Riley Smith. *Green Book*, p. 28.) The words comforted LeGrand and Ina.

Difficult as it was to carry one child and lose another, Ina had many responsibilities to immediately consume her time and energy. Her three remaining girls were seven, six, and five; baby LeGrand was just over a year. Their needs were ever before her, and the time of the new baby's arrival drew near. He was born January 17, 1918, and they named him George LaMont. This was the child whose later perceptive understanding would help to ease his parents' hearts when sorrow came to them again.

As Ina worked to meet the needs of her family, LeGrand turned to the pressing demands of his business, which, F. Orin Woodbury writes, "was geared to brokerage, negotiating sales of residences, farm lands, and occasionally, commercial properties. It also sold fire insurance." In addition, it was keyed to services. "No fees were charged for developing, financing, appraising, investment advice, or managing properties." Although in the early years the sales force was small, Orin states that "commission income generated by LeGrand's personal sales was substantial, adequate to enable the firm to operate profitably." Orin, who proved to be a top salesman and businessman in the company, gives good reasons for the company's success. "LeGrand was a symbol of integrity, a strong force in improving the quality of real estate services, in stimulating membership in real estate boards, and enforcing compliance with a code of ethics." (Letter to author, December 29, 1980.)

Joseph Cutler, who later came into the business, discovered this integrity of LeGrand's through a personal experience. He drove down from Idaho, seeking to trade his farm for some Salt Lake property. He was shown what the firm determined they could reasonably trade. The man asked, "Would you make the deal if you were I?"

Businessman LeGrand Richards flanked by sales and office force of LeGrand Richards Realty Company.

LeGrand replied, "Well, you shouldn't ask me that question, because I've never seen your farm and I don't know what it's really worth, but you do. You've seen both properties, so you ought to make the decision."

Cutler still said, "Well, I want to know if you'd make the deal."

Pressed for an answer in this way, LeGrand said, "Now then, you tell me what would be the lowest cash price you'd take if you were selling instead of trading your farm." When the man gave the figure, LeGrand asked, "You mean it's actually worth that in cash?"

"Yes," said Cutler.

"Then I would not make the trade."

The commission from that transaction would have been an almost-new automobile and several thousand dollars. It made no difference. As LeGrand had earlier told a Dutch friend who questioned whether a man could be honest in real estate, "If I couldn't be as honest dealing in homes as I could selling either the gospel or shoes, I wouldn't be in the business."

His cheerful optimism was another asset to the company, and it was infectious in the office and out. A former secretary, Evaline Peterson, says there was a congeniality of spirit between him and his employees that made working for him a pleasure. Another employee, Royden Weight, remembers the trust his boss had in him as office manager and how he would work to please him. A low-producing salesman responded to his employer's suggestion that some other line of work might be more beneficial to him. "But I enjoy working with you and I'd like to stay on," he said, and he did.

Clients felt it too. One man came in response to an ad. It was a wet and drizzling day when LeGrand drove him to see a west side property. As luck would have it, a tire went flat. At that time, a flat meant a mending job on the spot, so while the man sat under cover in the car, his realtor whistled and sang as he sloshed about in rain and mud to remove the damaged tire, repair it, and replace it. The client was so impressed that he turned a lot of business the company's way.

Underlying and adding strength to his pleasant joviality, however, was a vigorous dynamism that people found hard to resist. He always told his missionaries, "If you go to get turned down, you *get* turned down." He expected positive results whether in proselyting or in business, and more often than not he got them. When one of his notes fell due, the bank sent word that they didn't wish to renew. "The dickens they don't!" was LeGrand's response. He put on his hat and walked out of the door and into the bank. Courteously but firmly, he said, "I've come over to renew my note." "Just a minute, Mr. Richards," the cashier answered, and he wrote out a new note to be signed.

It was his forceful certainty of how things ought to be done and his ability to see that they were which gave him a preference for managing his business as an individual entrepreneur rather than in partnership with others. This preference is clearly stated in a story he tells of Heber J. Grant's visit to him. The President offered to invest money in his business if LeGrand would take his son-in-law in as a partner. The younger man was faced with something of a dilemma, but he made an honest appeal to his important friend. "Well, President Grant, I'd do most anything for you, but partnerships don't always work out, and I'd be lots happier working alone. As much as I love you, please don't ask me to do that." There was understanding between them, and the matter was dropped.

The success of LeGrand's business was largely due to his unique personality. Central to it were openness, fairness, and a desire to serve. When Orin Woodbury was later president of the Utah Real Estate Board, he told the realtors in a meeting that LeGrand Richards had trained him in the business and had counseled his salesmen that "no deal ought to be made unless it would be of benefit to both parties." In line with his own advice, he always tried to point out any problem or flaw in properties he dealt with. For instance, LeGrand never sold a home in the Forest Dale area (before sewers were in and drainage problems were solved) until he told prospective buyers that during summer irrigating the basement would get water in it. Thus if a client bought from him, it was with full knowledge of the property's bad points as well as its good ones. His willingness to place the other man's interest before his own did not always pay off financially, as one instance shows. A certain man was about to be dispossessed of his home, and LeGrand gave up his total commission to reinstate him. Later on, when the man prospered, he did nothing to repay his debt.

While the war in Europe continued, and occasional reports of it arrived from his father and brother, LeGrand felt most fortunate that his company had grown to the point of necessary expansion. In April 1918 he moved his office to 75 West South Temple, where he joined the Ashton Improvement Company in renting the property where Temple Square Hotel now stands. They remodeled the old blacksmith shop for their offices, subletting the balance so that they cleared their rent and had twenty dollars a month to spare.

In June LeGrand sold his house on Tenth Avenue, moved to 325 K Street until October 1, and then traded for a home at 1064 Hollywood Avenue in Sugar House Ward, near the property he had purchased for the proposed lumber company before his second mission. Within weeks the ban necessitated by the flu epidemic was imposed, and all Church, school, and public meetings were discontinued.

On November 11, 1918, the Armistice was signed, which officially ended the terrible conflict in Europe. Headlines on the front page of the *Deseret News* read, "Glory to God in the Highest and On Earth, *Peace*." A holiday was declared, thousands jammed the streets, and the noise was deafening. "The whole town went wild," LeGrand says, "and so did we." In Liverpool, his father recorded that he and his son George F. Jr. took a ride to the pier head and back, witnessing the seething mass of humanity on the streets singing and hollering. The bells rang, guns were fired, flags flew there. In the United States there was jubilation as well as a macabre form of celebration. In towns, cities, and suburbs, straw effigies of "Kaiser Bill" (the German emperor) were burned. Sugar House was no exception, and some of LeGrand's children remember watching the spectacle there.

The flu ban was still in force when President Joseph F. Smith died a few days later, on November 19, and it was announced that only a graveside funeral would be held. The date was set for November 23, the same day that Heber J. Grant was sustained and set apart as President of the Church. He retained the former counselors, Anthon H. Lund and Charles W. Penrose. He also spoke at President Smith's funeral.

LeGrand was there, feeling keenly the personal loss of President Smith's death. This was the uncle in whose home he had been a frequent guest as a youth, and whose sons Willard R. and Hyrum H. were particularly close to him. This was the Church President who had taken him into his arms at the end of LeGrand's mission, the prophet whose spiritual power had often moved him to tears. As he stood on the cold ground with its thin covering of snow and listened to President Grant pay final tribute to the dead leader, using quotes from William George Jordan's *The Power of Truth*, LeGrand's thoughts were upon President Smith's remarkable life. Son of the martyred Hyrum, he had driven his mother's oxen across the plains when a mere boy, was orphaned at fourteen, was called on a foreign mission at fifteen, and during the course of his life served six other missions. Legislator, apostle, counselor to three Presidents, he succeeded Lorenzo Snow as President on October 17, 1901. LeGrand felt a great affinity for the man and for his mission.

For his own part, since his return from the Netherlands LeGrand had accepted every assignment that came to him. He counseled his elders upon their release from the mission field to serve well in "small jobs," and he had done just that. (He defines "small jobs" as those with a limited sphere of activity or with little or no carry-over or follow-up.) In the two years he lived in Ensign Ward he taught the parents class, was secretary of the 176th Quorum of the Seventy, and supervised one district of ward (now home) teachers, achieving 100 percent of visits for the full time. This of course meant that if others did not make the visits, he did.

His popularity as a speaker had grown steadily from the time of his return in July 1916, when he was invited to occupy all the time in the Sunday afternoon meeting at the Tabernacle, an

honor he "little dreamed would ever come" to him. (These Sabbath services were held on a regular basis and featured guest
speakers.) There was no public address system then, but
LeGrand's resonant and compelling voice was easily heard as he
talked about the importance of the Book of Mormon to the restoration of the gospel. He recorded (as he always did when he
had been so blessed), "The Lord surely sustained me." Anthony
W. Ivins, who conducted the meeting, gave high praise to the
young mission president just home from the Netherlands.

From then on he was in constant demand for talks in numerous wards, at funerals, at stake priesthood meetings, and at the
Dutch conferences. At one two-month count, he had filled ten
ward speaking assignments of various kinds and given a funeral
talk and a Christmas talk. Ina once said to him, "I don't think
you know how to say no," to which he replied, "How can I, and
still be a servant of the people?"

Upon moving into Sugar House Ward he was first called as
teacher of a girls' class, then as supervisor of a district of ward
teachers. The flu ban was still in effect, and with no meetings
being held the ward teachers and the Relief Society helped the
bishopric keep in touch with the members. LeGrand tells of his
experience during this period.

> I went around in the ward and helped administer to a lot of
> sick people, and then I took the flu. I had it so bad they took me
> to the hospital. They wrapped me in hot blankets and cared for
> me according to the current treatment for the disease. I signed
> papers deeding everything over to my wife, so if I didn't survive,
> she'd be taken care of. Many of my friends were dying. There were
> hardly enough coffins to bury them all, but the doctors pulled me
> through. Ina and the children also had the disease, but not as bad.

Ruth May Fox, general president of the YWMIA, heard of his
critical state and volunteered to come and help Ina while he was
hospitalized. The flu ban was lifted in February, but in March all
the Richards children came down with scarlet fever. Ina was
quarantined in with them and LeGrand was quarantined out.

His brother George and family had returned from England
on February 20, 1919. Now, while LeGrand's family was in quar-

antine, his mother left to join her husband in the mission field. After a separation of two years and eight months, her arrival in Liverpool on March 30, 1919, gave them "one of the happiest days of their lives." In May they had the pleasure of touring the Netherlands Mission in company with President John A. Butterworth, of visiting the places where LeGrand had labored, and of meeting some of the Saints he had known. Shortly after this George Albert Smith was appointed to succeed George F. Richards as European Mission President, and on July 26 the couple was again in Salt Lake.

In the meantime LeGrand's family had survived their serious illnesses, the hardship, and the separation during quarantine, but from then on for a number of years Ina's strength flagged. In addition to his usual help with the children at night, LeGrand took over much of the heavy home work for her—the washing, scrubbing, lifting.

In April his brother George came into the realty business with him. (Because of foot trouble and the difficulty of standing for long hours, he did not return to his dental practice.) In May, F. Orin Woodbury joined them. During that spring LeGrand filled assignments speaking in the wards of Granite Stake as a home missionary, and on June 29 he attended the Dutch conference at the Ogden Tabernacle along with visitors, Rulon S. Wells and Sylvester Q. Cannon, his former Netherlands Mission president. All three spoke. That evening LeGrand was in his home ward to be ordained a high priest and set apart as bishop of Sugar House Ward by President Charles W. Penrose of the First Presidency. The latter gave sound advice to the new bishop: "If we put forth all the effort we can, the Lord will make up the difference of our imperfections."

LeGrand's three years of service in so-called small jobs had given him ever-broadening experience on various levels of Church activity. It hadn't mattered where he served; it was his faithful attention to the work, his totally willing commitment to it, and his faith that the Lord would sustain him, which kept the spirit of testimony bright within him. He once said, "I never aspired to any Church position in my life. As long as I love the

Lord and his Church as much as I do, I'll always find someplace to serve." Now, as a bishop at age thirty-three, he wrote, "I believe with the help of the Lord we will be able to fill this appointment acceptably." (LGR *Journal*, vol. VI, p. 93.)

Bishop of Sugar House Ward

1919-1925

*B*ishop Richards sat in his office going over the priesthood rolls with his counselors. Like him, Elliott C. Taylor was a newcomer to the ward. Alexander R. Curtis had lived all his life in Sugar House, so it was mainly to him that the questions were directed.

"What about Brother A_____?" the bishop would ask.

"Oh, he's inactive. You can't get him to do anything," would be the answer.

Night after consecutive night they continued to review the alphabetical list, the bishop putting a check mark against all the "can't gets." When they had completed the survey, the bishop said: "Brethren, let's ask the stake president not to send us any home missionaries for a few months (only high councilors to check up on us), and let's ask each of these inactive men to speak in our sacrament meetings. By giving them twelve minutes apiece, we can have four speak every Sunday but fast day."

They visited each man on the list, became acquainted with his family, and invited him to speak, not upon a gospel subject but about what the Church meant to him, his family, and his pioneer ancestors. If the brother said he preferred not to give a talk, the bishop would smile and say, "Well, it's up to you, but on [giving a date about two weeks hence] we will announce you, and if you are not there we will tell the people that we came to your house and personally invited you, so they will know we didn't overlook you."

Almost to a man the inactive brethren responded, and with tears flooding their eyes and voices they would tell at the pulpit that in the twenty or thirty years since their mission reports, this was the first time they had been asked to speak in sacrament meeting. This experience taught Bishop Richards that "you can rehabilitate a man better spiritually by putting him at the pulpit than in any other way." His aim was to apply Granite Stake's motto, "Everybody Working," and this reactivation project was a significant start.

In Sugar House Ward, "everybody" meant approximately eleven hundred members, a large portion of whom were poor. There were many widows and elderly people and a large number of big families that were struggling to keep going. To get the greatest possible number working required considerable motivational and administrative skill. The Sugar House period gave the young bishop experience which further prepared him for later positions of greater responsibility and wider influence.

Another area of experience was in the realignment of ward members in callings, out of which came LeGrand's oft-used phrase, "a round man in a round hole and a square one in a square." Its first application was in the matter of the ward choir. Support for the choir was weak and attendance poor, and it received no invitations to sing at conferences. It became clear that a new director was needed. "You'll break his heart," one counselor said of the present leader. "I don't think so, if we put it to him straight." "Straight" to the bishop meant directness, in the spirit of Paul's words, "Except ye utter by the tongue words easy to be understood, how shall it be known what is spoken? for ye shall speak into the air." (1 Corinthians 14:9.)

Together, the bishopric called on the brother and asked if he had confidence enough to sustain them in moving the members around like checkers on a board and using them where the bishopric felt they would best serve the ward. The brother said he did, so they put him in charge of entertainments and dances, where he did an excellent work. To lead the choir they called a man who had recently moved into the ward. He was not a better man than the other, only a better musician, and he had ability to draw people to him—even those who did not know they could sing. "What's happened to Sugar House?" people asked when the choir performed at a conference. It was simply that "a round man had been placed in a round hole."

Another aim was to build spirituality through greater attendance at sacrament meetings at a time when, Churchwide, this was markedly low—only 8 to 12 percent. The bishop wrote on the flyleaf of his Bible, "Let's make these meetings as practical as possible so we can take away with us something to do." Just *hearing* the word would not expand the spirit; only *doing* could. So the members were constantly encouraged to give, to serve, to sacrifice for the Church. Also, while this is not generally possible in today's vastly expanded Church, Bishop Richards occasionally invited his prominent friends to speak. Among those speakers recorded in the ward minutes are James E. Talmage, Frederick J. Pack, George F. Richards, and Stephen L Richards. These of course gave ward meetings almost the stature of a conference and increased attendance notably.

Of the youth with whom he worked, LeGrand says, "They were my friends." The bishop functioned at their level in friendliness but gave concentrated attention to their spiritual development as he groomed them for their missions. Mark B. Garff was a deacon then, and he tells that for outings and conferences the bishop loaded his Allis-Chalmers car so full of Aaronic Priesthood that the wheel spokes broke.

The young men thought he could do anything, yet they were always on the lookout for ways to get the best of him. Mark thought such a moment had come when, at fast meeting, one of them gave him a bottle of oil to be consecrated. It had the old-fashioned tight-fitting cork pressed flush with the bottle top. "All right, bishop," the boys whispered, "let's see what you are going to do now." Matter-of-factly, the bishop whipped out his pocket knife with a fold-down corkscrew and neatly pulled out the cork. "Oh, no," they groaned, "he did it again!" Their pleasure in him was as great as his influence upon them, and in many cases it proved to be lifelong. During the sixty years of his close association with LeGrand, Mark affirms, "his bishop" has never disappointed him.

*Bishop of Sugar House Ward with his sons LaMont and
LeGrand, Jr., on fathers and sons outing.*

Other youth were the distinguished sons of his counselor Alexander R. Curtis, who have been mission and stake presidents and who admit to his powerful influence upon their lives. One was named LeGrand for him. Another, Lindsay R., M.D., wrote to him, "Our early association with you has been a forcible incentive for us to serve the Lord honorably. Our family owes you a deep debt of gratitude for a relationship with which few families are blessed." (Letter, June 15, 1965.)

Not only did he have a solid following among the youth with whom he worked, but he evoked a singular loyalty from their elders. Long before Belle S. Spafford knew him as Presiding Bishop, she heard of him from her sister, Tessie S. Johnston, who served as organist in Sugar House Ward. Tessie resided there in an old home that was left to her and her husband by his mother. A bit impatient, Belle would say to her, "Why don't you move to a newer, more modern home?" "What? And leave my bishop?" came the emphatic answer. "I wouldn't move any place as long as we have LeGrand Richards for our bishop."

Mark Garff's mother believed, and frankly told her children, that someday their bishop was bound to be a General Authority. As adult members of his ward passed on stories about him to their young children, these children grew up feeling that they knew him too. Herman Zobrist, a prominent Las Vegas businessman who received his blessing as a baby at the bishop's hands, says of his father (also Herman), "Had the bishop asked him to jump off a New York skyscraper, he'd have done it and never asked why."

In spite of his strong ward following, there came a time when a block of opposition arose which caused the young bishop and his counselors much heartache. It started soon after the building program was begun. Sugar House was an old parent ward which had cut across the lower part of Salt Lake from State Street to the mountains and which had been divided twenty-three times by 1930—more times than any other original ward in the Salt Lake Valley. The chapel was "an old rattletrap with dirty outside toilets attached to the back of the building." It had been old when LeGrand had attended dances there as a youth. So when

Brother Lund, a high councilor who lived in the ward, said to
LeGrand about the new meetinghouse, "You can't build it, our
people are too poor," the bishop responded, "Then we'll die
trying, because if we don't do it the ward will die, and we aren't
going to let that happen."

President Frank Y. Taylor of Granite Stake gave his full support to the project, saying, "If you people will go to with your
might, it will be accomplished, and you will never feel poorer for
your giving." They went ahead with their plans. Three months
after LeGrand became bishop, he and his counselors began their
campaign for the new building. In September 1919 they presented the priesthood with a plan to sell the present chapel and
purchase other property in the area. The bishop asked for their
response. The brethren expressed their support, and a Brother
Hoare made the motion to sell the present building, buy a lot,
and organize a finance committee to begin gathering funds. The
motion carried with only one dissenting vote.

The site selected was on Twelfth East near Westminster
Avenue, but there was no direct access from the east, where
many ward members lived, and these would have to go north to
Seventeenth South or south to Twenty-First South and then
backtrack. So the bishopric got permission to have an access
street opened—actually an extension of Westminster Avenue
between Twelfth and Thirteenth East streets—which would
provide the people with a more direct route to their meetinghouse. This meant, however, that for the city to improve the
necessary land, the property owners whose lots were affected
must be assessed a moderate sum. Bishop Richards requested
that his property be assessed as an example to the others, although it was not part of the affected area and represented a 147-
foot frontage compared to the others, whose lots ranged from 25
to 90 feet across.

About twenty-five ward members opposed the action so
strenuously that it was taken before the mayor and the city
council for a hearing. The mayor, Charles C. Neslen, said,
"Bring us a petition signed by those who oppose it." But a coun-
cilman openly objected, explaining that the need for the street

was obvious and there was no need for the petition; whereupon the mayor upheld the decision to go ahead and the street was cut through.

By spring of 1923 funds had been raised to purchase a well-situated site, different from that first proposed, and the work went forward. Ward members willingly accepted their building assessments of money and labor. Of special note was the contribution of William J. Dean, contractor, and his son, Vernon, who took over the building supervision at no profit to either of them, donated generously in addition, and allowed credit for every hour of labor that ward members could provide.

The plans had been procured from the Church Architect's Office, then under the direction of Brigham Young's sons Colonel Willard and Don Carlos Young. Bishop Richards hoped for a building similar to those now current, in which the chapel opens to the recreation hall for expanded seating. The colonel was adamant for a separate chapel and amusement hall joined by a spacious foyer. As he and the bishop verbally sparred to reach an agreement, the colonel said, "You know, we Youngs have strong minds of our own"; to which the bishop answered, "Well, that's all right, as long as you don't tangle with a Richards." In the end, however, the younger man acquiesced and the work proceeded according to the Church Architect's plan.

As they struggled to raise money they occasionally reached a standstill, and the bishopric solicited additional funds. They called upon a nonmember storekeeper and asked if he would like to help get the work going again. He hesitated, then went to the back of his store and wrote out a check for two hundred dollars. Many years later LeGrand learned that the man had given the last money he had with which to meet his obligations, but that later the same day he had received that exact amount in payment for a bill he had written off as noncollectible.

It was August 1924 when ward members congregated on the site of the new meetinghouse and President Taylor dedicated it. The cornerstone was laid, and into it were placed "A History of the Building Operation," prepared by Bishop LeGrand Richards, several books, and a list of the ward members. By this time the

Board of Education had bought the old chapel for ten thousand dollars and stipulated that they were to take possession in September. An extension of time must have been granted, for it was January 1925 when the first event was held in the new amusement hall (a party and a dance), and it was April 12 of that year when the members met in the old chapel for the last time. While the balance of the money was being raised and the building completed, all meetings were held in the amusement hall.

While these events were taking place, there was another interesting development. The street which had been cut through in the face of such strong objections proved to be such a convenience to those who had been assessed that one by one they found their way to the bishop and asked his pardon for their original opposition. From the experience LeGrand learned a lesson in administrative technique. It became his policy from then on to give the opposition time to reconsider first, thus allowing the ripening process to precede the action. This procedure, he notes, tends to foster unity among men. Hence his saying, "It is better to be united on a poor policy than divided on a good one."

While he was proving himself an able administrator on the changing, growing ward scene, changes were taking place in the Richardses' home life. The year after he became bishop, LeGrand engaged the Ashton Improvement Company to build a more spacious firebrick home on his Eleventh East property, and he sold the smaller Hollywood Avenue house to F. Orin Woodbury.

On February 8, 1921, daughter Nona was born. To Ina he wrote the following note: "Of all my joys and happiness at this glorious time, the sweetest joy to me is the preservation of your life. For this priceless gift I thank my Heavenly Father." A year and some months later, on July 5, 1922, their son Alden Ross arrived.

These two children were to complete LeGrand's and Ina's family of eight children. Perhaps no other accomplishment of Ina's was so consistently praised nor so deeply appreciated by her husband as was the bringing into life of their sons and daughters. In each note or letter he wrote to her, that theme is central. One from this period accompanied a money gift with which she was to purchase "a new winter outfit" for her thirty-eighth birthday.

> Even though the years of your life that have passed since first we met have been hard indeed, I am sure, when you look upon your accomplishments in that time, you must feel that your life has been rich in works of righteousness. When we have fought the good fight together, and finished our work . . . we shall continue to live in the children you have mothered into this world, and for which you have given your life's blood and strength. You truly are a noble little mother. (Letter, September 14, 1924.)

Ina, too, had a birthday gift for him. She replaced his well-worn Dutch Bible with a small English copy, bound in fine leather. A constant student of the scriptures, he used it heavily. All of the twenty-seven formerly blank reference pages are filled with his closely written notes on gospel subjects, wherein he gives the reference and follows with a terse summary of its contents. To mention only a few, areas of his research and study include: Judged by the Gospel; Faith and Works from Teachings of Christ; Need of Scriptures; Apostasy; and the Restoration. His studies reveal his ever-growing interest and mastery in "fitting the pieces together" into one vast and comprehensive whole.

The partnership LeGrand and Ina had begun sixteen years previously had held firm through varied and demanding circumstances and experiences—her childbearing, their mission, serious illnesses, a child's death, and consistent, heavy demands in the work of the Lord. Theirs was not, however, a long-faced, grim adherence for duty's sake, but rather a glad, good-humored devotion to Church, family, and each other, in that order. She held true to their original partnership terms and never stood in his way where service to the Lord was concerned. (She also served; now she was teaching Gleaner Girls and working in the PTA.) LeGrand for his part was bound by covenant and promise to place the work of the Lord first in their lives, with Ina and the children running a close second.

From the Sugar House period when their father was bishop, the children have some vivid recollections. One says, "Father began his days with faith, enthusiasm, and gusto. We were awakened by his calling from the stairs, 'Rise and shine. Get up and put on your beautiful garments.' " The sound of water in the shower or from the hose outside was accompanied by his "less-than-melodious voice," one continues. "In true operatic fashion he serenaded us with such songs as 'Nellie Bly Caught a Fly and Tied it to the Sky'; 'She's Only a Bird in a Gilded Cage'; and 'Two Little Girls in Blue.' " He was missed when he was away, and his vibrant zest for life filled the home when he returned at night. He would literally burst in with his "Well, I've finished the Lord's work for the day, now what can I do to make my family happy?" They often called him "Busy Shop" instead of bishop.

At a time when tithes and offerings were paid not often by check but in silver, occasional gold pieces, and "greenbacks," he would gather the children about the kitchen table and let them help him stack and count the coins and bills. They were proud to be included. Many experiences were related and many lessons learned as the money was carefully recorded and placed in bags for delivery to the bank the next morning. One child remembers that "Father always put the bags in the pan cupboard overnight, saying that if anyone tried to take them, at least he would be sure to hear."

The children's inclusion in Church activity was evident in Sunday meetings as well. It was not uncommon to see the bishop with one or two of his little ones seated on the stand beside him, while the others sat with Ina. As the new meetinghouse took form, the children were "permitted" to donate their war bonds to the building fund and thus pay for a bench in the chapel. They carried lemonade to the workmen at the site and delivered Ina's pies to the carnival held to raise money. They were proud of their father's position, but they sometimes chafed at being reminded that they must set good examples as befitted the bishop's children, or in following Ina's injunction, "We owe it to Daddy always to look nice."

Although of a loving and tender nature with his family, the bishop could take a firm stand with the children when it was needed. Once when they coaxed and cried to see a Saturday matinee in Sugar House, he said no. The decision held, but then, unhappy over seeing their vast disappointment, he ordered the same film for a ward show and both they and their friends had the pleasure of viewing it.

He could be firm without relenting, too. One time when Ina was not well, he engaged a young Dutch woman to come into the home and help. In an already full house, it was necessary for one daughter to share a double bed with her, a requirement that displeased the child. She took her blanket, pillow, and sensitive feelings out of the bedroom and settled herself under the dining room table, presumably to spend the night. The incident touched correspondingly sensitive feelings in her father; namely, his compassion for his Dutch friends. The spanking he gave was brief and his direction final—that his daughter return promptly to bed.

The Dutch Saints continued to absorb his attention at the office and even in the ward, where two of his friends from the Netherlands now resided. (Abram Dalebout and B. Teimersma, who had published *De Ster* during LeGrand's first mission.) During the time he served as bishop, LeGrand continued to meet in their conferences, and he entertained a large group in his own ward.

His real estate business adequately supported his family, provided funds with which to help others, and now allowed for investment expansion. Midway in 1921, his counselor Elliott C. Taylor moved from the ward. Upon his release, E. T. Ralphs succeeded him; however, the association between LeGrand and Elliott continued through the years and touched their business lives as well. That fall they combined resources with George F. Richards and Heber C. and Moses Taylor to purchase the old Beverage Ford Agency at 309 East 300 South and to establish the Taylor-Richards Motor Company at 161-165 Social Hall Avenue. The 1922 city directory lists the officers of the firm as George F. Richards, President; George F. Jr., Secretary; and Heber C. Taylor, Treasurer. However, George F. Jr. managed the business, with Elliott's brother Heber C. assisting.

From the time he returned from England in February 1919 until the formation of the new company in September 1921,

George F. Jr. worked with his brother in real estate, an experience of which he wrote, "It is glorious to be engaged with LeGrand, and I do appreciate it." (GFR Jr. *Diary*, March 17, 1919.) George later enumerated in a letter to LeGrand (June 18, 1933) the latter's qualities as observed at close range. He saw him as "by nature a wonderful man, blessed with endowments, admirable tendencies, high aspirations, and almost unlimited ambition for the things worthwhile in life."

In all phases of his ward work the bishop gave tirelessly of himself, always in a spirit of camaraderie. As he gave, others were led to give, and because so many were poor, their giving required the exercise of faith sufficient to make sacrifices. This bound them to the ward, to him, and to each other. Although money was scarce and the building program drained the ward members, a steady flow of missionaries accepted calls and went out to labor. At a time when bishops could suggest where their young people could go, he recommended at least five for the Netherlands. One missionary's call which required sacrifice was that of F. Orin Woodbury. Orin had continued in the real estate business with LeGrand until, as their bishop, the latter sent him on a mission to Germany. His wife, Nina, who was also LeGrand's young sister, was an excellent secretary and she worked in his real estate office until her husband's return. That period for the couple was difficult but rewarding.

It was a sacrifice soon to be matched by the bishop and his family. During the opening session of October conference, 1925, President Grant called for a thousand men—one from each of the "thousand" (985) wards in the Church—saying that he wanted "men of mature years and sound judgment who have had experience in the preaching of the gospel . . . who are financially able to go forth and labor in the mission fields of the United States, Canada, and Mexico for at least six months, at their own expense both going and coming." His call was powerfully reiterated by President Charles W. Nibley in the same session, and by Elder Melvin J. Ballard the next day, emphasizing that "bishops and stake presidents will not excuse themselves . . . and indeed no one should feel himself exempt." (*Conference Report*, October 1925, pp. 10-12, 124.)

The call penetrated the heart of Bishop Richards with great force. A visible tremor shook him as he silently committed himself to do the will of the Lord. His counselor E. T. Ralphs, who sat next to him in the Tabernacle, said, "I get it. You're going!"

Chapter 9

Short-Term Mission

1926

Soon after general conference Bishop Richards faced President Frank Y. Taylor of Granite Stake with these words: "You heard what President Grant said. Financially I am as able as any man in my ward to go on such a mission, and I am not the kind of man to pass the buck. So if you want me to go, I am willing to do it."

"I will take up the matter with President Grant," President Taylor responded.

He did, and with no hesitation President Grant said, "Send him." A short-term mission call to the Eastern States soon followed, with instructions to leave on January 6, 1926.

LeGrand set his affairs in order and prepared to leave at the appointed time. He arranged with F. Orin Woodbury to manage the real estate firm in his absence—a wise choice, for Orin kept the business stable so that it provided for Ina and the children, for LeGrand's mission needs, and more.

On November 15 LeGrand was released as bishop and was promptly set apart as an alternate member of the high council in Granite Stake, with the promise that, because of his willing sacrifice, the Lord would bless him, his family, and his business, and that he should have great influence and power for good.

Only he and Ina knew the extent of the sacrifice which was now required of them. It was the first time since their marriage that a call from the Lord would separate them; but by the terms of their partnership it was now required, and they simply submitted to the terms and trusted the Lord to make them equal to the demands imposed.

That winter was cold. Ina was not well, and the thoughts of caring for their seven children without him—her constant support and mainstay—chilled her. Even when he was absent for a day she missed his exuberant, vital presence in the home; now, the six lonely months stretched out even before they had begun. Weighted with apprehension and heavy with reluctance, still she neither complained nor attempted to restrain him, and he loved her all the more. There was a soberness about the children, too, as they faced additional responsibilities and restraints just when their youthful natures were inclined toward greater freedom and more good times. As for LeGrand, he was ever solicitous for Ina's welfare, and he was drawn to her and to each of his children with deep and tender feelings. He knew that he must carry some tangible reminder of them to sustain him during his absence from them, so on December 30 the family posed for a photograph.

On January 6, 1926, LeGrand boarded the train at Salt Lake City's Union Pacific Station at 8:30 P.M. Ina was sick in bed, and LeGrand Jr. stayed at home to care for and comfort her. The other children, with friends and relatives, saw him off in company with five other Eastern States missionaries, among whom was Elder Carroll L. Wadsworth, a twenty-two-year-old from Idaho Falls, who was later assigned as Elder Richards's companion.

After the long train journey to New York City, they reported first to the mission president, B. H. Roberts, a member of the First Council of the Seventy, at 273 Gates Avenue, Brooklyn. He assigned them to the Boston Conference (*conference* was a term then used for a mission district, and there were ten in this mission) under President Eldon Wittwer. President Roberts's instructions to Elder Richards were "not to get in the way of the members or the full-time missionaries, but just show them how to convert." These words proved to be the mission president's only personal communication to Elder Richards until he approved his release six months later.

Upon their arrival in Boston, President Wittwer assigned Elders Richards and Wadsworth to New Bedford, Massachusetts, the once-famous old whaling center located some fifty miles due south of Boston on the Acushnet River and Buzzards Bay and immortalized by Melville's *Moby Dick*. Now it was a cotton-mill, glass, and tool-factory town. In winter, storms from the Atlantic blew into the vast inlet with fierce and relentless fury.

The new missionaries found a room to rent, apportioned their housekeeping duties, and went to work. Two lady missionaries were laboring in New Bedford, and soon the two elders visited some of the families with them. They found that the sisters were faithfully making visits but were not proselyting as such. Elder Richards asked them how long it had been since the last convert baptism. "Sister Marchant was the last," they answered. The records showed that to have been five and a half years previously. Yet for most of that period there had been four full-time missionaries working in the area. Part of the reason for the absence of conversions became apparent almost immediately. The region was as spiritually resistant and cold as the bitter weather that assailed it.

Late in January a blizzard hit, with gales "blowing to beat the band." As the elders attempted to tract, literally clinging to doorposts, women would neither stand to talk with them nor invite them in, so they were obliged to find refuge in the public library and pass the time in study. "My, what a life!" LeGrand wrote Ina, "to be transferred from so many cares and responsibilities to where I have to create work to keep busy. I have all my life felt guilty if I were merely studying. I felt that I should be working."[1]

The following Sunday was a bitter day, and only a handful of the thirty-three branch members attended the sacrament meeting. Elder Richards bore his testimony in the cold building and then took Elder Wadsworth and the lady missionaries out to dinner—an infrequent event, for most of the time the elders ate in their rented rooms, where Elder Wadsworth was cook and Elder Richards "kept house." On a later Sunday evening, he wrote to Ina: "How would you like to have joined us for dinner. We had a can of beans thinned with water and eaten with bread

---

[1] In this chapter, all correspondence quoted is in LGR *Personal Letter File* (1926) in his possession.

and butter." That meal was saved, however, because of a delicious cake Ina had sent. Throughout his mission she supplemented their plain fare with such treats from home.

On February 4 Elder Richards recorded that there arose that morning "the worst storm I have ever seen. It blew a perfect gale, sending the snow in all directions, and continuing all day." The missionaries were forced to remain in their rooms. The next day they again tried to tract, but the snow was so deep that everyone was busy shoveling out. The next day they got in to talk with a Baptist minister, who listened to their message, was receptive to it, but was afraid to commit himself and jeopardize his pension receipts "even if we had the truth." They talked with another minister who would not listen at all because he was "already saved."

Shortly after the great storm a gracious lady allowed them entrance to her home and listened intently. A Mormon at heart, she said, "If we were in Salt Lake City we'd join your church tomorrow, but we just don't have the faith to do it here. My husband is in business, and should we join so unpopular a religion we would surely lose out."

Day after day, between storms, the elders worked. A common response to their message was, "Well, we are Baptists, but if we were to move to Providence, Rhode Island, and our friends were Presbyterians, we would join that church." "The people here are not religious," Elder Richards recorded, "except as a matter of form and social standing, seeing no relation between religion and the requirements of salvation. They are not hunting after truth." Evidently the attitudes were not peculiar to New Bedford, for in Boston President Wittwer wrote for the *Liahona* (February 6, 1926), "While people are rather indifferent toward religion, we are getting into a few homes and interesting people." While his statement was only mildly negative, the last convert baptism in Boston had taken place several years previously.

Whether or not spiritual apathy and coldness were widespread in the mission during that period, they presented a powerful deterrent to the work in New Bedford. Capable and seasoned a missionary though LeGrand was, the conditions threatened to dishearten him and make him wonder if, indeed, he could possibly find success and have the "great influence and power for good" which President Taylor had promised in his pre-mission blessing.

One contact who contributed to his wondering was an unmarried teacher of culture and high education, who welcomed the two missionaries often to her home, listened attentively, applauded and approved while they were there, but had no conviction to motivate her to any kind of commitment. Elder Richards wrote of her, "She is like a ship without a rudder. She seems to have no foundation." He added that it was "oh, so hard to make them feel any need of changing. They think if they just try and live a good life, that should be sufficient, and they can do that with their friends without accepting Mormonism."

There were times when he longed to "take a boat to Holland and work with the religious, Bible-reading Dutch strangers again." To Ina he wrote: "Sometimes it is hard to keep from deserting duty and everything else. When I look ahead, it seems a long time. . . . I just have to take a day at a time." Then as the elders pushed their way though further disappointments and deep snow, Elder Richards worried about Ina. "I can't fancy that you had to shovel snow with so many large children," he wrote, "or didn't you ask them to help? How I wish I could get up nights for you when you are not well." He then made a plea to the children to be their good selves and handle the snow, furnace, and heavy jobs "so things will not be too hard for Mama."

The letters he received from Ina were of inestimable worth to him. While she described the normal tenor of life at home, plus the challenges of carrying on without him, she did not complain but admitted that she didn't "see how he used to do so much before going to work." She reported a child's comment. "Little Alden says, 'You stay too long, he's tired of waiting.'" She sent a Valentine from his "little sweetheart, Nona":

> Some folks I like,
> And some I don't.

> And some I will,
>> And some I won't.
> And one I like
>> Enough for two.
> This favorite one,
>> Of course, is you.

And Ina poured out her love for him. "I tell the children how I love them, but Daddy stands above all and seems like life itself to me."

Her words sustained him as he struggled to gain a foothold in the discouraging and bleak spiritual terrain. Not able to make any headway at all with strangers, the elders worked to reactivate members who had dropped away. One family, the Birdwells, had not been to church for two years, and the conference president said the missionaries need no longer visit them; but not wishing to miss any possible opportunity, Elder Richards and Wadsworth did go out into the country where the family lived, found them, had a fine visit, were brought home in the man's car, and obtained a promise from him that his family would begin attending church again. It was one heartening experience.

They made four attempts before finally contacting the Hadleys. Through them and certain others they tried to set up cottage meetings. No was the answer in every case. After several such answers the elders returned to their rooms feeling how unpopular Mormons really were. Elder Richards placed his family's photograph before him, reread all his letters from home, and wrote to his family: "This is a day when I belong there more than here. I'm loving you all from your picture. My, what a fine little crowd." He then advised Ina in her concern over the fact that boys were hovering about their teen-aged girls: "You must lay down the law to them. Have the boys come in for proper visits, and not expect to see the girls outside." To Norinne he wrote a special letter, saying, "I want you to meet lots of boys and associate with different young people, and then you will be better able to make a good choice. You deserve the very best the land produces, and if you are careful, I am sure that is what you will get." (March 31, 1926.)

*1925 family photo Elder Richards took with him on his short-
term mission to the Eastern States.*

As if acute homesickness and near total discouragement were
not enough to try his faith, Elder Richards's eyes went bad on
him, as they had in Holland. He could not read at all. He
recorded, "The feeling is just like seasickness—severe headache,
nausea." As it turned out, however, his eye trouble led him to
Dr. Rothwell on Spring Street, who had once practiced in
Murray, Utah, and who became a good friend. He and his wife
welcomed the elders for meals and visits, although they were of
the same spiritual disposition as most of the people and did not
receive the gospel even from their friends the elders.

In the hopes of breaking down the spiritual barriers, Elder
Richards decided to try another approach. Drawing from his
experience as mission president in Holland, where he increased
attendance by adding an evening meeting to the existing Sunday
School and hour-long sacrament service, he asked President
Wittwer for permission and funds to rent a hall to hold such
meetings. The matter went to the mission president, who didn't
object to the additional meeting but said no funds were available.
Accordingly Elder Richards located a hall and paid the rent from

his own pocket for the duration of his mission. In this way, formerly inactive members and friends (made through continued tracting) were attracted and began slowly to join some of the most faithful members. The Birdwells were some of the first to respond. Elder Richards reported to Ina: "I have fully made up my mind that I must content myself with the thought that the work here is different than in Holland, but I am satisfied that I am doing considerable good here. . . . Our Sunday evening meeting is going to help us a good deal."

For the most part, the responsibility to initiate and lead out in the work was upon Elder Richards. Although older than present missionaries when first sent into the field, Elder Wadsworth was inexperienced. Sometimes his older companion conducted sessions in which he let the young man explain the gospel to him. Elder Richards would then correct, suggest, and fill in as needed, so Elder Wadsworth could feel more comfortable in talking with strangers. For all that, the young elder was a fine man, conscientious, totally compatible, and he lent his wholehearted support to whatever his forty-year-old companion initiated. They were both encouraged that on a certain Sunday forty-four people had attended the evening meeting. Elder Richards preached a powerful sermon, and Mr. Marchant, nonmember husband of the last convert (five and a half years previous) was there and said, "It is a crime. Such an address should go to hundreds, not just to these few."

With these results the elders took heart, although they still felt that much of their efforts were expended in what was virtually a spiritual wasteland. Frequently they met with icy receptions as well as apathetic expressions and even blatant rebuttals to doctrinal persuasions. Upon visiting with a woman who had six bright, healthy children, they were touched by the family's eternal potential, and with characteristic skill Elder Richards explained the principle of celestial marriage as taught by the Church. To this the mother replied, "Well, I've had enough of their father in this life that I wouldn't care to put up with him in the next." For Elder Richards, who cherished his wife and family and was so loved in return, such a view was incomprehensible.

With the prevalent atheists there was no base upon which to touch ground. "It is hard where there is no measuring rod," he wrote. And with Catholics there were basic differences in doctrine which made the going most difficult. One day Elder Richards discussed with a woman of that faith the origin, need, and merits of baptism by immersion. Concerning his explanation, she challenged, "What in thunder difference does it make?" He left her door with a heavy heart. "I knew when I was whipped," he said. Then, in that moment of deep disappointment, his fighting spirit surfaced and he saw and felt something he'd never seen or experienced before. "Well, what in thunder difference *does* it make anyway, unless I can first show the importance of the gospel restoration itself and the mission of the Prophet Joseph Smith in it." He recorded, "I decided that I must convince those people that I had the greatest thing in all the world or I should be home with my wife and children and with my business." (*Blue Book*, p. 67, and interview.)

The light of comprehension which came at that moment illuminated his whole being. Suddenly his years of gospel study, his lifelong committing of scriptures to memory, his preaching of the word, his faithful prayers, his seeking after spiritual excellence, his giving of self, and even his present cold disappointment and struggle—all these fused together in a burst of inspired comprehension and knowing. He had caught brief glimpses of this on his previous missions, when he taught the Apostasy and the Restoration, but now bits and pieces, segments and splinters, merged together in their true perspective and wholeness. Never again would he expect any person to understand and accept the gospel unless he first laid the foundation, built the structure, put on the roof, set windows and doors in place, and furnished the whole to the last detail. After all, could anyone sell a house if the client saw only a hole in the ground, the studs in place, or the window frames? Of course not!

So overpowering and deep were the convictions of those moments that they became both base and star out of which evolved his later great contribution to the missionary effort of the Church—his book *A Marvelous Work and a Wonder.*

That Easter, in a letter to Ina, he expressed the depth of his feelings:

> I have been blessed this day with thoughts of sincerest grati-
> tude to my Heavenly Father for his mercies and blessings unto me.
> I think I have never before entered so completely into the spirit of
> the Savior's crucifixion, and the events preceding and following.
> . . . And when I realize that the gospel, as we have it, has come
> to the earth to prepare the way of his coming . . . I feel that it is a
> glorious thing to be numbered among those who have given so
> freely for its establishment upon the earth. I would not want to be
> unworthy of the companionship, eternally, of those who have
> borne the burdens in the heat of the day. I pray that whatever else
> may come to me in life, that my humble efforts may receive his
> divine acceptance, for I do want to be worthy of his love. . . .
> (April 4, 1926.)

From then on the work seemed to be imbued with a special spirit. One of the lady missionaries, Sister Madsen, said, "Missionary life seems entirely different to us now." She realized that she and her companion had neglected their duty by just visiting people rather than diligently teaching them the gospel.

In March, Elder Richards and his companion scoured New Bedford to determine a suitable place to hold street meetings. Finding one, they visited the chief of police and gained permission to hold them, not in the center of town where they would cause congestion on the narrow streets, but out at the South End in a suburb which Elder Richards compared to Sugar House in Salt Lake City. To celebrate their success in obtaining such permission, the elders spent that Saturday afternoon with the sister missionaries going through the famous Bourne Whaling Museum on Johnny Cake Hill.

Hard tracting continued, becoming a little easier as the weather eased off. President Wittwer came down from Boston one weekend to check on the work and to speak in the evening meeting. He was more than pleased with the work and encouraged them to go ahead with the proposed street meetings. Just as he left, a sudden late snowstorm hit which continued for a day and a half. Because of lingering cold weather it was actually

April 14 (the nicest day since they had arrived) before the elders
and sisters held their first street meeting.

"I didn't know how it would work," LeGrand reported to
Ina, "for I didn't know whether I could talk to a moving crowd
or not. . . . After we had sung, and I called them in and prayed,
Sister Madsen spoke first, but two dogs kept chasing each other
through the crowd, and she had a hard time to keep her thoughts
centered, so she turned it over to me. Well, I got warmed up, and
got the spirit of it, and held a crowd of about eighty for forty
minutes, and at the very best of attention." In his journal he expressed great appreciation for the Lord's sustaining Spirit, and he
admitted that he had enjoyed the experience very much. Thus,
with his mission two-thirds over, he finally found an effective
medium in which to carry on the work.

It proved to be the breakthrough they had been struggling
for. The next day they left for Boston to attend a conference
priesthood meeting and were met by President Wittwer. While
there, Elder Richards helped the Boston elders with their street
meetings. Both on Boston Common and at Pemberton Square he
spoke to crowds in excess of a hundred, after which the various
elders split up with small groups to answer questions, explain the
gospel in more detail, distribute tracts, and sell copies of the
Book of Mormon until the police cleared them out at 10:00 P.M.
"I got quite a thrill out of it," Elder Richards recorded that
night.

That Sunday President Wittwer asked him to talk to the
missionaries, and the Lord blessed him to speak with great
power. Again in Lynn, Massachusetts, he was given all the
speaking time in sacrament meeting, and he wrote that he "enjoyed the Spirit in such an abundance" that he lost all track of
time, "as did the audience." Greatly pleased, he recorded that
"more than ever before, my labors are appreciated."

By no means, however, had he and his companion seen the
end of opposition, for when they returned to New Bedford and
held their next street meeting with a good crowd listening, the
Gospel Hall people (a noisy, extreme sect) dismissed their meeting up the street and came to heckle the missionaries. Elder

Richards took over for the younger elder and said to the disturbers, "Now, you folks would like to be gentlemen, wouldn't you? I'll tell you what we'll do. You give us twenty minutes to finish our meeting, and then we and the crowd will remain a half-hour and listen to you." To this the opposition and the crowd agreed. When the opposition got their turn, it was only to tear down the Mormons. One said, "Why, if you would let them, these Mormons would bind the Book of Mormon in the same cover with the Bible and ask us to take it and like it."

Not wanting the meeting to close on that note, Elder Richards said, "You wouldn't mind if I make an announcement before the meeting closes, would you?" No objection was raised, so he addressed the crowd: "If you will come back next Tuesday at seven-thirty, I will tell you why we would bind the Book of Mormon in the same cover with the Bible and ask you to take it and like it. Bring your Bibles with you, for you will have no further use for them after that day, if you are not willing to accept the companion volume of scriptures which the Lord promised he would bring forth and put with your Bibles."

His announcement provided effective bait for the crowd. The next week they came with friends they had brought along to see the fun. The missionaries sold sixteen copies of the Book of Mormon and gave another to Mrs. Hendricks, a Portuguese woman, who had no money with her. She had been prepared spiritually by a dream to receive such a book and she was hungry to be taught. "What a joy to teach those whose hearts the Lord has prepared," Elder Richards wrote in his journal that night. By May 2 he was finally feeling encouraged that his mission would not, after all, be a failure. The next week their calendar was completely filled with appointments, and other visits were scheduled for dates further in the future.

One visit was to the McDonald home, to which the elders would return a number of times. The man was confined to his bed; and his wife would never come in and listen to the elders, but instead went into an adjoining room, left the door opened, and ironed. Elder Richards made it his business to speak loudly enough that she could hear what he was telling her husband.

Mr. McDonald had never joined any church, but every time the elders left, he would say, "I guess I have been a Mormon all my life and didn't know it."

On the last visit of his mission, Elder Richards said to the man's wife, "Mrs. McDonald, won't you come in and listen to me today? You have never so honored me, and you may never see me again in this life." She came in, and he asked her husband to let her follow along in his Bible, a thing he liked to have people do so that they would not think the missionaries were using different Bibles than theirs.

They had just started their discussion when the couple's son, a student at Harvard, came in. His mother said to him, "You are just in time. You have a trained mind. You sit down and show us how this man is trying to lead us astray." The elder discussed the promise to Joseph of a new land in the utmost bounds of the everlasting hills, where that land is, and the two records which the Lord commanded should be kept. The son followed along in the family Bible.

When Elder Richards was through, he closed his Bible and said to the young man, "Please tell your mother how I am trying to lead you astray." The young man turned to his mother and said, "This man isn't trying to lead you astray; he is teaching you the truth."

As the missionaries prepared to leave, Mrs. McDonald said, "Mr. Richards, even if I don't believe what you are trying to tell us, there is something about you I can't help liking. Won't you pray with us before you go?" Her heart was closed to the truth; and the men also, although convinced of the truth of what they had been taught, did not join the Church. (*Blue Book*, p. 66, and interview.)

Before the elders left for a mission conference in Boston, however, others showed great sincerity and real promise as repeat visits were made and the gospel was more fully taught to them. The conference was to be presided over by Church President Heber J. Grant, and President B. H. Roberts would of course be there. There was a good deal of anticipation of a spiritual feast, and Elder Richards looked forward to seeing again his friend

President Grant. At the conference he would also learn of his mission release. It was disappointing, however, that after the public announcements made and the encouragement given to the people, attendance at the meetings was poor and there were few strangers there. New Bedford had a better showing than most of the branches. There was no explanation for the poor attendance except that many members were not sufficiently committed to make the trip and that people in general were "simply not hunting for the truth."

That night Elder Richards stayed in the home of a member in Lynn, Massachusetts. With the disappointment of the poorly attended meetings fresh in his mind, he drifted off to sleep and had this dream, which he recorded the next evening, Monday, May 10, 1926. (LGR *Journal*, vol. VIII, p. 89.)

> I had a very beautiful dream last night. I dreamed that while we were met together in priesthood meeting, the Savior appeared [in a pillar of light], and immediately we began to sing "Hosanna, Hosanna, Hosanna to our Lord." It was a most wonderful feeling, and I awakened with the thought that, though the world doubted his coming, I had actually lived to see it. It was a sweet and beautiful climax. I do hope I will be worthy of him when he does appear, for I do know he shall come. (Retold in interview with a minor correction to journal entry as indicated in brackets.)

While still at the conference, Elder Wadsworth had been instructed to report for the month-long training school to be held at mission headquarters in Brooklyn. Elder Richards was to have a new companion for the remaining weeks before his release, which was set for June 14. Realizing the critical need for follow-through on his now considerable number of investigators, and with the termination of his mission imminent, he told President Wittwer that if he did not send a good, capable elder to follow up on his investigators when he left, he would never forgive the president in this world or the next. "It has cost me too much in time, effort, and means to fill this mission, and I cannot afford to see my efforts fail and my work go back to seed." (*Blue Book*, p. 66.)

President Wittwer took no offense at the strong words but

fully understood what was at stake. As Elder Wadsworth's replacement he sent Elder Thomas K. Bailey, a capable, twenty-
seven-year-old schoolteacher from Arbon, Idaho. This elder
labored faithfully to become acquainted with each investigator
and to assist fully in the wind-up of the work so painstakingly
begun by Elder Richards and his earlier companion. After three
weeks of whirlwind activity, Elder Bailey told President Stonely
of the Providence, Rhode Island, Branch, "I had not previously
known what missionary work really was."

On May 14 LeGrand reported his release date to Ina and
firmed up plans for her to accompany his former counselor
Elliott Taylor and his wife to Detroit, where he would join them
at the close of his mission. Then, remembering their anniversary
due on May 19, he wrote, "It would be hard to get nearer
heaven than the night I first held you to my heart as my own
darling wife."

When Ina's answering letter came, it was a contrast in joy
and sorrow. She was elated with the news of his release and the
plans for the trip. "I am like a youngster," she wrote. "I can't
wait. If I once get hold of your coat again, I am just going to stay
with you." But she was obliged to tell him of the sudden death of
Katherine Curtis, young daughter of his other former counselor,
Alex Curtis. The same day a letter came from George, LeGrand's
brother, telling of his son's lingering illness and of the despair he
felt. Elder Richards recorded, "I lost myself and had a good cry."
That night he wrote letters of comfort to both sorrowing families
and then stayed up late to call Ina long-distance—a rare
occurrence for that time. Ina was both frightened and ecstatic.
"How I did shake. . . ." she wrote to him, "but I was so thrilled, I
still love the looks of the telephone corner."

Hard as it was, Elder Richards turned his thoughts away
from home and family. The elders' days and nights were now
filled with visits to investigators. Time and again Elder Richards
recorded eight- to ten-hour days of talking until his "jaws
ached." One elderly lady told him that it would be a shame for
him to leave the mission field and that the Church should support his family so he could remain in New Bedford to teach the
people.

While tracting one day, the missionaries came to a door where the lady said, "Mr. Richards, what are you trying to do anyway? Are you trying to make Mormons out of us all?" He replied, "Well, we will never ask you to join the Mormon Church, but if I can show you how you can trade one dollar for five, I won't have to ask you to do it, will I?" She replied, "I get you." She was one of the contacts Elder Bailey was able to successfully follow through on. After Elder Richards went home, she wrote to him expressing her appreciation for the challenge he had given. "I decided to trade the one dollar for five," she said. "I was baptized last Friday."

With applications for baptisms beginning to come—Mrs. Hendricks; the nonmember husband of Sister Roberts; the Hadley mother and daughter—Elders Richards and Bailey looked for a suitable place to hold a baptismal service. They went to the YMCA and requested the use of the pool during hours it was not scheduled. "No!" said the man in charge. "Would you please state your objections?" they asked. "Well, you're Mormons aren't you?" was his curt and final reply.

The only alternative proved to be Buzzards Bay, the vast inlet from the Atlantic. They went out to select a possible place and decided on Harbor View, where cottages were not yet occupied and there was a measure of seclusion. On Saturday, June 12, Elder Richards baptized four adults and two children— the first convert baptisms for New Bedford in six years. The next day the six were confirmed. Eighty people were present, of whom twenty were investigators—nearly all of them found during the six months of Elder Richards's mission. In gratitude he recorded that night, "The Lord has sustained me in my last effort." And true to his trust, Elder Bailey labored untiringly for the remainder of his term; and the Lord sustained *him* to bring an additional fourteen of the twenty into the Church during the following year. A visiting member of the Twelve later told Elder Richards that the New Bedford effort was one of the greatest pieces of missionary work he had ever known.

On the Monday following the confirmations, the newly baptized member, Brother Roberts, drove Elder Richards into Boston to catch his train for Detroit. Of the journey, LeGrand wrote, "It would be hard to express my feelings as I neared Detroit. I arrived at 1:25, having *so* looked forward to this day. I found Ina . . . and my joy was full."

That evening they visited with Elliott and his wife, Mame, and the next day they took delivery on a new Chrysler for Elliott at the factory. They also ordered one for LeGrand to pick up two weeks later. For the intervening time they toured Eastern Canada and Upper New York and visited Church history sites, New York City, and Washington, D.C., returning then to Detroit for LeGrand's Chrysler Crown sedan. The couples lunched, said their good-byes, and started home separately.

LeGrand and Ina visited more Church history locations on their way; but when they reached Kansas City on July 1 it was unbearably hot. In those days neither cars nor hotels had air conditioning. Ina was weak and felt ill, so to spare her strength LeGrand drove her to Topeka, Kansas, put her on the train for home, and continued on alone. On the Fourth of July family members met him in Parley's Canyon, and as many as could pile into the new car rode the rest of the way home with him to Sugar House.

As he contemplated getting back to work, he felt a little like the man in the lines:

> Home from his journey, Farmer John
> Arrived this morning safe and sound,
> With his new clothes off
> And his old clothes on,
> "Now I'm myself," said Farmer John.

> (*Blue Book*, p. 70.)

Chapter 10

California: Bishop and Stake President

1929-1933

LeGrand quickly picked up the strands of life at home. President Frank Y. Taylor promptly reinstalled him as a high councilor in the Granite Stake. Under his resumed personal direction his business continued to prosper. He sold the Sugar House property, buying and moving his family to a larger, lovelier home on Harvard Avenue in Normandy Heights—where the president of Liberty Stake, Bryant S. Hinckley, soon called him again to the high council.

Ina was in poor health as a result of physical setbacks received since his return—a full-term stillborn baby girl, then later a miscarriage—but the lovely new home, developing friendships, and happy environment had raised her spirits and there was hope for her recovery. Life indeed looked good.

But another change was on the way. In December 1929 LeGrand's father came to his Main Street real estate office. "President Grant wants to know," George F. said, "whether you would be willing to move to California and serve as the president of Hollywood Stake."

"Well, Father," LeGrand responded, "I have my business here with a dozen people depending upon me for their jobs. I don't know what I'd do for a living in California. We have a lovely new home where Ina and the children are happy. Our daughters are at the mating age and have many fine friends." Then he said, "You'd better tell the President that I think enough of the Lord, the Church, and him that if this is what he wants, I will go down and look around to see how I can earn a living."

George F. reported LeGrand's response to President Grant and soon told his son, "The President says for you to go down and look around." So on January 30, 1930, after selling his business and putting his home up for sale, LeGrand left by car for Southern California, telling his eldest son, LeGrand A., that he was "now the present man of the house, and to see that Mama is well cared for."

It was the tag-end of winter with its slush, snow, and bleakness when Ina, saddened over the necessary move, began to supervise small repairs, show the home to prospective buyers, and sort and pack less-used items—tasks which seemed mountainous in her weak condition.

For his part, as soon as LeGrand passed from the snow and cold into the California sunshine, he was full of enthusiasm for the area and could hardly wait to bring his family there to enjoy it with him. He wrote to Ina, "I need you and the kiddies now to make this a perfect home." He stayed in a modest hotel in Glendale and made contact with his former friends Alex Nibley and Preston Cannon, who suggested that he work with them selling real estate in Rossmoyne (a residential development largely owned by President Charles W. Nibley). In the face of the Great Depression, which had begun to get a stranglehold upon the country since the market crash of the previous October, LeGrand prepared to join them.

He studied nightly for his California Real Estate Board examinations, which he later passed, and worked diligently to get into a position to bring his family to California. He counted heavily upon the sale of the Harvard Avenue home for expenses and reserve. He encouraged Ina with his letters and sent a picture of a handsome Spanish-type house which would be within their price range when the Salt Lake house was sold. But up in Salt Lake, Ina's spirits lagged. She was confined to her bed part of the time, and Marian, now seventeen, was missing considerable school to care for her and help with the younger children. Marian wrote a poignant letter to her father. In part it read:

> I'm afraid this letter is going to be a little lectury, but I love
> you a lot, so pardon it, please. Mother is awfully blue . . . I find

her in tears every time she gets a letter. . . . She wouldn't tell you, but I can see what's happening, so I am. Please don't hold it against me 'cause I love you lots. . . . You know you're my only Daddy and we're terribly lost without you. (January 1930.)

LeGrand's answer to them was one of understanding, promise, and encouragement. To Ina he wrote, "It does look like I'm a traitor to run off and leave it all to you, but my desire is to share the burden with you. It would be such a joy to help you again." In answer to his daughter, he said, "Tell Marian I will just love her forever, teach her to drive the car, and do most anything to please her if she will just settle down and look after you so you will not break under the strain. She has it in her to make up her school easily."

In his next letter to them he wrote, "I am afraid if I don't come for you pretty soon, you will not want to come." Accordingly he decided that even if the Harvard Avenue house stood empty, he would get his family together again. He took over the lease on a Glendale home and brought his family there to be with him again. The older girls remained in Salt Lake to finish the school year—Mercedes teaching and Norinne attending the University of Utah.

In late May LeGrand returned to Salt Lake, finally to sell the Harvard Avenue home, pay all debts (which left him only a modest reserve), and bring his older girls home. Before he left Salt Lake, Joseph Grant Iverson, a favorite of the family, met with LeGrand and told him he had asked Mercedes to be his wife. Her father shook Grant's hand and assured him that there was no other man in the world to whom he would rather say yes for Mercedes.

In California the family attended Glendale Ward, which met in Stepper Auditorium, and entered into its activities. These were limited when compared with the stimulating ward and stake from which they had come.

It was not long before the president of Hollywood Stake, not having been informed of the reason for the move to California, called LeGrand to be bishop of Glendale Ward. When the information reached President Grant he wrote the stake leader that, since LeGrand had previously been so tied up with Church work and was just getting established in business, it might be best to let him get his feet on the ground before being called to so demanding a position. LeGrand heard of it and wrote his father with total frankness and uncommon sensitivity to the local situation:

> Father, Glendale Ward is down on everything, and I think I'd better *be* bishop while I'm getting acquainted. If I am appointed stake president now, there will be an insurrection on the part of the leaders down here to think that a man was sent down from Salt Lake when they have so many talented men here in the stake. If I could lift Glendale Ward up, that would be my approach to the other appointment. (Letter and interview.)

George F. so informed President Grant, who in turn sent word to the stake president that they had reconsidered and it would be all right to appoint LeGrand as bishop.

Nothing happened, however, until late in June when George F. happened to be on a brief vacation and visiting in Glendale. It was decided that he and LeGrand would take a trip to San Diego, which LeGrand had heard was a beautiful place, and while they were gone the stake president came to Glendale Ward and released all the ward officers and had LeGrand sustained as bishop.

LeGrand and his father returned from San Diego and learned what had taken place. In sacrament meeting the next Sunday when the new bishop met with his ward, he said to the congregation: "Well, I guess I'm the only man in the ward with a Church job. Now, all of you who are willing to sustain the officers as they were before they were released last Sunday, except the former bishopric, please indicate it." All were willing, so he put them back to work.

He chose as his counselors William D. LeCheminant and Nephi L. Anderson. The new bishopric held their officers' training meeting and there received assurances of support in making any new assignments they wished. It lifted them to a new level of activity. Reed E. Callister, who was appointed Young Men's

Mutual Improvement Association president, said that Glendale had been a "dead ward into which was breathed new life."

Under the new leadership the ward (home) teachers were reorganized and reassigned for greater coverage and efficiency. The bishopric worked to activate, strengthen, and prepare the youth of the Aaronic Priesthood for their missions. They encouraged the Saints to hold family home evening. His journal shows that the bishop faithfully observed it in his own home as an example.

Most ward members were from out of state, with a predominance of Utahns, and they needed sociality with each other; yet the ward was eight hundred dollars in debt, hard times were upon them, and public entertainment was out of reach for most. Long before the system became Church policy, the bishopric met with the priesthood and had them approve a budget system which would provide for maintenance and amusement expenses, with provision also to pay off the debt.

In the ward was a gifted man whom the bishop had earlier considered for a counselor but who could not serve in that capacity because of a Word of Wisdom problem. "Bishop Richards," this man said, "I'd do anything to help you that I'd be permitted to do." The Bishop answered, "Would you take over the ward finances, other than tithes and offerings?" "I will," was the ready response, and the man was totally faithful and effective in that position. The debt was paid, maintenance payments were met, and money was provided for the monthly ward party held— dinners, dances, socials—with no additional charge for member admission. These events were so successful that it was humorously related that people attended church to learn when the next party would be held. Commenting upon the finance chairman, Bishop Richards said, "What a waste of manpower it would have been to keep that talented man from performing so important a service just because of a physical weakness he had not yet found strength to overcome!"

His estimate of this brother was typical of Bishop Richards. He sought always to reach for a man's potential and then lift him to attain it. To aid him in his already keen perception about

people, the bishop kept a little notebook, and when he observed
someone who was gifted or adept at something, he made an
entry to that effect; then, as particular needs arose, he had a
ready reference to consult. He used this technique not only for
party planning but for more serious Church functions and for
assigning workers. He was committed to delegation and to finding those who could perform services in a superior manner.

One day when he visited the stake center, located in Wilshire Ward chapel, Sister Kathrine Higginbotham, who acted as
receptionist for visitors there and also did much of the detail
work for the stake clerk, said to him, "Bishop, how do you get all
your members talking about you and your ward?" "Just put them
all to work and show them a good time," was his breezy answer.

By Christmas of 1930 the ward was welded into a smooth-
running, harmonious unit. On the home front too changes were
taking place. In the fall Marian had gone to Salt Lake for a
promised year at the University of Utah. Norinne worked at the
First National Bank and Trust of Los Angeles and had received a
proposal of marriage from Reed Callister. The older boys were
active in school and sports and had part-time work. Nona and
Alden were now acquainted in their school but happy for the
holiday break. Ina was still somewhat homesick for family and
friends in Utah, so when they went to Salt Lake for Mercedes's
wedding on January 1, 1931, it was with pleasure not only at the
temple ceremony performed by LeGrand's father and the Hotel
Utah wedding breakfast and reception, but to be in Salt Lake
again among old friends and many relatives. It was with some
reluctance that Ina left her two daughters and returned to California with LeGrand.

He came back to his bishop's responsibilities with new enthusiasm. He noted in his journal that the spiritual progress of
the ward was reflected in the tithing receipts for the first quarter
of the year. They had doubled over the same period of the previous year, and this in spite of the deepening economic depression. He was still aware of the call that could come to him at any
time, so to assist him in becoming better acquainted with the
stake leadership, Bishop Richards and his counselors invited the

stake presidency, the high council, and all the stake officers with their spouses to a chicken dinner and entertainment.

For the latter, they had a man dressed as St. Peter. A committee of sisters checked with the wives of the stake leaders and obtained personal information concerning each of these brethren, so that when they came before their judge, St. Peter was able to ask them questions about things which greatly surprised them. This caused such interest and merriment that the party was long remembered.

On April 25, about 1:00 P.M., the bishop received a telephone call from Elder George Albert Smith asking that he come into Los Angeles right away and meet with him and Elder Joseph Fielding Smith at their hotel. This he did. They explained that they had been appointed to attend the Hollywood Stake conference and reorganize the stake presidency. The presiding authorities had selected Bishop Richards to be the new president of the stake. In his journal the bishop recorded that he had had a long and very pleasant discussion with the two Brethren concerning the affairs of the stake and had explained that, despite "the understanding I had previously had with the Presidency, if there were some other man better qualified to take the place, I would be perfectly satisfied to continue as bishop of Glendale Ward, which labor I had enjoyed very much."

In his talk with these Brethren, the bishop learned that the high council and stake members were circulating a petition against the release of their president. In subsequent suggestions to the Brethren, Bishop Richards demonstrated a wise appraisal of both men and situations. He suggested that they might submit the matter to the priesthood leadership of the stake and ascertain their feelings. The Brethren agreed, a vote was taken, and Bishop Richards received about the same number of votes as the first counselor to the stake president. It was enough of a showing in his favor that the apostles decided to go ahead with the reorganization and install the bishop as president.

They asked whom he would like for his counselors. Guided by inspiration, he said, "For my first counselor, I'd like the man who headed the petition." "I don't believe he would accept,"

George Albert Smith commented. "I don't think he would either," LeGrand responded, "but it would stop him from leading any activity against me." The brother did refuse to accept. Bishop Richards's next choice was the second man on the petition, David A. Cannon, who accepted. (After he had served for a few months, he thanked his new president for selecting him, saying that he could feel himself growing under his leadership. Although this was unknown at the time, he was progressing toward later leading the stake himself.)

The visiting Brethren then offered to release all the former high council members so that the new president could start with a clean slate. "Oh no," LeGrand said, "I don't want them standing on the bank saying 'Watch him swim.' Just give me the high council as they are, and within a year I will have them all for me or release them one by one." As a result of these careful moves, that leadership body "never had a riffle."

Charles H. Norberg was selected as second counselor and was set apart with Presidents Richards and Cannon at the conference on May 3, 1931. Sister Kathrine Higginbotham continued doing the detail work of a stake clerk until quarterly conference in October of that year. President Richards always had a high regard for women and their ability to do important work, and with President Grant's approval he had her sustained and set apart as clerk of Hollywood Stake.

One of only 104 stakes in the Church, Hollywood had a membership of 5,891, with its Melchizedek Priesthood divided as follows: 203 high priests, 111 seventies, and 597 elders. There were fifteen units, which included wards and both independent and dependent branches.

The immediate concern of the presidency was fourfold: to overcome rifts and factions, to weld the stake family together, to harness the talents and abilities of its members, and to build spirituality. Two slogans were adopted to implement new approaches to old issues: "Not failure, but low aim is often our greatest sin," and "Work for everyone, and everybody working." In order to understand and appreciate what was accomplished, conditions at the outset of the new presidency's tenure need to be considered and a close look taken at the new president as he led the way.

A competent observer, Wilford G. Edling, still living at this writing (1982), was a young member of the high council under President Richards. Having a part in the actions and decisions of that body, and later serving as stake president, he had insight into both the nature of the men involved and the conditions that obtained in the stake at the time. Says he:

> Deep-rooted factions in the stake involved members of the presidency, the high council, and other leadership, and President Richards found himself in a position where drastic changes of attitude, of organization, and social patterns were imperative. To see how these matters were brought up in the high council, the questions he would ask, the penetrating review that he would make of persons' individual concepts, was a wonderful experience. Implementation of actions often called for changing officers, sometimes releasing them without assigning other duties, sometimes shifting them from one office to another by reason of association, friendships, communal activities that would foster and supplement changes for good; and he did it with the end result not only of holding friendships but building them. Some who had been quite critical of him turned out to be his best supporters. In many cases he was able to change their whole concept of the gospel and its application in their lives. Things that had been important ceased to be so; others that were not, because they were not clearly understood, now came to the fore and became powerful motivating factors by which the members could live.

Brother Edling becomes even more precise in his observation of President Richards as he continues to tell about the latter's dealings with the council.

> He always came to the high council meetings with a clear-cut program. He knew exactly what he wanted to discuss and how much time should be devoted to any one subject, and he didn't hesitate, in his very friendly, kind, but positive way, to bring us back if we got off or took too much time. He was always in command, but it was by way of directing and leading, not commanding us. I have never seen him say or do anything that would cause a person to think less of himself. Instead, he had the ability to build each one up in his own eyes as well in the eyes of others.

Inside, he was always firm. I have never seen him change his mind because someone disagreed with him, but I have seen him change it, and then lend his total support to an issue, if, after further evidence and explanation, he was convinced of its greater merit.

There were in the stake at that time a few highly educated and professional people who had not given the same attention to getting and keeping a testimony as they had to their secular studies and professions. For instance, one member of the high council, a doctor, said, "President Richards, I don't know that the gospel is true." "But you *can* know it if you want to," was the president's answer, "and you *will* know if you will just give a fraction of the time to find it out that you gave in getting your medical education, and then add a little earnest prayer." Shortly after this the man filled an assignment to one of the wards with his president, and there he bore fervent testimony concerning the Prophet Joseph and the restoration of the gospel. "Well, you found out, didn't you!" the president said after the meeting. "I certainly did," the doctor replied.

It will be seen that in many different ways President Richards liked to challenge people to do better, to be better, and to work for the highest good. For instance, parties then being held by stake leaders reflected the social status of some of them. In the beautiful lounge of the Wilshire Ward chapel entertainments were held for which formal dress was required for men and women alike. In connection with this practice, the new president gave his view. He too enjoyed wearing a tuxedo, but until the least member of the most distant ward bishopric could comfortably afford to wear one, formal dress would be optional and he would wear his Sunday suit. Yet because he was a great believer in the value of parties and socializing among the members of the Church, he fostered and enjoyed them. Monthly, two high councilors and their wives were assigned to plan an entertainment for the stake officers and their companions, and at Christmastime a party was held for all stake and ward leaders and their spouses. These events did much to promote unity and closeness.

Having equitably settled the matter of formal dress, the president promptly had another divisive practice discontinued—the ribboning off of front sections of the chapel to reserve seats for ward and stake leaders at conferences. Thereafter, those of the general membership who made an effort to come early took whatever seats they wished.

As changes were made and individuals were won over to consider the good of others, an increasing sense of unity prevailed, first in the stake family but also reaching into the wards. This was achieved partly by the president's inviting members of the high council and stake auxiliary boards to attend ward conferences along with the presidency at a time when this practice was not yet standard Church policy. Each was to come prepared to make a spiritual contribution but no one was to be disappointed if he was not called upon, for the president would keep track and see that each had an opportunity in his turn. Some wonderful ward conferences were held. The stake leaders were built up by the testimonies they bore, and the ward members felt the spirit of the stake visitors. When bishoprics saw the support the stake leaders gave their conferences, they in turn pledged the support of their memberships at stake conference. The result is reflected in attendance figures for the first conference after LeGrand became stake president, as compared with those of eighteen months later. (At that time, three Sunday sessions were held.)

July 11, 1931   1) 236   2) 993   3) 481
January 21, 1933   1) 503   2) 1562   3) 1538

(Hollywood Stake *Historical Record*, LDS Church Archives.)

Not only was growth reflected in numbers, but increased activity resulted from the philosophy that there was something for every man, woman, and child to do. Drawing upon his experience in Sugar House Ward, President Richards and his counselors met with bishoprics early on ward conference Sundays and went over priesthood rolls with them. As he had formerly done, they now placed check marks by the name of each inactive brother, saying to the bishop, "Now, the next time we come to your ward we would like these same rolls, and we want to know what you have asked each of these inactive brothers to do and what his response has been." Then, in the general session of the conference, the president would challenge the people that if any of them wanted to work for the Lord and help build his kingdom and they did not receive an assignment, they were just to let the presidency know and they would receive one. What with ward and visiting teaching, genealogy and temple work, missionary effort, and youth activity, there was something for everyone in addition to regularly assigned callings, and the members were encouraged to sense the importance of each area of need, not forgetting to include the young people.

"President Richards well understood the critical transitions in the lives of Aaronic Priesthood holders," says Brother Edling, whose assignment on the high council was particularly with the youth. "If a young man could make the transition from deacon to teacher happily, then he had a better chance of doing the same as he moved from teacher to priest. The president's aim was to infuse into them some of the same enthusiasm for their priesthood activity that they had for the demanding athletic program of the Church." Not only the Aaronic Priesthood bearers but also the corresponding-aged girls were encouraged to prepare for leadership and missions. President Richards told his counselors, "We've been pouring it into them, now let's take some of it out."

Accordingly the youth were invited to speak in ward and stake conferences about what the Church and the priesthood meant in their lives. In addition a spirit of sociality was encouraged through fathers and sons outings (in which President Richards participated with his own boys), and youth parties. An annual M-Men and Gleaner banquet and entertainment was held, and the young people would vie with each other to make each one more attractive and successful than the last.

One year the young lady chosen to take charge of this event said, "Oh, President Richards, I'm frightened to death." "Who are you afraid of, me?" he asked. "No," she answered. Again the question, "Are you afraid of President Cannon or President Norberg?" She again answered no. "Then you are just afraid of afraid," the president told her. "When you are conducting or announcing, why don't you look at one of us that you're not afraid of and then go ahead as if no one else were there?" She did that and got along just fine. The advice he gave her then became a guideline to him in later, more far-reaching assignments which required him to speak before immense audiences. Says he, "I fix my eyes on a friendly face in the audience, someone who is nodding approval, and I speak to him. That way I feel no fear."

In no Church assignment did LeGrand ever feel he was reaching fulfilment unless he was promoting the missionary effort and building up membership in the Lord's kingdom. Stakes were then functioning without stake mission presidents, and appropriately the missionary work was carried on through the seventies quorums. President Richards called many stake missionaries from among them, encouraged cottage meetings, and spoke at many of these meetings. Following the January 1933 stake conference, the visiting authority, Elder Melvin J. Ballard, remained for four evenings of missionary training sessions designed to motivate the Saints to open their doors to non-members so that the stake missionaries could effectively teach the gospel under favorable circumstances. Attendance at the four meetings was gratifying—837, 1127, 859, and 1218. Elder Ballard, who had a fine voice, delighted his audience by singing "The Seer" and preached powerful sermons. Other speakers, including President Richards, gave great impetus to the missionary effort. During the ensuing year, 486 cottage meetings were held in the stake and there were 140 convert baptisms; and this was achieved without the assistance of full-time missionaries and at a time when it was thought that investigators must be thoroughly indoctrinated in gospel principles and that it took six months to prepare one for baptism.

As new members came in and branches grew in activity, several new wards were created from them. As these new units were created and former ones grew in membership, the stake held leadership conventions to train new and old officers and teachers for greater effectiveness in their callings. At one of these

President Leo J. Muir of the neighboring Los Angeles Stake was invited to speak for an evening session. Under his inspired leadership his area had achieved an enviable record in spirituality, with special emphasis in genealogy and temple work. His stake regularly sent busloads of members to the nearest temple, in Mesa, Arizona. Up till now, Hollywood Stake had not sponsored any temple excursions; nevertheless President Muir, being an admiring observer of the general progress and varied achievements of his rival, said at the conference, "President Richards, we will have to give you credit for outdistancing us."

It wasn't long until Hollywood Stake gave special attention to the genealogical and temple effort in which they had been lacking. To head the program, President Richards had a certain brother in mind, a prominent and well-respected doctor. In his call we see a unique characteristic which had been evident in varying degrees since LeGrand's first mission but now had become an effective tool in recruiting and "about-facing" capable men to help build the kingdom. It was a breathtaking but guileless audacity which first startled the person, then challenged him to think, to evaluate, to choose, to change, to grow. It is apparent in his bold suggestion that the proud and pompous Mr. de Rijke attend church to see for himself what the Mormons have to offer; it is seen again in his assigning inactive priesthood bearers in the Sugar House Ward to talk in sacrament meeting; and it is observed often on his short-term mission in his blunt statement of his position to heckling crowds or resistant contacts. But however audacious, blunt, or bold his approach, it is always tempered with faith in and love for the individual. Even his opposition is led to think it over, to reconsider, to come around, and usually to lend support, so that in late years he can answer the question, "Did you ever have an enemy?" with, "I don't believe so; I think I made them all my friends."

One man who felt the force of his bold challenge and allowed it to shape him for everlasting good was the doctor mentioned above. When President Richards suggested his name to his counselors, they said in unison, "But, President, you can't do it. He smokes." "I know it," was the answer, "but he has a lot of good in him." In meeting with the high council the President repeated his request, to which members made the same response: "You can't do it; he smokes." To this he said, "I know it, but we can clean him up all right." The council reluctantly agreed that, were this to happen, the appointment would meet with their approval.

With that much encouragement, President Richards invited the doctor and his wife into his office and told them what he had in mind. He did not mention the smoking. The doctor tipped back his head and said, "President Richards, I'd do anything for you and the Lord." Although he didn't realize it, the president had him. "I knew you would, and that's what I told the brethren." Then, continuing: "Now, there's one little thing we'd have to ask you to do. We couldn't have a man at the head of our genealogy and temple work who is using tobacco" (the doctor's face colored as if he had thought the president didn't know about his cigars), "but I told the brethren that you'd quit it to do this important work for the Lord." The doctor put his head down on the desk for a few moments; then, raising it, he said, "I'll quit."

About a week later, the doctor took a busload of Saints to the temple at Mesa, the first that had ever gone from that stake. President Richards went with them. They spent nearly a week working there. One morning they held a testimony meeting in the little chapel before going through sessions, and the doctor sat there with tears running down his cheeks. Even though he was an experienced speaker and toastmaster, he couldn't speak before the group. But as they walked into the lobby, he put his arms around his president and said, "Brother Richards, where do such feelings come from? I've never felt anything like this in all my life." "Oh, I think the Lord is just letting you know how much he appreciates your giving up your cigars and taking on this important work for him," was the ready response. The doctor did an excellent job in his assignment. Always liked and respected, he later became one of the most loved of bishops in the stake.

The growth, the unity, the training, and the increased activity of Hollywood Stake under LeGrand Richards's guidance was impressive. Elder George Albert Smith, in reporting to the

Brethren in Salt Lake, said that for 1933 it led the Church in leadership; but perhaps of greater significance was the resultant increase in spirituality. Wilford Edling felt it. He says: "There was a change in the spirituality. As a result of what President Richards did, those of us that succeeded him found ourselves in friendships and conditions of understanding that never would have been there except that he had set the pattern and led the way." He adds: "Everything that happened in my life after I had felt the spirit of LeGrand Richards, and had seen how someone could subscribe completely to the will of the Lord, was colored by the experience."

The effect upon Brother Edling was shared by others. Kathrine Higginbotham, who continued to serve as stake clerk after President Richards left, was one who sensed it. She comments: "Those who followed him worked hard to maintain the level of spirituality which he and his counselors achieved, but they did not surpass it."

No area of need appears to have been neglected. LeGrand's journals (volume VIII, beginning at p. 143, and all of volume IX) show that he traveled the long distances to his wards with punctual regularity; he visited the sick, the troubled, the sorrowing; he initiated a program in the interest of the old folks; yet he stayed close to his own family.

At any time his would have been a distinguished achievement, but it was particularly so when viewed in the light of general conditions and of the personal loss and tragedy they produced. The country was in the depths of the Great Depression, when thirty billion dollars in stock values had vanished, a third of the country's banks had failed, and unemployment had reached fifteen million, with many more millions earning only starvation wages. New apartments just off Wilshire Boulevard in Los Angeles could have been bought for fifteen to thirty cents on the dollar of the first mortgage after wiping out the second. Nobody could finance the buildings because people could not pay the rent. There were those living in hundred-thousand-dollar homes who could not pay their utility bills.

No one knew the conditions better than LeGrand, who depended upon real estate (the business he knew best) to make a living. He could make sales, but people could not get financing to complete transactions. He recorded, "Everyone is having a struggle, and we are not spared." For all his adult life he had been on the giving, providing, helping end of things—for his family, his relatives, his ward members, and his Dutch friends. Now he found himself unable to make even his best efforts financially productive enough to buy a home for his family or to purchase such things as he had always provided to make them more comfortable. Even necessities were scarce, and occasionally it was not certain where the next meal would come from. Had he not come to California with some reserve resources, his circumstances would have been even worse.

Since he was the stake president, he and Ina often hosted General Authorities in their home as well as friends and relatives who came from Utah to visit. Even with her culinary skills, it was difficult for Ina to do as she would like for them. One time when President Grant was with them, she inquired what he might like for breakfast. He would enjoy a poached egg, he said. There were but two eggs in the house, and she had never poached an egg before. One she broke, the other made it safely to the President's plate. In addition to the home visits of President Grant and his own father, LeGrand noted in his journal those of J. Reuben Clark, Jr., Anthony W. Ivins, Melvin J. Ballard, Rudger Clawson, Stephen L Richards, Sylvester Q. Cannon, and Bishop John Wells, and he remarked that he had "enjoyed each one and learned much from them." His friendships with these great men were an encouragement to him as he carried his heavy Church responsibilities in an atmosphere of economic disaster.

That period was crushing to many a man's spirit. Some who found no work, or worked tirelessly with practically nothing to show for their labor, despaired, turned dishonest, left their families, took their lives. When his brother George F. Jr. wrote LeGrand to come home to Salt Lake and take over his business again, adding that the Brethren surely did not realize what a sacrifice LeGrand had made to leave all he had and go to California, he answered, "I will be a much bigger and better man in ten years if I do what the Brethren have required of me, than if I were to come home."

He expressed his feelings on the subject even more forcefully in his Christmas letter to Ina that year. In part he wrote:

> The last year has been a very trying one for you, in having been taken away from your loved ones and friends and having to adapt yourself to new conditions. . . . I appreciate very much your loyalty. . . . The Lord has a work for us to do. The Patriarch said I "had not come here upon earth by chance, but in fulfillment of the decrees of the Almighty to do a great work in the building up of his kingdom."
>
> My one great ambition is to not falter in that mission, so that another will be required to do my work; so I am happy when you are so willing to face all these changes and losses so cheerfully. Ours is a real partnership, neither can succeed without the other. . . . (LGR *Personal Letter File* [1931], in his possession.)

Ina's ability to work with shortages and deprivations without complaint was a great aid to LeGrand's work, and he was grateful for her adapting to them, but there was one phenomenon to which she could not adapt—the earthquakes. They terrified her. The first big one came on March 10, 1933, while they were entertaining President and Sister Grant, Bishop and Sister David P. Howells of Wilshire Ward, President and Sister Antoine R. Ivins, and Kathrine Higginbotham. LeGrand wrote: "Ina, Sister Higginbotham, and I were in the kitchen and it felt like our home would be twisted in two. Everything that was loose began to roll around." Outside, the sidewalks rippled, waved, and cracked. Young Alden, who had been out, said, "Mother, it looks like someone is playing with the Fox Theater at the corner of Wilshire and Western." One hundred forty-seven lives were lost, and the reported damage was thirty million dollars, with the most severe losses in the Long Beach area.

The quakes continued intermittently until the end of the year. LeGrand described the October tremor. "At 1:00 A.M. we were awakened by windows and dresser drawers rattling, [and] the apartment rocking in a most vigorous manner. Ina was so frightened she almost lost herself. . . . I am afraid I will not be able to keep her here in California if these things do not cease." (LGR *Journal*, vol. IX, p. 290.)

As well as being subjected to the Depression and to natural upheavals, the family suffered personal tragedy. Just a month after he became stake president, LeGrand and his counselor, David H. Cannon, were driving along Los Feliz Boulevard when they saw a large crowd gathered. Brother Cannon went ahead to see what it meant. He found LeGrand's daughter, Norinne, lying on the grass. A drunken policeman had run into Reed's car head-on, and she was severely injured about the face. Her nose was broken in two places, and her cheek "looked like she had been hit with a golf ball which had been embedded there," LeGrand recorded. "The bone had been broken and driven up under the eye socket, and had drawn the flesh with it." At the hospital she underwent an operation. President Cannon, as attorney, later got judgment for two thousand dollars against the police officer, but he was never able to pay anything.

By late summer of 1932, LeGrand and Ina's three eldest daughters were married. Mercedes had become Mrs. Joseph Grant Iverson on January 1, 1931; Marian became the wife of Harold R. Boyer on December 19 of the same year; and Norinne married Reed E. Callister on March 9, 1932. Now in August, the family were together for a rare visit. Marian and Hal were working in California earning money for school the next year, and Mercedes and Grant had come down for sports events.

On August 4, LeGrand A. and LaMont went to Santa Monica Beach with some of their friends. While there, LeGrand A. was riding a surfboard, and as he came over a high wave one end of the board caught in the sand and the other end dealt him a blow across his stomach. This caused internal hemorrhaging, and he started to cough up blood. They took him to the hospital, where the doctor performed an operation in an attempt to stop the bleeding; but after two transfusions a clot formed, causing his death the next day. LeGrand A. was the eldest son and the family's pride. They were desolate in spite of the many friends and family members that tried to comfort them. Ward and stake leaders and members responded with concern and compassion. Thirteen of LeGrand's and Ina's family members came from Salt Lake, including their parents. President Grant, who was in California at the time, deferred his return to Salt Lake so that he could attend the funeral and speak words of solace. LeGrand A. was buried in Forest Lawn Cemetery.

In his *Blue Book*, LeGrand wrote about his son and expressed his feelings for him.

> At the time of his death, LeGrand stood six feet tall and weighed 150 pounds. He was a teacher in the Aaronic Priesthood. The principal of his high school in Glendale came to the house and told Ina that LeGrand was the finest boy he had ever had in his school. I used to take him with me on my visits to the various wards of the stake, and returning home, he would say, "My, Daddy, I don't see how anyone could listen to you and not believe the gospel is true."
>
> In his little pocket memorandum he had listed the names of his girl friends with their telephone numbers, and then passages of scripture that impressed him, such as the promises of Jesus that we should become joint heirs with him of all things, through our faithfulness, and the words of Mormon, advising to let no man be your leader except he be a just man, walking in the way of the Lord and keeping his commandments.
>
> LeGrand was a wonderful son, so free from vice and meanness of every kind, and so considerate of his parents. He loved the gospel and had a fine voice with which to defend it. He and his mother were such pals that it will take a long time for her to be happy without him, and I loved him dearly. (*Blue Book*, p. 74.)

Later, LeGrand's father, George F., performed the temple work for his grandson. In a letter to LeGrand he wrote, "I was ordained and endowed for LeGrand last evening in the Temple. President Grant and President Clawson were in the company of 164. . . . I am sure LeGrand was ready to receive these saving ordinances, and I am happy to have had the privilege of representing him in that sacred work." (LGR *Personal Letter File* [1932], in his possession.)

As LeGrand had stated, it would take a long time for them to be happy without their son. Ina grieved as only a mother can.

Those who were close to LeGrand said that he was quiet and mourned inwardly. He pleaded with his counselors to try to find some answers to the "Why?" in his and Ina's hearts. If they could just feel that there was divine purpose in his death, he said, comfort would come; but if, by choosing a different course and not coming to California, or by leaving earlier, they could still have had their son, then there was no comfort.

As it happened, it was neither counselors nor other friends who found the answer they sought. It was fourteen-year-old LaMont to whom the Lord gave inspiration. One day LeGrand was taking Ina for a little ride and asked LaMont if he would like to come along. He declined, and while they were gone he studied and compared the patriarchal blessings which had been given to him and LeGrand A. just a year before on the same day by Hyrum G. Smith, Patriarch to the Church, who was not acquainted with the boys. That evening when they had returned he sat on their bed with the blessings in his hands and said, "You have not understood these."

From LeGrand A.'s, he read, "You shall be privileged to preach the gospel in strange lands to strange people." Then from his own, "You shall be called to preach the gospel at home and abroad." He then explained that his refers to this world, but LeGrand A.'s to the other. Again he read from his brother's blessing (which, incidentally, was the first of the two the Patriarch gave to the brothers): "In the own due time of the Lord, your home will be the fit abode for the spirits of your loved ones." He explained that this meant in the hereafter, when LeGrand A. would have spirit children. But in his own it said, "You shall be privileged to see your children grow up around you and honor you in the same manner that you have honored your parents." This had unmistakable reference to this life, LaMont told them. (*Patriarchal Blessings*, LDS Church Archives.)

LeGrand says of his son's explanation: "It brought us great comfort, for we felt that with it we could hardly reach any other conclusion than that the Lord had not intended to leave LeGrand with us for long on the earth as he had LaMont." To his counselors and the leaders in the stake, he could say, "The

Lord has been good to us, he has let us know," and peace could enter into his mind and heart again.

For Ina, it was a longer time coming. While she was in Salt Lake to await the arrival of their first two grandchildren nine months later, she was still struggling for emotional equilibrium. She wrote LeGrand: "Life and sickness are so uncertain, I seem to have lost most of my courage. Maybe with study and prayer I can rebuild; we have much to be courageous about." Then the babies were born. Marian's Barbara Ruth arrived on April 17, 1933, and LeGrand recorded in his journal, "Became a grandpa tonight at 11:15. . . . our first grandchild." Mercedes's Carla Ann was born on May 27, after which her mother wrote greetings (in the baby's name) to "Grandpa and Uncles LaMont and Alden, even if they don't deserve it for wishing I was a boy." (LGR *Personal Letter File* [1933], in his possession.) With the birth of the babies, Ina began to find happiness again.

It was at the April conference while Ina was in Salt Lake that LeGrand's former teacher and friend, J. Reuben Clark, Jr., was sustained as second counselor to President Heber J. Grant, an appointment which pleased LeGrand very much. (President Clark was just completing a very successful assignment as United States Ambassador to Mexico, 1930-33.)

Shortly thereafter, LeGrand was invited to a banquet given by the California Bar Association at which Ambassador Clark was the invited guest and speaker. Will Rogers, the famed humorist, was also to have spoken, but he was away at the time, so he sent a lengthy telegram to be read for the occasion. LeGrand remembers that among other things Rogers said, "If we ever get into trouble with Mexico, we will have to turn back to J. Reuben Clark, Jr.; so God bless him, and make him a Democrat or a Republican as the situation may require." LeGrand remembers the further tribute paid his old friend when, at the same event, the president of the Bar Association introduced the Ambassador. "The time may not have arrived for Utah to propose a presidential candidate," he said, "but this man Clark is of the kind of timber from which great presidents are hewn."

By this time in his life, LeGrand could count most of the General Authorities as personal friends who had touched and influenced him. One of these was Elder James E. Talmage, about whom LeGrand wrote at the time of the apostle's death. (The journal entry is dated July 27, 1933.) "Aside from my own father, I believe Brother Talmage has had a greater influence than any other man," he said. "I had the privilege of attending his class as a young man at LDSU Sunday School. I have had many letters and books from him. He inquired daily as to my welfare when I had smallpox. He was a great man."

In the fall of 1933 another great man, Charles A. Callis, was released as president of the Southern States Mission and called as a member of the Council of the Twelve. LeGrand had a presentiment that he would succeed him in the South. When he voiced his impression to Ina, saying, "How would you like to go down to the Southern States with me and preside over the mission there?" she retorted, "You mustn't think so much of yourself." His feeling about the matter intensified, however, and when President Grant and President Clark came as the visitors to stake quarterly conference, he was even more certain. He showed them around on Friday and, with his counselors, hosted a reception for them that evening. They held priesthood meetings on Saturday and the morning session on Sunday. No word was said nor any indication given about the purpose of their visit. They were tense hours for President Richards.

After the morning meeting, the visitors met with LeGrand, his counselors, a bishop, and a missionary who was in difficulty. When the business was taken care of, President Grant requested that the others withdraw, as he and President Clark wished to speak with LeGrand alone. When only the three men remained, he asked LeGrand, "How would you like to go down and preside over the Southern States Mission?"

At this point LeGrand remembered that he had originally been called to the South for his first mission but that his bishop had intervened and he had gone to Holland instead. He now thought it a fine opportunity to fulfil that early request. To the

Brethren he said, "I'd be happy to go to the South if you want me as the mission president, but if you are asking me to go because you know I'm having a struggle financially and the mission president's living allowance would help, I don't want to do it." President Grant assured him, "I don't know another man in the Church I'd rather turn that mission over to than I would you." "All right," LeGrand responded, "then I'd like to go."

At the time, he said nothing to Ina about the call. The afternoon and evening meetings were held, attended by 1725 and 1325 people respectively. When LeGrand got home, he said to his wife, "Ina, how long will it take you to get ready to go to the South?" She said, "Daddy, I don't think I'm well enough to do it."

Although she felt unequal to it, the pattern of their lives had been set and Ina began preparations to go. Both she and President Richards went to the patriarch George Bowles—a man of great prophetic power, who, according to some, seemed to have the Lord's arms about him all the time. In a blessing to Ina he promised her the health she required, "even to the coming of an angel" to buoy her up. He also pronounced a great blessing upon the head of his stake president. In part, he said,

> In the past thou hast desired to have the voice of an angel to declare unto mankind the restoration of the gospel of Jesus Christ. That gift is yours and shall be henceforth a fullness thereof. Thou shalt be mighty among the children of men. (*Blessing*, December 16, 1933, Hollywood Stake Tabernacle, in LeGrand Richards's possession.)

Many hearts were heavy at their leaving. Parties, wishes, and gifts were given them and farewells were said. President David H. Cannon, who succeeded LeGrand as stake president, spoke for the members of the stake when he said: "He came to the office with such devotion to the Church and to its ideals and with such a fervent testimony of the gospel that his influence was immediately felt. He has stimulated spiritual growth throughout the entire stake." He told of LeGrand's abilities, his knowledge of Church government, his courage, his fine sense of justice, his understanding, and his deep humility which "had endeared him to them all." He paid tribute to Ina for her support to him and for "her cheery, comforting words and benign influence which would not soon be forgotten." (*Hollywood MIA Stake News*, vol. 1, no. 2, Nov. 5, 1933, p. 4.)

The family said their good-byes, and by December 21 they were in Salt Lake City to prepare for and spend Christmas with Mercedes, Marian, their husbands, and the babies. The next day LeGrand resold his home on Eleventh East at half its original sale price. (It had been necessary to repossess it after the former buyer had defaulted.)

For the next several days he met with President Grant and various others of the General Authorities, and since the weather had turned unseasonably warm, he played golf with his father and mother. On December 29 he was set apart by President Heber J. Grant; and Ina, by President Anthony W. Ivins.

Before they left, LeGrand sat at lunch with President Grant and some of the Brethren, one of whom said, "LeGrand, if they keep you as long as they did President Callis . . ." but he didn't finish the sentence before LeGrand quickly interjected, "But they are not going to keep me as long as they did President Callis. I love missionary work, but I will take mine in shorter terms. I don't believe in long missions." President Grant nodded and said, "Neither do I." LeGrand then asked, "How long will you expect me to remain in the South?" The President answered, "Three to four years."

As LeGrand's family prepared for their journey, a snow storm threatened; so, with Ina, LaMont, Nona, and Alden, he drove to Panguitch, Utah, on December 31, 1933. There, in the town's only hotel, they saw one year out and looked ahead to what the New Year might bring. Heavy snow fell all night, and in the morning they were obliged to follow the snow plow in order to proceed. With only minor delays, they made the trip south and across country safely and according to schedule.

Chapter 11

Southern States Mission President

1934-1937

It was January 6, 1934, when LeGrand and his family arrived at the mission headquarters, located at 485 North Avenue, N. E., Atlanta, Georgia. They were met by Elder Charles A. Callis and his wife, Grace. The next day President Richards preached a sermon in the Atlanta Branch, and on January 8 he left for a tour of the mission with Elder Callis, mission president since August 26, 1908, a period of almost twenty-six years. Elder Callis was greatly loved in the South. He had been the great evangelist whose faith had healed many and whose preaching had helped to bring hundreds of converts into the Church.

After two weeks of constant travel the two brethren returned, and on January 20 a program was tendered the departing president and his wife. They responded with words of farewell, and President Richards paid tribute to them in a talk which was reported in the *Liahona*. (February 27, 1934.) In part, he said: "President Callis has been an earnest champion of the truth and has been wholehearted in his devotion to the work. He has inspired those laboring with him and gained the love and respect of all who knew him."

On January 31 the Callises left for Salt Lake, where he would take his place as a member of the Quorum of the Twelve, and President Richards took over his responsibilities as president of the Southern States Mission. The ecclesiastical jurisdiction to which he fell heir included eighteen thousand members in nine mission districts located in Alabama, Mississippi, Georgia, South Carolina, and Florida. This is an area which at this writing, 1982, encompasses five missions, twenty-five stakes, ninety-one wards, and thirty-three branches. There were no local district organizations or district boards; no youth programs except one branch MIA (Mutual Improvement Association) in Atlanta and another in Jacksonville, Florida. There was but one local full-time missionary, James R. Boone. Almost no families had had any part in the Church school program or in the blessings available to those attending the temple.

President Callis had labored faithfully during periods of strong prejudice against the Mormons; in fact, one county was still closed to proselyting. His philosophy had been one of decentralization. He had kept his missionaries out in the country among people of humble circumstances and away from urban centers, where he felt temptations were great. President Richards, on the other hand, as a former bishop and stake president, saw the future of the Church in the South in terms of wards and stakes located in towns and cities, yet felt that their influence would naturally spread out into the countryside. From his previous experience as mission president he also knew the value of proselyting not only the poorer people but also the better-educated middle-class men and women. These would more readily give credibility to the message of the Restoration and could eventually take over the branch and district leadership in the South, thus releasing the missionary leaders to spend their time finding contacts and bringing them to conversion.

The new president saw the vast human resource among the youth of the mission, saw how greatly they needed missionary experience, training, and cultural development, which were available to youth in the West. He longed to help them, to lift them through the organized programs of the Church. His aim was to harness them for the Lord so that His blessings could become operable in their lives. With clear-cut goals, an indefatigable taste for work, and the will to drain heart, mind, and strength in carrying out his new responsibility, he moved ahead.

His first missionwide communique was to the effect that if his administration was going to be outstanding for any one thing more than another, it would be for everybody working. Then, on February 25, he set out by car with members of his mission staff for his second tour of the nine districts, one of three such tours a year he made during his tenure as president. Distances were great—the Mississippi tour alone was 1743 miles. Between district visits he would return to Atlanta to handle matters at the mission home and his correspondence. He wrote that he was "grateful for the dictaphone." His journal shows that he dictated five to nine rolls at a time as he worked late into the nights. With his great propensity for balance, he also gave quality time to Ina and the children. Then he would be off again with a new set of missionaries to preach and teach the new doctrine of growth and opportunity to the Saints.

Typical of his challenges to "get to work" is the following. At a conference he attended in one district, the Relief Society served lunch on the lawn between meetings, and this gave the president opportunity to circulate around and visit with the people. He went up to one brother, put his arm around him, called him by name, and said, "How long have you been a member of the Church?" "Forty years," the man answered. The president then asked three questions.

"What are you doing in the Church?"

"Nothing."

"Do you hold the priesthood?" He did not.

"Have you quit your tobacco?" He had not.

President Richards queried again, "What Church did you belong to before you became a Mormon?"

"The Baptist Church," the man responded.

"Why don't you go back to it?" the president continued. "You would make a good Baptist, and I don't see that Mormonism has done a thing for you." He then proceeded to teach him the parable of the talents and the statement of the Savior, "Every tree that bringeth not forth good fruit shall be hewn down and cast into the fire." (D&C 97:7.) It was a turning point in the brother's life.

One faithful Saint who did "bring forth good fruit" was Samuel Taylor Blue, chief of the Catawba Tribe and branch president of the Catawba Indian Reservation near Rock Hill, South Carolina. During the days of persecution, he had carried the missionaries across the river on his back to protect them from the mobs. Under his leadership 97 percent of his tribe came into the Church. The *Church News* of October 10, 1981, featured him in an article.

In 1950 his friends paid the fare for him and his wife to attend April conference, where President George Albert Smith asked that he speak. "I have tasted the blessing and joy of God," he told the conference audience. "I have seen the dead raised. I have seen the sick whom the doctors have given up . . . restored to life. . . . I know that the gospel is true." (*Conference Report*, April 1950, pp. 141-42.) It was the highlight of his life. While in Salt Lake, Chief and Sister Blue visited with President and Sister Richards in their home and talked of their mutual efforts to further missionary work in the South.

To the Saints all over the mission the president said: "You are as much entitled to missionary training as our boys and girls out West. If you work for it, save for it, and pray for it, your sons and daughters can go on missions. We ought to have one from the South for every one we have from the West." It was only a matter of weeks until there were sixty-eight full-time local missionaries in the field. Some could afford to go for only three months, or six, or one year, but after their missions they returned to the branches and appreciably helped to staff and strengthen the local Sunday Schools and budding MIAs.

It was in the area of MIA that some of the most drastic changes were necessary. A total break with tradition was required. When the president told the people that they were going to teach the young people to dance, some of the brethren said it could not be done in the South, for if they let them dance in Church buildings the local inhabitants would burn the buildings down. To this he said, "Well, if they do, we will build them up again, only we will make them larger so more can dance in them." (One chapel was burned down—whether from arson was not established; but another larger one was built to replace it, and successful dances were held there.)

Emotions ran high. One good brother in west Florida said, "President Richards, if you let them dance in our building I will have my father's body removed from the cemetery next to the

Church property." As the Lord's representative in the mission's program for the youth, President Richards told the man not to worry, they would not force him to dance in that building; but he added, "Before I leave this mission you will be dancing in it yourself and enjoying it." And he was.

Not only were the young people invited to attend the dances, but the girls were to come in party dresses. This was to foster a sense of refinement and self-worth, so that even country girls (many of whom worked barefoot in cotton fields) could hold out higher standards to the boys and not marry the first one that came along. One branch president who opposed the idea at first, later attended an MIA dance where the girls wore party dresses and danced the graceful patterns taught them. He told his members to get their daughters pretty dresses if they had to sell the chickens to do it.

For the boys, the standard of no-smoking was encouraged. In a tobacco-raising country, its use in those days was prevalent even among Church members. It wasn't just the youth of the Church but adult members too who were addicted to tobacco. President Richards began with them. He was approaching the steps of a chapel when a brother extended his hand saying, "Welcome to our mission, President Richards."

"Who are you?" the president asked.

"I am the superintendent of the Sunday School."

Noting the strings hanging from the man's shirt pocket, the president lifted out the pouch of tobacco and said, "I haven't been accustomed to seeing these things used by Sunday School superintendents, but we will talk about it later."

In his instructions to the members he now reminded them that "as with the priest, so with the people," and he taught them that the leaders and the parents would have to set the example. He then gave them a little time to straighten up. If a leader did not do so after a reasonable time, he was released.

There was great need for leadership training among the local members. President Richards had been in the mission field only six months when he organized a mission leadership convention in Jacksonville, Florida. To it came the missionaries and local leaders for three days of instruction and help. Departments were held for the auxiliaries, and the leadership was told that qualified women could take full part in the work of the mission. Then the leaders worked to help the women qualify, by teaching them to give talks, open and close meetings with prayer, prepare lessons, and serve as branch clerks. So implicit was the president's faith in a good woman's ability to serve that he encouraged them in any area of Church activity not specifically requiring the priesthood.

In addition to departmental instruction, general sessions and testimony meetings were held. The convention gave great impetus to the work of the mission as the participants returned to their areas fortified with knowledge of how to do things more effectively and fired with enthusiasm for the doing. These conventions were thereafter held annually.

Not only was it thought imperative to hold training sessions for the local people in order to prepare them for greater responsibilities and calls, but the missionary district presidents needed to catch the vision of their part in the total picture. They needed to see districts as junior stakes and themselves as junior stake presidents who would be superseded by local stake presidents when the time was fully ripe. It was a new view for mission districts. In order to implement the program, semi-annual seminars were held. To these came the nine presidents of the districts; four or five prospective presidents; the mission staff; mission heads of auxiliaries; and President and Sister Richards. Three three-hour sessions were held during each of three days, or twenty-seven hours of meetings in all.

President Richards made up the agenda covering every aspect of leadership in the mission. He then assigned to each attending member a segment of the work for thorough advance preparation. At the meetings, each presented and discussed his portion of the program. One of these agendas has survived the years. It is complete, comprehensive, and practical.

After such a seminar, President Richards felt that his leaders could have gone back into the various districts and supervised the district affairs without him. Transposing instruction into practical action, however, did not come easy to some, and it required infinite patience and constant guidance to bring each man up to the potential his president envisioned for him and for the work he had to do. After one of the seminars, a district president came to President Richards and said, "It is time to plan our next conference. What do you suggest?"

"Well," the president replied, "do you want this to be my conference or yours?"

"I guess I want it to be mine," the elder said.

"I thought you did. Now you figure what you feel we should have and then I will be glad to go over your suggested agenda with you."

Accordingly, for the conference the elder planned a program for Friday night with a dance following, and left Saturday and Sunday for leadership meetings with missionaries and local leaders as well as for general sessions for the Saints. For the Friday program he asked each branch in his district to furnish a number. When the program was presented, President Richards sat through it gritting his teeth. Nearly every number was a Negro stunt, and some were in highly questionable taste.

The district president came to the president afterwards and said, "President Richards, I daren't ask you what you thought of the program."

The president replied, "Oh, I think it was wonderful."

"You don't mean that, do you?" the surprised elder asked.

"Yes, it was wonderful because it showed us what our starting point is, but if you ever have another one like it while I am president of the mission it will be just too bad for you, my boy. Now, you will have to get out in the branches and censor what they are going to put on. They have to be taught that music is the voice of angels, but it is also the voice of hell-holes and dives, and they have to discern the difference."

Both the president's reprimand and his instruction to the missionary were received without offense, yet he had been firm and he was in character. The incident reveals again one of his most distinguishing characteristics—boldness tempered with respect for the individual, but crystal clear as to what was intended and what was needed in the way of change or improvement.

In all his labors with his missionaries President Richards aimed at being father, friend, and guide to them. That he was successful is attested to by many who, at the time of this writing, are still around and serving in positions of leadership and responsibility. One says: "He seemed to know our thoughts, and he had feelings of love and compassion for us in our great weakness. I loved and admired the president and felt understood by him as I had never felt understood by mortal man. His will was my pleasure, and with joy I gave my best effort to the work, taking him as my hero."

Another elder later sustained a hurt which he confided to his president by letter after returning home. "I'm afraid I have some sliver in my heart," he wrote. "I'll either have to get the rest of the arrow or continue on thus afflicted. If I had not always been able to confide in you so completely, I would not dare tell you my secrets, but you and Sister Richards have been like parents to me, so my confidences can be yours."

In all areas of mission life President Richards worked to keep the missionaries close to him. When he traveled he took some from the mission home with him, picked up others en route to ride from town to city, left them to work, and picked up others to continue on. He talked with them, listened to them, ate and lodged with them. In Atlanta, between trips, he allowed Saturdays for recreation time with them and his family. They gathered at the park for a picnic and games—softball and other games of prowess and skill, including Indian leg-wrestling, for which Elder Richards is noted. He surprised even the strongest and most powerful by throwing them.

Not only did President Richards work and play with his missionaries, but when they had troubles he did not merely write letters but went to them. One elder lost both mother and father during his mission, but to honor his mother's dying wish he remained in the field when she passed away. LeGrand took the news to him and remained several days. When the father soon followed his wife in death, the president brought the son to the mission home for a period. Upon his release, Elder Richards gave him a blessing, promising that if he so desired he would be able to earn enough to bring him back for an additional short-term mission. This the elder did, and it helped alleviate the sorrow and aloneness he so keenly felt.

President Richards was not without problems where his missionaries were concerned. There were car accidents and operations, sickness and discouragement. In each case he treated them much as he would his own children. He tells the story of one discouraged elder:

> I received a letter from a missionary in South Carolina telling me he just couldn't take it, that he wasn't cut out to be a missionary, that he would be willing to furnish the money to keep a missionary in the field for two years, if I would just release him. [President Richards immediately caught a train and went to him.] I told him that I thought the Lord was pleased with his expressed willingness to furnish the money to keep a missionary in the field for two years, but I said, "If I were to release you and let you go home, you would never forgive me. In the future when your own sons were old enough for their missions, what would you say to them?" I said, "I will help you any way that I can, but you make a success of your mission. It will get easier day by day." To make this story short, he did his best and then some, and became a district president and one of my finest missionaries. (*Just to Illustrate*, p. 216.)

Everywhere he went the president preached, and his sermons then, as now, were punctuated with stories from his missions. (*Just to Illustrate* contains no less than forty-two oft-told ones from the Southern States alone.) One might ask how these and others can be heard dozens of times without tiring his listeners. James R. Boone (who served as a district president and at this writing is a patriarch in Jacksonville, Florida), gives us his view: "I once traveled with President Richards for nine days and heard him preach twenty-seven times. I feel that I have heard some of his stories at least a hundred times, but he has been so full of the Spirit that I still enjoy each telling." In saying this he touches truth. One of Elder Richards's favorite scriptures in connection with his preaching is, "The letter killeth, but the spirit giveth life." (2 Corinthians 3:6.) This is the principal reason why he never uses notes. He must communicate eye to eye, and freely, enthusiastically—even loudly—pour it out.

Stories help him to put his message across, just as they did the Master Teacher. A story holds the attention, teaches a lesson, is remembered. Elder Richards's never-ending store of them, gleaned from actual experience and told in simple, earthy style, creates a bridge between him and his listeners, whether young or old. He relives them and enjoys recounting them. He puts as much of himself into the hundredth telling as he put into the first, and somehow the hearer does not weary in the retelling any more than he tires when a friend says, "I love you." In essence, that is what Elder Richards is saying to his listeners. "I love you. I want to reach and teach you, bless and lift you, and help you become all our Lord intended you to be."

Feeling President Richards's spirit, his Southern audiences, although reluctant at first, soon took him to their hearts. President Callis had been a powerful and popular preacher, and many found it hard to shift allegiance. Noting this when he visited the South early in Elder Richards's presidency, Elder Melvin J. Ballard made a helpful statement to the people. A former missionary there, Francis L. Urry, reports that statement: "You people have looked to President Callis as your father, but he is now your grandfather. President Richards is your father; look to him." And they did. As one brother said, "We wondered if he would ever fill President Callis's shoes, but we soon found that he had boots of his own."

Not only the people of the South heard President Richards preach during the period he remained there, but the body of the Church heard him as well. By invitation of the First Presidency he attended all seven semi-annual conferences within the three and a half years of his mission and was called to speak in each. These talks are of record. According to some who heard them, his style of delivery, then as now, was informal and familiar, yet the sermons are tightly organized. He did not write them, but, as is now the case, he mentally formulated them with purpose, theme, and summary. Because of the freedom with which he speaks, his sermons seem almost extemporaneous, but in reading them we find the careful organization unmistakable.

In connection with President Richards's preaching, there is a charming bit of advice from his father, George F. Richards. The apostle visited the mission during the fall of his son's first year in the South, and as he observed the breakneck pace at which the president was driving himself in order to attain goals he had set for the mission, he worried. When he returned home, and periodically thereafter, he wrote of it. "I wonder, son, if you are undertaking to do more than you have strength to carry you through," one letter said. "I wish I could convince you to slow up a little and thus check old age which is creeping on." He continued, "Perhaps you like your work so well and do it so successfully that it does not tire you as much as like work tires some others of us. One way to ease up is to not put so much effort into your preaching, i.e., do not think you have to speak louder than is necessary to be heard in order to emphasize what you are saying." (LGR *Personal Letter File,* in his possession.) Ina, too, thought he could tone down his dynamics to good advantage.

To please them both, he tried, but he was not entirely successful. Amusingly, he uses scriptural support to justify that which, in all probability, is a naturally amplified voice, born of his boldness, his conviction, and his much experience in preaching both indoors and on the streets. One elder said that when the president spoke at a street meeting on Lord's Corner in Atlanta, he could be heard a block away. In addition to the scriptures which instruct the elders to "declare my word with loud voices" (D&C 60:7), LeGrand likes Doctrine and Covenants 42:6. "And ye shall go forth in the power of my Spirit, preaching my gospel, two by two, in my name, *lifting up your voices as with the sound of a trump, declaring my word like unto angels of God.*" (Emphasis added by LGR.)

Throughout the mission were numerous chapels and rented halls of varying quality. The president preached in them all. Some had not even outhouses on the premises, but allowed the dense woods which crowded close to the buildings to serve such natural requirements. President Richards felt such conditions to be deplorable, and he set about to remedy them. As the mission's first building project, neat and sturdy outbuildings were constructed for each meeting place that lacked them. The next project was the painting and renovating of neglected buildings. The erection of new buildings soon followed. Early in his tenure, President Richards appointed a mature missionary who had had construction experience to supervise the building program— S. D. Pearce from Vernal, Utah. This man was so successful that following his release the Church called him back to the South to work full-time in that capacity. He returned with his wife and his brother, the latter to help him in the work.

Notable among the new chapels were those in Liberty, Mississippi; Augusta, Georgia; Orlando, Florida; and Columbia, South Carolina; the last named being dedicated on October 28, 1934, by Elder George F. Richards while on his tour of the South already mentioned.

Just as his father was worried that President Richards might break under the strain of his work, so was his mother. Added to her concern over his health was her worry that he would not find time for his family. "Ina and the children need some of your company," she wrote him. It was true that his work took him away with never-ceasing regularity and that, with three children yet at home, the mission staff, and a constant influx and outflow of missionaries to look after, Ina had her hands full. As a result she did not often travel with her husband. Nevertheless it was a fulfilling time for her.

After her years of illness, the blessing given Ina by the patriarch George Bowles before they left California had been honored of the Lord, and she was finally well. She headed the mission Relief Societies. She managed the mission household with efficiency and grace and saved hundreds of dollars through her careful buying and her culinary skills. While being a loving mother to her own children, she was also friend and confidante to the young men and women who served their missions in the South. Whenever the opportunity afforded, she also concerned herself with instructing them in manners, grooming, and the art of conversation. As always, President Richards appreciated her with a depth of feeling that constantly found its way to expression. He told Mable Chapman, his secretary, that her most important assignment in his absence was "to keep Sister Richards happy." In letters and in his journal are written words which he often expressed in person. "Ina has been a beautiful companion," he wrote on January 1, 1937. "She is all I could ever have asked for —so sweet and lovely and helpful—and her influence with the children has been wonderful. She has greatly strengthened me in my ministry because of the love and respect the people bear her." (LGR *Journal*, vol. XI, p. 3.)

Despite the load he carried, he did not neglect Ina or the children. As in earlier assignments, he could break away from his work for brief periods to give them his undivided attention. "I've finished the Lord's work for this hour, now what can I do to make my family happy?" His journals from the mission period are full of entries showing that he took time with them at every opportunity. With Ina there were shopping times, lunches, a lecture (Carl Sandburg), a concert (Lily Pons); with the children there were school events, games, birthday celebrations; and he took them all to the movies (*Maytime, Seventh Heaven, Magnificent Obsession*). (LGR *Journals*, vols. IX, X, XI.)

He regularly wrote to his married daughters, receiving special letters in return. Such an answer from Norinne brought him satisfaction. She wrote, "May my life someday bring me (through intense joys, suffering, and progressing experiences) some of your wisdom and spirituality. Is it possible, Daddy?" He also wrote to his son LaMont when he served a three-month mission in the South between his junior and senior years in high school, and later when, after graduation, he left for work and further schooling in Salt Lake.

The night before LaMont left home for the longer period, his father spent the evening with him. President Richards recorded in his journal: "Had a long talk with LaMont tonight until after midnight. Discussed my confidence in him and expectations of him. Also his program for future, including college, mission, and marriage." (LGR *Journal*, vol. X, p. 73.)

As he counseled his own children about such important matters, he also extended fatherly advice to young people in the mission. One of his stories from west Florida shows him doing this.

A recent convert, a lovely young woman school teacher, came up to me and said, "President Richards, I am going to get married. What do you think of that?" I replied, "Wonderful. Do I know him?" She answered, "No." Then I said, "Is he a member of the Church?" She answered, "No." Then I said, "Well, you are a beautiful, clean young woman, and you could no more find happiness with an unclean man than you could mix oil and water. In your courtship with him you will know whether he is motivated by clean and holy desires, or whether he would take advantage of you if he could." Then I added, "And he must be a prayerful man with a faith in God, for, as wicked as the world is, I would not trust any man to be true to his wife and children who does not believe there is a God and that someday he will have to answer to him for what he does here on earth. Also, he must be willing to let you raise your children in the Church, for knowing as you do that the Lord has restored his truth to the earth, you would be a very unhappy woman if you could not teach your children the truths of the gospel." Then I added "Let me know when he joins the Church." I didn't dare tell her not to marry a nonmember of the Church, for I didn't know where she could find a young man in the Church, except our missionaries, and we had "hands-off" signs hanging all over them.

I didn't hear anything more from her until the next conference about four months later. Her train was late, so she came into the morning meeting late. After the meeting she came up to shake hands with me. As she put out her hand I said, "Name, please." She replied, "Oh, I am still Miss So-and-So." I said, "What became of your anticipated marriage?" Her answer was, "He did not come up to your specifications." (*Just to Illustrate,* pp. 23-24.)

Working with countless individuals on a one-to-one level as well as his responsibilities on a missionwide basis kept President Richards going at a relentless pace. Always an early riser, he did not often finish his day until late hours. But it was as his father said: Even with the load he carried, he enjoyed his work, and it seemed not to tire him in the same way it might have done another. In laboring full-time for the Lord he appears to have tapped the source of renewal spoken of by his beloved prophet, Isaiah: "Even the youths shall faint and be weary, and the young men shall utterly fall; but they that wait upon the Lord shall *renew their strength*; they shall mount up with wings as eagles; they shall run, and not be weary; and they shall walk, and not faint." (Isaiah 40:30-31. Emphasis added.)

On his fiftieth birthday, February 6, 1936, the president recorded, "I am enjoying wonderful health. I feel like a young man." (LGR *Journal*, vol. X, p. 19.) For that same birthday he received a letter from his father which in retrospect is seen to contain a prophetic statement. He wrote: "The thought that a half-century has passed since you were born makes me feel quite aged. May you have many returns of the eventful day of your birth, and *another half century at least*." (LGR *Personal Letter File*, in his possession.)

As the days passed, the president was careful to record in his journal not only near-at-hand events but also those that affected the Church, the nation, and the world. He noted that temples were to be built in Idaho Falls and Los Angeles; that the Pioneer Cemetery at Florence, Nebraska, was dedicated; and that George F. Richards, having served so many years as Salt Lake Temple president, was called in April 1937 to supervise all temples and at the same time was sustained as acting Patriarch to the Church. President LeGrand Richards also recorded the reelection of President Franklin D. Roosevelt; the death of King George V of England; Edward VIII's abdication of the throne to marry the American divorcee; and the coronation of King George VI—four events that captured headlines in many parts of the world.

The Southern States Mission, too, had a flurry of excitement over the official visit of a famous man, Elder Reed Smoot, member of the Quorum of the Twelve and recently senior member of the United States Senate. He toured the South with President Richards from the third to the eighteenth of December, 1936. There was considerable publicity as he met with distinguished people and the press and spoke over various radio stations. Everywhere in the South he was paid homage as a notable

With visiting apostle Reed Smoot at Columbia, South Carolina, 1936.

With Chief Samuel Blue.

public figure, but there is a story which shows him quietly performing a humble service in private.

After the morning session of conference in Orlando, Florida, a brother came to President Richards and said, "My wife is lying at death's door. She'd be thrilled if you and Elder Smoot would visit her before she dies." "How far is it from here?" the president asked. "Thirty miles," the man replied.

President Richards told Elder Smoot of the request. "What do you wish to do about it?" Elder Smoot inquired.

"Well, I would like to go out and see her," was the reply.

"Let's go," the senator agreed.

They drove the thirty miles, located the home, and upon entering the sister's room found her lying on a low bed. Elder Smoot lowered his towering frame to kneel beside her. He placed his hands on her head, gave her a blessing, and then kissed her good-bye. (LGR *Journal,* vol. X, p. 173, and interview.)

Both the visits from General Authorities and President Richards's attendance at semi-annual conferences in Salt Lake added a special dimension to his years in the South. His rail trips west afforded him opportunity to keep perspective, review progress, plan ahead, refresh his spirit, and pour out his soul in thanksgiving for his many opportunities. Gratitude is central to his character. He often recorded his prayers of appreciation to the Lord for his "standing and part in this gospel dispensation"; for the manner in which the Lord had sustained him; and for the outpouring of the Lord's Spirit which "is the greatest witness of the truth of this work." He observed that "at times, the Lord seems so near and the veil so thin." On March 29, 1936, he wrote as he traveled, "Had a lovely day reading and thinking over my work. Outlined report for mission presidents' meeting. Also planned what I might say if called to speak in general conference. In spirit and thought, I lived the day very near to the Lord." (LGR *Journal,* vol. VIII, p. 44.)

He did speak at that conference. He took as his text the eleventh chapter of Isaiah, concerning how the Lord would "set up an ensign for the nations, . . . assemble the outcasts of Israel, and gather together the dispersed of Judah from the four corners of the earth." It was a subject upon which he gave much thought at the time; in fact, some months later he expanded his thinking upon it to freely explore (on five pages of typed manuscript) ideas which he felt might be helpful to the Church in becoming an ensign to the nations. He covered such areas as council meetings, stake presidents' conventions, separation of Church and business, court and arbitration committees, Church-owned property, and missionary surveys. His grass-roots experience, his familiarity with Church administration and procedures, his wide vision, and his originality are evident in each area upon which he deliberated.

At the next general conference, October 1936, President Richards had an opportunity to speak with President Grant upon two matters, both of which had been discussed prior to his mission in the South. The first pertained to the Church President's stated hope that he might visit the Southern States during President Richards's term there. When reminded of it, he said with a twinkle, "Oh, I tell that to all the mission presidents." Not to be put off, President Richards said, "But we have counted on your visit, and we have a mission conference planned for next June at which you are the drawing card. Our people are saving their money to come, and we expect a wonderful time." Persuaded, President Grant said, "All right, I will come."

The second point for consideration was the duration of President Richards's mission. "I am willing to remain as long as you want me to," he said, "but when you come in June I will have been in the South for three and a half years, so if you still feel as you did when I went down there, it would be better for me to be released in the summer. That is a better time to restart my real estate business so that I can make a living, and it would also be a better time for my children to change schools." He continued, "Now, I have my work all planned six months in advance, and I wouldn't like to read about my release in the newspaper, so you might like to bring my successor with you." His longtime friend smiled and said, "All right, I will." (LGR *Journal*, vol. X, p. 140, and interview.)

As it happened, Merrill D. Clayson, who was appointed

Mission President LeGrand Richards and Branch President Homer Yarn greet Church President Heber J. Grant, Charles A. Callis (rear), and Le Roi C. Snow (right) on their arrival in Atlanta.

President Richards's successor, was unable to meet the earlier date (May 1, 1937) which President Grant set for the mission visit, and he planned to go in June when his work as principal of South High School Seminary was completed for that year. In the meantime, Elder Charles A. Callis and LeRoi C. Snow accompanied President Grant to Atlanta, Georgia.

A very full two days of activity had been planned for the Church President's visit. After the missionary session on Saturday morning, Ina served a beautiful luncheon for the guests and mission leaders. Social calls and sightseeing filled the afternoon until dinner. Then in the evening nearly a thousand people gathered at the Women's Club for a reception, a program, and a mission Grand Ball with the presentation of nine district queens. It was a culmination of three and a half years of intensive work with the mission leadership and youth.

President Grant was delighted with the experience, and Elder Callis said that had he known it would be so grand he would have brought his wife. The press covered the evening events, and there were favorable comments in the newspapers concerning it and President Grant's radio address. Many city officials and dignitaries came, and they carried away like impressions of the Mormons and their influence in the Southern community.

On Sunday three conference sessions were held at Bass Junior High auditorium. The visitors were invited to do most of the speaking. President Grant was at his charming best, even singing for his audience. President Richards's young son, Alden, who had a sweet, clear voice, also sang. President Callis, happy to be back among the people of the South, warmed to the occasion and immensely enjoyed speaking to them again. It was a memorable event for Saints who had worked and saved to attend. A Sister Powell from South Carolina said, "President Richards, it was worth it even it I did have to sell my cow to come." For Brother Richards it was a deeply satisfying time and the realization of his dreams. He recorded that night: "Now I am anxious to turn the mission over. I have completed my plans with few exceptions." (LGR *Journal*, vol. XI, pp. 122-29, and interview.)

One of the exceptions was the setting up of districts under local leadership, which the president had not yet completed. During the intervening month before President Clayson's arrival, he worked to accomplish it. Before he left, three local district presidents with full district councils and boards were installed and functioning. He told them, "You are like the prophet of old, who one day was called Jacob and the next day, Israel. Today you are districts and branches, but soon the Brethren will come and change you to stakes and wards. You will be the same people, but your names will be changed."

As he traveled from place to place, President Richards jotted down in his notebook everything he thought would be helpful to his successor—businesses the mission dealt with, proposed chapels which needed to be built, men he had in training for positions of leadership, and those who would want to be advanced in the priesthood who were either not ready or not yet worthy. This information he typed and had ready to turn over to the new president.

President Richards had yet another important work to do before he left, a work which he had neither anticipated nor planned but which had far-reaching and undreamed of import. In his journal are recorded the steps as this work progressed and was completed.

On May 24, 1937, at Gaffney, South Carolina, the missionaries put questions to him "about the order of procedure in presenting our story to the people." Extemporaneously he took an hour and a half doing this. In nearby Greenville on May 27 he "took an hour in scripture class, covering eleven evenings of instruction, and gave proper presentation of our message to investigators—in systematic order." On June 6 he "commenced the write-up of our message [to be given] once a week for six months." He worked all day on the outline on June 7 and completed ten pages. He continued on June 11 and then helped the elders hold a street meeting. We know that between that day and June 16 he completed his outline, "telling our story in order to properly present our message," because on that date he mailed copies of it to all the elders in the mission under title of "The

Message of Mormonism." (LGR *Journal*, vol. XI, pp. 145, 152, 160, 162, 167.)

The importance of this labor cannot be overemphasized, for this was the outline that later served as the basis for his book *A Marvelous Work and a Wonder*, which he and many others consider to be his greatest contribution to the missionary effort of the Church. As shown, the groundwork for it was laid during the time when his mission in the South was essentially over.

In the light of what he had just accomplished, and what its future was to be, it seems significant that in his last general conference address as president of the Southern States Mission (April 1937), he said, "I believe that when the Lord announced to the Prophet Joseph Smith that a marvelous work and a wonder was about to come forth among the children of men, the work was to include many important things." He then delineated some of those things, including the Word of Wisdom and the Book of Mormon, and added, "*In the analysis of every phase of our work, to me, it is a marvelous work and a wonder.*" That thought, that actuality, was deep in his consciousness, even though it would be many years before his book would be written and before its title would be "found."

President Clayson arrived on June 18, and LeGrand "was very well impressed with him." He and Ina showed him about the mission home (which they had had freshly painted and refurbished with new curtains and other niceties). LeGrand discussed the affairs of the mission with him and gave him the notes and suggestions he had prepared. (President Clayson later told him they had served as his "Bible.") Then with full confidence that his successor was capable of moving ahead on his own, he and his family left Atlanta. (LGR *Journal*, vol. XI, pp. 167-68.)

By the evening of June 19 they were in Paducah, Kentucky, 455 miles on the way home. That night LeGrand wrote that he had completed his work in a manner satisfactory to himself, and he hoped to the Brethren and the Lord. (LGR *Journal*, vol. XI, p. 168.)

It was not many days until they were in Salt Lake City and he was reporting his mission to the Twelve assembled in the temple. He told them that he had filled in all the report blanks they had sent him, adding, "and goodness knows you've sent plenty; but there is no place on them to report what we have accomplished which I feel was of greatest importance to the mission—the individual growth and development that came as a result of harnessing the members and putting them to work."

He then told them that many from the mission had traveled west to receive the ordinances in the Salt Lake Temple; that young people had saved to attend BYU; that local youth had served missions; and that no missionary had been sent home in disgrace. He spoke of the three districts now under capable local leadership; of the full functioning missionwide MIA; of sites purchased, buildings remodeled and built, with others in the planning; and of the expanding membership which would occupy them and carry on the extended Church programs in the South.

It had been a different mission for President Richards. The missionaries had proselyted many, and converts were numerous, but his own efforts had been exclusively devoted to administrative work, to his missionaries, and to lifting and building up the members already on the books. He had faithfully and effectively enlarged and strengthened the foundation—begun by others before him and continued by those following—upon which the numerous missions, stakes, and wards of the south have come into being. And from his outline "The Message of Mormonism," written during the last weeks of his mission in the Southern States, he would later write the book which has reaped a vast harvest of converts for the Lord.

Chapter 12

Bishop of University Ward

1937-1938

Within a few days of LeGrand's return to Salt Lake City, Orin Woodbury, with whom he had had such a long and agreeable business association, offered him a half interest in the very successful and lucrative Woodbury investment and brokerage firm. LeGrand thought it over, and his reply was typical: "Orin, I think it is wonderful for you to make me such an offer, but I have never been second man in business. If I were to come in with you, that's what I would be, and I don't think I could be happy in that position." He continued, "I have confidence that I can reestablish my business as I left it when called to go to California by the President of the Church, and that I can retrieve some of the fortune I lost as a result of the Depression." So it was settled.

With characteristic vigor, he immediately set about rebuilding his real estate business. On June 26, 1937, he took his examinations at the Utah State Capitol, secured his broker's license, and began lining up prospects. On June 30 he rented office space for thirty-five dollars a month in the Columbia Trust Building at 125 South Main Street—"a fine building with marble halls," he recorded. On July 1 he commenced his business activities, and that day he closed his second real estate deal. He also moved his family into the George Lloyd furnished home at 545 DeSoto Street for a two-month period.

On July 3 he obtained eighty-eight real estate listings, ordered a new suit, and wrote in his journal that the *Deseret News* and the *Tribune* had "run a nice announcement with his picture." That evening he took Ina to the temple. During the month of July, he rented a Kodak and took pictures of his listed homes, bought new office furniture, ordered a neon sign for his window, obtained his multiple listing membership for $250, and began to build a sales force of six.

While his weekdays were filled with his many business affairs, he was instantly in demand as a speaker on Sundays. Four days after his return from the South, he spoke in the Salt Lake Tabernacle at the afternoon service under the direction of the Ensign and Liberty stake presidents. His talk, "The Worth of the Scriptures," appeared in the *Church News* of July 24. His KSL radio address of August 8, "The End of the Journey," was printed in the August 14 issue of that newspaper. Sometimes he preached two or three times on one Sunday. On July 16 he addressed the area's Dutch Saints for forty-five minutes in their own tongue. His years away had not estranged him from them. Their welcome was warm, genuine, and tearful when he greeted them that night at the Fourteenth Ward chapel.

For the next six months the days had to stretch in order to encompass his rigorous schedule. He began building a large new home at 925 South Thirteenth East with an adjoining triplex apartment. While it was being completed, he moved his family from George Lloyd's home to an apartment at 227 South Thirteenth East within the boundaries of the University Ward. It was while he was living here on a temporary basis that President Winslow F. Smith of Ensign Stake called him to be bishop of that ward, even though, when his home was built, he would be moving from the area.

When President Smith asked him about counselors, the new bishop chose Devirl B. Stewart as his first counselor. Brother Stewart had a background of ward experience, having served with the previous bishopric under Bishop Arthur T. Burton. In the brief time he had known him, Bishop Richards had come to respect Devirl and to enjoy his fine spirit.

For his second counselor, the bishop requested John L. Firmage. "But," said the stake president, "he is not active in Church affairs and has not performed any ordinances. I wonder if you are not making a mistake. There are a number of returned mission presidents in the ward who would make excellent counselors." But the bishop had a clear purpose in requesting this particular man. He explained it to the president. He had felt of Brother Firmage's sweet spirit when, after a trip from the East, he had borne his testimony in fast meeting. The bishop said also, "I think, because of Brother Firmage's standing in the financial and educational community, we will have a better connection with the wealthy, influential, and educated people in Federal Heights (which makes up a large segment of our ward) than if we take someone without his prestige."

The president was dubious, but after some deliberation and inquiry he was convinced that Brother Firmage was a good and a generous man and he and his counselors approved the appointment. The new second counselor proved to be an outgoing, friendly, and effective leader to the Aaronic Priesthood, in financial matters, and in positive influence which helped to build ward unity.

The ward was in close proximity to the University of Utah, and because of divergent views propounded by some of its educators and other men of influence, ward unity suffered over the issue of orthodoxy versus liberalism. A common question among members was "Are you a fundamentalist?" Shortly after the new bishopric was sustained on January 23, 1938, Bishop Richards attended the Sunday School Gospel Doctrine class. There the issue was freely discussed—and, of course, not resolved before the lesson period was concluded. The teacher asked the bishop if they had his permission to continue the discussion the following Sunday. "By all means," Bishop Richards replied, "but I should like to have the last ten or fifteen minutes to address the class."

The next Sunday brought a lively class discussion of such "controversial" issues as that the vision of Joseph Smith is not provable; that the Book of Mormon was not literally translated from golden plates; and that Christ was the Savior, not because he hung upon the cross but because he taught saving principles. The interchange of opinions and talk was terminated in time to allow Bishop Richards to address the class.

"The things I have heard in these two weeks of free discussion are not Mormonism," he told the group. "Now, as long as I am bishop of this ward, we are going to teach fundamental Mormonism in this building. That means that Joseph Smith indeed received a vision of the Father and the Son (and it is provable by personal testimony), that he did indeed translate the Book of Mormon from the golden plates which he received from the Angel Moroni." He continued, "In that book, we read of the vision shown to Nephi by the angel, of Mary with child, of the child growing to manhood, of his choosing twelve apostles, and of his being crucified for the sins of the world. Now, that is Mormonism."

The power of the bishop's office was upon him when he challenged: "Now, if any of you do not approve of fundamental Mormonism, why don't you go and organize a church of your own and teach what you want to. There are so many churches now teaching the precepts of men that one more won't matter." He then turned to Elder Joseph F. Merrill of the Council of the Twelve, who was in attendance as a member of the ward, and said, "Now, if I have said anything of which you do not approve, please correct me while the people are here." Elder Merrill responded, "I approve of every word you have said."

It was a sober class that filed out of the room. Some were jubilant. Lester F. Hewlett, who would shortly become president of the Tabernacle Choir, reported to President Grant that day that he had shed tears of gratitude that the Lord had sent them a man who could hold his own with the liberals. Some, however, were disturbed and thought the bishop to be severely orthodox. A few were angry.

For his part, the bishop soon went to his office and, sitting at his desk, put his head in his hands. The ward clerk, Joseph Toronto, who sat at a small table in the same room, remembers the bishop saying, "Oh, did I pour it on too strong? I hope I haven't put them from me. I have wanted them to love me so I could help them to love the Lord."

Feeling the intensity of the opposition and knowing the schism which could result, Bishop Richards was not surprised when the following anonymous and vitriolic letter came to him.

LeGrand Richards:

Do you know what you are doing with your narrow-minded Dogmatism? You will send the intelligent Mormons to the Unitarian church where they can have freedom of speech for which the Pilgrims came to America. . . .

We believe in revelation, but we want to clarify our ideas if you don't mind. . . .

You will be tempted to read this letter in Sunday School, but you won't. Why let the simple-minded that just take the dictation of orthodox fanatics know why you were made Bishop of this educated ward?

> One of Many who believe this is still
> the land of the Free and the home
> of the Brave.

February 26, 1938

Bishop Richards read the letter thoughtfully and pocketed it. He was determined to win the support of his opposition.

Shortly after this incident he met with one of the most influential liberal educators in the area. By way of introduction, Bishop Richards told him about the words of his prominent friend in Atlanta, Georgia—a Doctor Sutton, who was also in the field of educational philosophy: "If I were to have my way, I would not award a doctoral degree in a university. We make them doctors. Doctors of what? Doctors of memorization. I would wait until they get out of the university and prove that their education has made them leaders in their fields, and then I would give them a doctor's degree." The bishop continued, "Now, by that standard, I am as much entitled to a doctor's degree as are you. You are a Doctor of Philosophy and I am a Doctor of Religion. I know what religion will do for the member, for the convert, for the missionary. I have proven it from every angle, and I feel that I can speak as a Doctor of Religion." From that point on, the professor and the bishop were on agreed equal footing. They had a great discussion and parted friends, but not before the educator had invited his bishop to attend an Exchange Club luncheon as his guest.

The bishop's interesting analogy of academic and religious skills implies the distinction he has always recognized without question. Only in the field of religion does he equate his training with that of a Ph.D. In all other areas—literature, the arts, philosophy, science—he defers to scholars who are academically his superior. (The three honorary degrees which would later be awarded to him perhaps justify that earlier assessment of his hard-won mastery over the complexities of applied religion.)

Another staunch liberal leader became both friend and cooperating member of the ward community when Bishop Richards had him supervise an outstanding program and party to which President Grant was invited. Knowing the man's liberal tendencies, the President questioned Bishop Richards's judgment when he became aware of the party chairman's identity through the bishop's personal invitation. In defense, the bishop said, "But President Grant, you've not questioned my judgment before. I want to make friends of my opponents, and I've found that a person catches more flies with honey than with vinegar. Now, I figure that I will do better working with them than opposing them. I'm not asking this talented man to teach a doctrinal class, but I don't think it will hurt to have him put on a great entertainment."

"Well," said the President, "I guess you know what you are doing." The President attended the party, enjoyed the evening very much, and complimented the educator who had made the event so memorable and the bishop who had made so wise a choice.

By such means the bishop brought to the troubled waters of that period a seasoned judgment, a personal warmth, and a sure confidence in the ward members which they found hard to resist.

He assiduously studied members' names, faces, and identifying detail so that he readily came to know them all, and his remarkable powers of recall made it possible for him to make his greetings and conversation with the people personal and meaningful. His long-standing success formula—plan, delegate, follow through—brought blessings of activity to every ward member willing to respond. He discontinued the practice of bringing noted outside speakers for sacrament meetings and instead called whole families to provide talks and music for the services. As in similar previous situations, his notebook kept track of each family's turn.

He was supportive of activities. One member recalls that when the choir prepared for a special program, the bishop attended each rehearsal, even though according to him he "couldn't sing a note." He wanted the members to know he was with them each step of the way. He also initiated ward temple excursions, attended them with the members, and at one time arranged for the temple president, Stephen L. Chipman, to speak to the group about the meaning and purpose of the clothing, the ordinances, and the saving work the members were doing. As always, his central aim was to increase faith and spirituality in those over whom he presided.

It was just two and a half months from the time LeGrand became bishop of University Ward that he was attending April general conference. After the morning session of the third day, he stayed to visit with missionaries and parents on the north side of the Tabernacle, where signs indicated meeting places for the various missions. When his Southern States group dispersed, he walked down to his real estate office on Main Street and found President Grant and his father, George F., seated there. As he walked in, the President hung up the telephone and said, "Oh, here he is now."

"It looks suspicious to see you two men here," Bishop Richards said.

"It is," the President responded. "We're going to change the Presiding Bishopric this afternoon, and we'd like you to be Presiding Bishop. Who do you want for your counselors?"

"Well, President, you've about taken away my thinking powers. Who can I have?"

"Any man in the Church you want," the President assured him, then pleasantly added, "We don't choose a man's wife for him, and we don't choose his counselors."

"How long can I have to choose them?" the new Presiding Bishop asked.

"Oh," President Grant replied, "we want to sustain them this afternoon."

The afternoon session would begin at two o'clock. It was now twelve-forty-five. Bishop Richards brought to the question all the power of concentration he could muster, then drawing upon his knowledge of Church procedure he said, "President, when you were deciding whom you wanted for Presiding Bishop, you had a list of men that were suggested by members of the Twelve. If you feel like entrusting the list to me, I think I could select my counselors from among them. They would be men that you Brethren of the General Authorities regard as having special qualifications for that office."

President Grant was pleased with this idea and wrote eight names on a slip of paper. He commented upon each, as did Elder George F. Richards. When the new Presiding Bishop checked the names of Marvin O. Ashton and Joseph L. Wirthlin, the two older men approved them.

"Are you going to tell them in advance?" the Bishop asked.

The President smiled. "No, we wouldn't have asked you if we hadn't had to consult you for your counselors."

"Well, now, President Grant," the Bishop said, "they may love the Church and they may love the Lord, but they might not feel that they would like to serve under me as Bishop. I'd feel much better about it if you would give them an opportunity to turn it down before their names are presented before the entire Church."

"Well," the President acquiesced, "if you feel that way, I will contact them." (LGR interview and GFR *Diary* account.)

The details of Bishop Ashton's affirmative response to his call are not known, but Bishop Wirthlin later told of his. President Grant phoned and said, "Is this Joseph L. Wirthlin?"

"Yes, sir."

"This is Heber J. Grant. We are going to change the Bishopric this afternoon. We'd like to know if you are willing to serve as a counselor to LeGrand Richards?"

"Well," said Brother Wirthlin, "there is so much involved. I have my business and I'm president of the stake. Can I come in and talk it over with you?"

"No," said the eighty-one-year-old President, "there isn't time. I have to have a little nap before the meeting. It will be all right, won't it?" It was.

The new Presiding Bishopric was sustained at the two o'clock session that day, Wednesday, April 6, 1938. (In those days, general conference convened for three days and always included April 6 in commemoration of the organization of the Church in 1830.) LeGrand was the last speaker before President Grant closed the 108th Annual General Conference.

Bishop Richards stood before the congregation deeply moved. At age fifty-two, he was now the seventh Presiding Bishop since the Church was organized. This would be his twelfth sermon from that historic pulpit, but never had there been such a time as this, for he now stood as a General Authority with the attendant responsibility of his call upon him. It proved to be his shortest talk to date.

He expressed his gratitude for the confidence of the Church leaders in him, and for the sustaining vote of the Church. He told of his love for the Brethren, the Saints, and the Lord, assuring his listeners that "there is not a place in the world I would not go, because of my love for and testimony of the gospel." He was grateful for every opportunity to serve that had ever come to him, but for that service, he said, "the Lord owes me nothing. All I have done in the Church, I have done because I love the Lord."

He talked of his predecessor, Sylvester Q. Cannon, who had been sustained as an apostle that same day. Since their days in Holland together, Bishop Richards had watched and admired his mission president. He recalled now that "it was as though the light of truth was streaming from [President Cannon's] eyes when he explained the glorious principles of the gospel to those who were seeking after truth." And he added, "I have always thought that this call [to the Twelve] would be, for him, inevitable."

The Presiding Bishop now addressed himself to the priesthood leaders with whom he would be working in his new assignment. With these encouraging words, he pledged himself to serve them without measure. "I hope," he said, "that you will never be afraid of me. I hope you will not hesitate to come to my office. I hope you will feel free to write, if there is anything I can do to help you. I am willing to give all I have, and all the Lord will give to me, to help this work roll [on] to the destiny which I know the Lord has decreed for it."

In his desire to render total service he reached out to the whole Church, but, as was his way, he remembered the needs of his family. To his children he said, "There is no achievement that can come to [you] that will be so pleasing to me as to know that [your] lives shall be lives of service to this great Church." (*Conference Report*, April 1938, pp. 119-20.)

George F. Richards was proud of his son. He wrote in his diary that day (April 6, 1938) that LeGrand's selection as Presiding Bishop had received among the Brethren a "unanimous vote"; that his son had "accepted [the call] in a proper spirit"; that he had "made a brief but splendid speech"; and that following the session "many people congratulated LeGrand and some congratulated me, including President Grant."

The next day Bishop Richards met with his University Ward counselors. His clerk remembers that he looked rather pale and shaken. A week later the new Presiding Bishop and his counselors were set apart in their respective callings. As the Brethren placed their hands upon his head and President Grant gave him a blessing, Bishop Richards remembered a dream, the significance of which had been withheld from him until now. He tells of it as follows:

> About the time I was to be released from the Southern States Mission, I had a dream. In it I met President Grant on the street in Salt Lake City and he said, "LeGrand, come to my office, I have a special blessing for you." I went, and he gave me a blessing. When I awoke, I couldn't remember a thing about what he had said, but only how his words had thrilled me. When he laid his hands on my head within the same year and set me apart as the Presiding Bishop of the Church, I knew why the knowledge had been withheld from my memory. It would not have been right for me to know it at that time. I had to wait until the call came and the actual blessing was given.

Between his setting apart on April 14 and his release as bishop of University Ward on November 13, a seven-month period, LeGrand Richards served in the dual role of ward bishop and Presiding Bishop of the Church. Even with the complexities of his new assignment, he did not neglect his ward responsibilities, one of which was to call young men into the mission field. It was during this period that he called his own son LaMont to serve in England.

The ward counselors, of course, carried a heavy load, but the majority of ward members had been won to unified support so that the work progressed smoothly, and this helped a great deal. In an evaluation of Bishop Richards's part in bringing this about, the ward clerk, Joseph Toronto, says: "He brought into University Ward a warmth, a love, a fellowship that was foreign to many of the members. It was the spirit of the gospel, the Spirit of Christ, and there was a unifying force felt there that lasted for a long time and left a lasting imprint upon the people with whom he served."

By the time Bishop Richards was released from his ward duties, he had already moved his family from the area. It had been a satisfaction to him that, since his return from the South, he had largely recovered his financial losses, had built a lovely home, and had returned his deserving family to their former gracious life-style. This home, with its beautiful canyon backyard, served as the family setting for the Presiding Bishopric years.

Presiding Bishop of the Church

1938-1952

W hen asked if there was a transition period between his call and his taking over the duties of Presiding Bishop, Elder Richards replied, "No, the next day Elder Sylvester Q. Cannon, who had been called as an apostle and whom I succeeded, walked out; and I walked in and went to work." It was of course necessary for the new Bishop to again terminate his real estate business. His counselors too had their business arrangements to make.

Of these men so hastily chosen that general conference day, Bishop Richards later said: "If I could choose over again I could not have made an improvement, nor would I have exchanged one of these grand counselors for any man that I met along the way."

He spoke of each of them in turn. "Joseph L. Wirthlin was a noble character, as true and loyal to the Church as any man I have ever known. If we ever questioned the instructions of the Brethren, he would say, 'Well, you know, if they asked that we put the Presiding Bishop's Office up on Ensign Peak, there it would go.' That is the kind of faith he had."

Marvin O. Ashton was LeGrand's brother-in-law, a man whom Ina had loved and admired since boyhood as a "magnificent character." Of him Bishop Richards said, "When we knelt in prayer every morning in my office as we commenced the labors of the day, Bishop Ashton, in his plain-speaking way would pray, 'Now, Father, give us the good sense to do what we know to be right to do.' He didn't think we always used the good sense that the Lord Almighty gave us, . . . that we didn't always step out of our way to do only that which ought to be done. He had a great heart, and he was one of the finest boys' men I ever knew."

They were strong men, with spirits to match the Bishop's own, a spirit which President Grant commended when he set him apart as Presiding Bishop on April 14. In part he said: "The Lord is pleased with your wonderful loyalty, love, and devotion to the work you have been engaged in from young manhood until the present and for the readiness and willingness at all times to respond to every call made of you, holding first in your heart and affections the gospel of the Lord Jesus Christ." He then blessed him that he would "increase in the love of truth and wisdom," and promised, "you will have the *ability to do more work with greater ease than you have done in the past.*" (*Blessing,* Heber J. Grant to LeGrand Richards, April 14, 1938. Used with permission of the Office of the First Presidency.)

In view of the pace at which LeGrand Richards had driven himself in all of his Church assignments, particularly in the Southern States, where even his father worried about possible effects on his health, President Grant's last statement indicates that he was well aware of the ever-widening responsibilities of the new Presiding Bishop and was further preparing him for his work through this special blessing. Now, with no further personal business concerns to dilute his efforts, Bishop Richards could spend all his working hours in service to the Lord. In this prospect he experienced great joy, as did his counselors. By commitment, direction, and temperament, the three were perfectly suited to work effectively as one in purpose and in loyalty to the Lord and to one another.

At the beginning of Bishop Richards's term of office, the total membership of the Church (figures for December 31, 1937) numbered 767,652, with 118 stakes, 1,101 wards and independent branches, and 36 missions. (*Conference Report,* April 1938, p. 76.) The majority of the members lived in Utah, Idaho, Arizona, and California. One of the early assignments from the First Presidency was for the Presiding Bishopric to tour these states and become acquainted with the Saints, their leaders, and the youth. In doing this they sometimes traveled with members of the Church Welfare Committee. Harold B. Lee, managing director of the Church welfare system, was one who accompanied them at various times. When they had covered the area,

Newly called Presiding Bishop of the Church with counselors Marvin O. Ashton (left) and Joseph L. Wirthlin.

the Bishopric were permitted to set up their own conference schedules. They aimed at visiting every stake conference (then held quarterly). When Lee A. Palmer later came into the Presiding Bishop's office to assist in administering the Aaronic Priesthood program, he also held some Aaronic Priesthood training meetings in some stakes to help ease the travel load. They traveled in all kinds of weather and mainly by automobile.

Since responsibility for the Aaronic Priesthood was central to their call, this segment of their work was of immense importance from the beginning. Elder Richards tells that when President Grant set him apart to administer the temporal affairs of the Church, that seemed to him a great task, but when he set him over the Aaronic Priesthood he was "truly humbled." That call he took most seriously, and he aimed to reach every boy. To accomplish this it was necessary to touch and influence their leaders.

One medium to accomplish this goal was the *Progress of the Church*, a bulletin sent out monthly by the Presiding Bishop's Office, its first issue appearing June 1939 (vol. 1, no. 1). It was a rousing challenge to bishops and stake presidents, and it bears the unmistakable stamp of LeGrand Richards. "Zion must arise and put on her beautiful garments," its editorial read. "We are custodians. The leader who can get ten men working is greater than he who does the work of ten men. All can be assigned to some useful service. Priesthood was given so that all men might be engaged in the work of their Father. This will still be true when the membership of the Church has increased to ten million." (The last issue of *Progress of the Church* [vol. 6, no. 8] was sent out August 1943 with the announcement that it would hereafter appear in the Church Section of the *Deseret News*, where it continued to provide regular communication between the Presiding Bishop's Office and the bishops and stake presidents.)

Once a year, stake conferences were devoted to the Aaronic Priesthood, and here again the Presiding Bishopric expended effort to motivate and teach. In preparation, a letter was sent to each stake president six weeks in advance. A suggested program approved by the Council of the Twelve accompanied it, wherein talks for a deacon, a teacher, a priest, and a bishop were assigned for the priesthood session and a talk for a young woman was added for the Sunday session. Study questions were included so that the youth could prepare his talk based upon sound information, and he was encouraged not to read the talk at the conference. Bishop Richards felt that when a talk is read, much personal benefit is lost to both speaker and listener. He has always set the example in this respect, and during his years as Presiding Bishop he extracted a promise from his counselors that they likewise would not read their talks.

With ward and stake leadership so instructed and encouraged through written media and regular personal contact with the Presiding Bishopric, a plan to involve the boys directly was initiated through the Individual and Quorum Award Program. It was particularly the Quorum Award which had a touch of genius in it, for through it a group spirit was instilled into the young men of the Church. This held them to one another in a bond of quorum loyalty which Elder Richards's associates say was unmatched before or since. It brought tremendous results. Many reports came in of boys on vacation who insisted that their fathers find the nearest church so they could attend their priesthood meeting and not let their quorum members down.

The Awards Program was challenging but not demanding beyond possible wide attainment. It required that the quorum must have the following: an average of 50 percent or more members at quorum meetings; 75 percent or more must fill a minimum of twelve priesthood assignments during the year; 75 percent or more must observe the Word of Wisdom; 75 percent or more who earn money must pay a full tithing; and 50 percent or more must participate in quorum service projects or Church welfare projects.

One priesthood assignment was the collection of fast offerings, which although not initiated at this time, was given great emphasis by this Presiding Bishopric. This one-to-one contact of the deacons with members helped to build spirituality in the boys and in the adults, and it greatly increased the fast offering funds, thereby blessing countless needy persons.

Other efforts to build spirituality were made through a specially designed Aaronic Priesthood manual, a songbook, and other books compiled under the direction of the Presiding Bishopric by Preston Nibley—*Inspirational Talks for Youth* and *Faith Promoting Stories* (Deseret Book, 1941, 1943).

Also under the direction of the Presiding Bishopric was an outstanding three-act pageant, "Prepare Ye the Way," in which six hundred Aaronic Priesthood bearers took part. It was presented to record crowds in the Salt Lake Tabernacle for three consecutive evenings. The prologue was spoken by Bishop LeGrand Richards, and a 450-voice Aaronic Priesthood choir, with Alexander Schreiner at the organ, provided the music. The production was endorsed by the First Presidency—Heber J. Grant, J. Reuben Clark, Jr., and David O. McKay—who charged the young men, "You have been given 'the keys of the ministering of angels.' See that you use these keys to open the doors to realms of high thinking and clean living, ever bearing in mind the injunction, 'Be ye clean that bear the vessels of the Lord.' "

It was not only through plans, directives, literature, and programs that the Aaronic Priesthood made such strides under Bishop Richards (the area in which he feels he made the greatest contribution during his term as Presiding Bishop), but it was his personal contact, and that of his counselors, with the boys themselves. Wherever they went they preached in a way that appealed to young men and of attitudes which benefited them.

Bishop Wirthlin said, "Boys and girls of our Church must have recreation. To provide for it, each ward and stake needs to set up a budget at once where no charge is made for ward entertainment. . . . where doors of the recreation hall stand open and the hand of fellowship is extended to all who wish to enter. No other requirement should be made for youth to attend ward socials than good behavior. Let rich and poor share alike." (*Deseret News*, April 8, 1940.)

Although there previously were isolated instances wherein forward-looking bishops saw the logic and were applying the principle (Bishop Richards himself had done so as a ward bishop), the setting up of a Churchwide budget system for ward maintenance and needs was initiated under this Presiding Bishopric. Elder Mark E. Petersen, as a counselor in Liberty Stake and then Sugar House Stake presidencies, witnessed the change-over. He says, "It revolutionized the whole concept of ward and stake financing and was very beneficial to the total Church."

Bishop Ashton, in his persuasive and powerful way, made an appeal for youth leadership. "There are some people . . . that have a thousand cattle on a thousand hills, and if you'd ask them for a thousand dollars, they'd get nervous prostration. The same people would hammer the stand and remind us where the young people are going. . . . We'll have less trouble if we just go with youth more. Thank the Lord for the fine bishops and stake presidents who have taken that philosophy and are going with their young people." (*Conference Report*, October 1946, p. 133-34.)

Bishop Richards pleaded with bishops to make sacrament services appealing to the youth. He remembered his boyhood in Tooele when he sat with his friends and listened to elderly, white-whiskered brethren wander through sincere but deadening talks which seldom varied from the last time, while the youth fidgeted and counted the long minutes until the last song was sung and the benediction lengthily pronounced.

At the time LeGrand Richards became Presiding Bishop, the feeling in the Church was that sacrament meeting was more for the older folks and that Sunday School and Mutual (MIA) were for the young. Elder Richards says: "Our average attendance at sacrament meeting was about 15 percent. We had many wards and stakes as low as 8, 9, and 10 percent. I told the bishops in the Tabernacle one day that I'd be ashamed to preside over a ward or a stake that couldn't get at least 25 percent of their people out to that meeting." He continues: "Many bishops took issue with us. They didn't think it could be done." In 1981 one stake president told him, "I was in your meeting when you made that statement. At that time our average attendance was 8 percent." During Bishop Richards's tenure in office, the Church average attendance at sacrament meeting reached 38 percent—an all-time high for the period.

In his leadership days in Liberty and Sugar House stakes, Elder Mark E. Petersen recalls, he not only observed the sharp increase in sacrament meeting attendance in those stakes but was impressed with "the magnificent work Bishop Richards and his counselors did with both the Aaronic Priesthood and the girls' programs in the Church."

While the Bishop reached out to youth in meetings, he also did this in every way he could personally touch a life. He sat one Sunday with a deacons quorum president and his bishop in personal interview. He said to the boy, "How many deacons are there in your quorum?"

"Twelve," the young president replied.

"How many attend quorum meeting?" he asked.

"Six," was the response.

"Now," said Bishop Richards, "you are a farm boy. If your father gave you charge over twelve of his sheep and one morning you found six gone from the corral, what would you do?"

"I'd go out and hunt them," the boy said.

"That's what your Father in Heaven expects you to do with your deacons, my boy." Then when the young man told him that they didn't have a regular advisor, Brother Richards counseled with the bishop on the crucial need for good priesthood leadership.

Another time he took his question about youth leadership directly to a group of boys. "What do you want most in a priesthood leader?" He got a direct answer. "We want someone who doesn't think boys are a pain in the neck."

That he as Presiding Bishop did not consider boys in this category is evidenced in the following two experiences. At the time he was Presiding Bishop it was thought that the General Authorities should do ward (home) teaching along with other priesthood holders in the Church. He obediently complied. From the experience, he tells this story.

I took a teaching beat in Yale Ward, and when I went into the home of a prominent attorney one night I found there only his son, a priest in the Aaronic Priesthood. In talking with him I learned that he'd quit going to his own Church and that he had been visiting in other churches. I wondered how I could get him back to where he belonged in his Church. I said, "How would you like to go ward teaching with me?" He said he'd be glad to. We made an appointment for the following Tuesday night.

We went to four different homes. In each, I talked to him via the families so he wouldn't think I was preaching to him. When we were through it was still early, so I said, "What are you going to do for the rest of the evening?" He said, "Nothing." I said, "Well, I live over there in an upside-down house. How would you like to come and see it?" He said he would, so we went and I took him through it. I had build it down into the hollow, and we had to go down to the bedrooms instead of going up.

After our tour, we went into the living room and sat down. I said, "Now, it's all right for you to visit other churches providing you know what you have in your own Church." So I took an hour or more and explained to him what we have to offer and what he could not find in any other church. When he left, I felt that I had him straightened out, so I called his bishop and said, "Bishop, I think I have another missionary for you." And he called him on a mission.

Bishop Richards's man-to-man approach with Aaronic Priesthood boys was appealing, even to one in his own family. He tells of an agreement he made with his son Alden, who at the time was too young to get a driver's license and yet had commenced going out occasionally with girls. One day his father talked with him in these terms:

"My son, . . . I have been thinking that I need a partner in my business. The more I think of it, the more I think you should be my partner, for I am going all around the Church telling brethren how to raise their sons, and my words would fly right back in my face if, when I was out at conferences, you failed to attend your priesthood and sacrament meetings."

Then I added, "And the more I think of it, the more I think you need a partner in your business, for you like to go out occasionally with your boy friends and the girls, and you do not have an auto nor a driver's license. I think I should be your partner, for I have an auto and I have a driver's license, so I can be your chauffeur."

Well, we agreed on this partnership. My desk calendar would show the appointments I made with him to take him and pick up his boy friend and then the girls. I would leave them at a show and inquire, "Shall I wait for you?" His reply was, "No, Dad, I will call you when we are ready to come home," so I would keep close to the phone awaiting his call. When he called it would usually be that they were at the confectionery store.

One Sunday, Mother and I were out of town attending a stake conference. As we neared home, I said to her, "I would give a dollar to know whether our son got up and got to his priesthood meeting, but I wouldn't ask him for anything. I wouldn't want him to think for one minute that I did not trust him to keep his agreement."

When we arrived home, he explained that although he had been out playing in his orchestra until midnight the night before, he had set the alarm clock and got up early and attended his priesthood meeting. This pleased me very much. (*Just to Illustrate,* pp. 211-12.)

Bishop Richards's personalized teaching has had far-reaching influence, and many prominent men who were then either Aaronic Priesthood leaders or young men comment upon that influence. President Ezra Taft Benson, then a counselor in the Boise, Idaho, Stake presidency, remembers "Bishop Richards's great enthusiasm for the Aaronic Priesthood and the emphasis he put on not losing any boy." He also remembers that the Bishop "was willing, even anxious, to meet with the young people whenever he visited there. He wanted to reach out, to touch each heart." These pre-conference 8:00 A.M. meetings with the youth are still part of his approach to reaching them. At age ninety-six (1982) he charms them and teaches them with his ever-ready fund of stories and experiences, so that they are not even aware of the learning process; but they remember him, and his stories remain with them to lift and motivate them to live better.

A man who felt the impact of his personal touch was Dallin H. Oaks, formerly president of Brigham Young University. "I was struck by how warm and loving he was. He was the Presiding Bishop when I was a deacon in the Aaronic Priesthood. I had to learn all the names of the General Authorities, and I remembered LeGrand Richards, Presiding Bishop of the Church. I always thought of him as *my* Bishop and I have always called him Bishop. I still have a kind of little boy's admiration for him."

When the influence of the Quorum Awards Program was being strongly felt in the wards and stakes, a sister went to President Lorenzo H. Hatch of Granite Stake and said, "President, you have done such a wonderful thing for the boys, why don't you do something for the girls?" So in that stake they developed for the girls almost a duplicate of the Awards Program. It was so successful in Granite Stake that it came to the attention of the Twelve, and George Albert Smith, then President of the Quorum, sent a letter to all stake presidents in the Church recommending it for adoption.

When Bishop Richards heard of this from Elder Joseph F. Merrill, he said, "It will never go over in the Church."

"Why won't it, Bishop?" asked Brother Merrill.

"Because there is nobody to promote it. Half the stake presidents won't know they've received the letter thirty days after they get it. You've got to have somebody to promote a program in the Church to have it take hold."

Elder Merrill then asked, "Would you brethren of the Presiding Bishopric do it?"

Bishop Richards answered, "We have plenty to do."

Elder Merrill pressed. "Would you brethren of the Bishopric do it?"

"We're not asking for any more work," was the answer.

"But, would you brethren of the Bishopric *do* it?"

Just a little impatient, the Bishop answered, "Now, Brother Merrill, we do anything we are asked to do by proper authority, and if we are asked to do this, we'll do it." And they did.

When Bertha Reeder became General President of the Young Women's Mutual Improvement Association she asked for the program, and she pledged at their YWMIA meeting in the Tabernacle that she would maintain and continue it at the level to which the Presiding Bishopric had taken it. As a result of her willingness and her pledge, the program was turned over to her organization to administer from that point on. It had great in-

fluence for good among the girls, just as the Aaronic Priesthood
Award Program did for the boys.

However demanding the organization, promotion, and
administration of the Aaronic Priesthood programs were, they
made up only a portion of Bishop Richards's administrative responsibilities. Bishop Wirthlin later wrote: "From the installation
of the first Presiding Bishop until the present time those who
have been called to [that office] have . . . received, distributed,
and accounted for the contributions and tithes of the people;
looked after the poor; comforted the weary; admonished and
exhorted to good works those who faltered; provided and maintained adequate places of worship; and accounted for the records
of membership, activity, and advancement of all members of the
Church." (*Improvement Era*, November 1956, p. 794.)

When LeGrand Richards became Presiding Bishop of the
Church, the wards and missions were retaining the money they
received for tithing, using what they needed for ward operational
expenses and remitting the remainder to the Presiding Bishop's
Office. There was no regular auditing system and no required
time for remitting the funds. It was a loosely structured system
which could invite problems. Under this Presiding Bishopric the
system was completely reorganized. Henceforth all tithes and
contributions, Churchwide, came to the Presiding Bishop's
Office first, and expense monies were then dispersed back to the
local units of the Church according to their size and needs.

Such a change was of great concern to the bishops, who were
fearful lest their operating needs would not be met. But one of
the things LeGrand Richards had promised bishops and stake
presidents in his general conference remarks was that they need
not be afraid to come to him. He was true to his word. Mabel
Jones Gabbott, who was Bishop Richards's secretary during this
transitional period, says: "Here was a man who could guide the
bishops to see what the Lord wanted. They would come in with
their problems and he would seat them across the desk and be so
considerate and kind. It was a big step, but he'd been a bishop
three times and a stake president and he understood their prob-

lems and their needs. He was never hurried, but he encouraged them that it was all right, that they'd get enough money to run their wards, and that this was the Lord's way of doing it. They would then leave with their fear and apprehension quieted and feeling that, in him, they truly had a friend."

Taylor H. Merrill was office manager for the fourteen years of Bishop Richards's tenure and found him to be a kind and loyal supervisor. He tells of the accounting methods initiated to handle tithes and offerings under the new rules: "Under this Presiding Bishopric all the tithing books and tithing receipts were numbered. When a ward wanted a tithing record book, they would apply. It would be sent out and a record kept of the receipt numbers. Every month these numbers would be checked off, and if one were missing, the stake auditor would be asked to find out where it was. A copy of every receipt issued came to the Bishop's office and it had to match the amount of money sent in because there were no deductions at the ward level."

Another innovation within the Presiding Bishop's Office came in the area of Church membership record-keeping. Elder Richards recalls: "If you wanted to find the record of a member, you'd have to write to the ward where he lived, and if it was not there, to the ward in which he lived before. There were no general membership records in the office at all. So we gathered in from all of the wards and branches the names and all the information they had about their members, and we built up a Church membership record."

Taylor Merrill adds further detail concerning the change:

> Membership cards written in longhand were coming in which could not be read. One ward clerk couldn't read the former's writing, so much of the information was nothing like that from which it began. The new Presiding Bishopric changed all this. Each ward was instructed to make a typewritten card for every person baptized or blessed, and thereafter the original card followed the individual wherever he went, but it passed through the Presiding Bishop's Office on its way to the member's new location.

Sister Ella Jack, a devoted and efficient woman, was put in charge of the Membership Department. A Church member from

California who came in to see Bishop Richards said, "They tell me you have a membership record now." "That's right," the Bishop responded. "Does it work?" the man asked. "Well, you give me your name and date of birth and we'll see whether it works or not." The man did so, and the Bishop called Ella Jack. She said, "Just a minute, Bishop," and in a moment she told him the ward in which the man was a member. "It works," the man said, as he walked away satisfied.

Brother Merrill tells of the changes also made in the Annual Reports (Form E) which the stake clerks were completing once a year, a complicated and tedious labor for which they were being paid. Under Bishop Richards's direction these forms were simplified and their statistical information was compiled and submitted each month instead of annually. The girls in the department put them on the calculating machine, lined up all the wards in a stake with a blank sheet at the end of the line, and ran them through, tallying the totals and copying the data once a month. This system provided a quick statistical check which was readily available for the April general conference report each year. It eliminated the previous payments to stake clerks and saved the Church thousands of dollars.

Under the Presiding Bishop's jurisdiction came both the Church building program and the Legal Department, the latter having responsibility for legal matters concerning Church real estate holdings. Bishop Richards's real estate experience enabled him to work closely with that department in initiating and supervising the analysis of individual records and from that the creation of a general, detailed listing of all real estate holdings. This general record, the first of its kind, was an invaluable aid to the building program.

During the war years (1941-1945) severe building restrictions were imposed, and wards that had raised money for buildings but could not proceed with their chapels were advised to send their funds to the Presiding Bishop's Office to be kept in trust and earning interest until such time as their buildings could be erected. To arrange these and other matters, the bishops came in to see their friend LeGrand Richards at general conference times.

Bishop Richards at work on Church building plans.

"We had bishops lined up two deep," he says, "trying to get to talk to us about their building matters."

As restrictions lifted, the building program went forward with renewed vigor, and 666 new chapels had been erected by 1952. Elder Richards recalls: "We had Brother Howard J. McKean come in to direct the building of chapels, and later Brother Frank Bowers joined him. We didn't have a crew out in the Church then, but we worked through local builders in their own areas." He adds: "I had to inspect many of the sites where they wanted to build. I traveled quite a lot for that purpose."

In addition to such trips for wards and stakes, he also was responsible for supervising the mission building program. He tells of one mission trip he made.

> The mission president from Mexico had been up to Salt Lake for general conference and talked with the First Presidency. He wanted to buy a building that he had inspected down there. The Presidency thought it would be better if I, as Presiding Bishop, were to go down and look at the property, so I went back with the mission president. We drove to the property. I said "Drive on."

"Don't you even want to see the building now that you've come all the way to look at it?" asked the president.

I said, "Well, I've seen the neighborhood that it's in." But I looked at the building, then I said, "Now let's see if we can't find a building where the middle-class people live—clerks from the stores, attorneys, doctors, and so forth. If you go to the middle class, the humble rich will come down to it and the poor will come up to it." So we checked with real estate men and we found a building that was less expensive than the one we had looked at, but it was in a nice neighborhood. We recommended it, and that was the one they bought.

Further commenting upon the missions, Bishop Richards says: "Mission presidents would come in scolding about not getting buildings. 'Shall I tell you whose fault it is?' I would ask. 'Whose?' they would respond. 'Yours,' I'd answer. 'You go out to the branches that want buildings, you write us, and then you forget about the branches until they bother you again, at which time you come and scold us.' " He then counseled them and taught them their duty. "You must take the lead. You've got to go to the branches and work out the details and decide what is standing in the way, help them work it out, and then encourage them to proceed. If the problem is lack of approval for the purchase of the land, get something that can be approved so they can go forward."

In this way Bishop Richards trained the men over whom he presided—not only mission presidents but stake presidents as well—in all matters pertaining to Church building programs. He often used the statement of the banker to a prospective real estate investor. "When you buy real estate," he advised, "there are three things you always want to consider. They are location, location, and location."

Another project having to do with Church properties was that of grounds beautification, begun in 1937 but given great impetus under Bishop Marvin O. Ashton. Many chapel grounds were not landscaped and were overrun with weeds or sagebrush. Thatcher Ward of Bannock Stake was an example. (*Church News*, July 17, 1937, p. 2.) When ward and stake leaders were counseled to plant grass, shrubs, and flowers, some resistant

bishops told Bishop Richards, "Our boys would pull them up."
To this he emphatically replied, "Your boys will be too proud of
their fine meetinghouse grounds to do any such thing." The
program went forward. The work pioneered in those early years
laid the foundation for the now beautifully landscaped grounds
associated with practically every Church-owned property in the
world.

There were other aspects of Church real estate in which
Bishop Richards was personally involved. His sound business
judgment made possible the buying up of investment property for
the Church which either saved or brought in hundreds of thousands of dollars. He negotiated for all the properties on the block
north of the Salt Lake Temple, except for one house on the
northwest corner of the block, as well as those on the east side of
State Street adjacent to the present Church Office block. He tells
of this last business transaction as follows:

> Elder Frank Evans and I negotiated for the purchase of the
> Bransford Apartments (now Eagle Gate) on the corner of State
> Street and South Temple, including the apartments on both sides
> of First Avenue. After we were given their lowest selling price, I
> asked the representative at the bank if it would do any good to
> make a counter offer. He said it would not, that they had other
> people interested in its purchase but that Mrs. Bransford had
> wanted to give the Church first opportunity to purchase it.
>
> After we had inspected the property, I said to Elder Evans, "I
> have a feeling that if we were to offer less than the price they are
> asking, that we would get the property." He agreed with me, so
> we asked President George Albert Smith if he would be disap-
> pointed if we didn't get it. He said, "You brethren understand
> these matters better than I do. You ask my counselors, and if they
> approve, you make the offer."
>
> They approved, so I called the officer at the bank and thanked
> him for giving the Church the first opportunity to purchase the
> property, but I said, "When building restrictions are lifted, there
> will be new apartments built, and it would cost nearly as much to
> remodel these buildings and bring them up to date as it would to
> build new ones, so we have decided not to accept your offer. Shall
> I return the abstract?"
>
> "No," he said. "You spoke as if you might be interested in
> making a lower offer." He then asked me if we would make such
> an offer.

I replied that I believed that our committee would be interested, but that I didn't want them to feel that we didn't want to pay what they felt the property was worth. He asked for time to take the matter up with his committee, and in two hours he called me and said they would accept the lesser offer. (*Blue Book*, p. 35.)

During the last year that he was Presiding Bishop (1952), LeGrand Richards was visiting in Glendale, California, and had a rare opportunity to procure another very valuable piece of property for the Church. He was visiting with a Dr. Walker, whom he knew well when he lived in California. The doctor told him of a widow named Jacquelin Lewis living in LaVern, California, who wanted to give her property to some charitable organization. She had no children. Elder Richards tells the story:

We decided to visit her, and this resulted in her giving the property to the Church on an annuity basis. [Mrs. Lewis later told President Vern R. Peel that the thing that made her decide to let the Church have the property was her meeting Bishop Richards.] We purchased some of the adjoining property and additional water rights, and in 1971 we sold about ninety-eight acres to the Metropolitan Water Company for cash. This returned to the Church all they had invested in the property, with a sizable surplus, leaving us with 385 acres clear of all encumbrance. Mrs. Lewis had died in December 1971, so we had nothing more owing her. I have been supervising the operation of this property for twenty years. We have some citrus groves and a number of buildings on the ranch. Some of the land has been sold.

In his position as Presiding Bishop, Brother Richards also served for years on the Board of Zions Securities Corporation (the Church's holding company for real estate), and for a long term as chairman of its executive committee. He also served as secretary and as director of Hotel Utah, director of ZCMI, and director of Beneficial Life Insurance Company.

On April 21, 1938, he was chosen president of the Board of Trustees of LDS Hospitals, and he had the supervision of all Church hospitals for the fourteen years of his term as Presiding Bishop. As such he was an advisor to the Primary Association for their Children's Hospital (later Primary Children's Medical Center). The hospital was then located at 40 West North Temple. It was Bishop Richards who located the site for the present building at 320 Twelfth Avenue and took President Grant up to see it. The President approved it, in fact he was thrilled with it; and when the businessmen of Salt Lake gave a banquet to honor his eightieth birthday and presented him with a thousand silver dollars to be used for some charitable purpose, he gave them to the Primary Association to help build their new hospital. President Grant thought that, for such a good purpose, the silver dollars could be sold for a hundred dollars apiece.

Later the dollars were made into paperweights and turned to the general president of the Primary, LaVern Parmley, and her counselors to dispose of. But nothing much was done beyond minor sales. One day in their hospital board meeting, Bishop Richards said, "Sister Parmley, do you know why you can't sell these dollars? You have never thought you could." When she asked for his suggestion on how it could be done, he said, "Just ask each Primary organization in the Church to sell one dollar to one, ten, or twenty persons." To show it could be done, he took the first paperweight to some members, told the story of the dollars and the purpose for which they were intended, and had no trouble in placing it. The Primary presidency took it from there, and they found they did not have enough dollars to supply the requests. A hundred thousand dollars came in from these sales, and this went a long way in those days to build the superb medical facility which was completed by 1952. (Church Section of the *Deseret News*, February 13, 1952, p. 12.)

Another beautiful facility which received the Bishop's careful attention was the Relief Society Building. As advisor to the Relief Society in their social work, he came often in contact with three great successive general presidents—Louise Y. Robinson, Amy Brown Lyman, and Belle S. Spafford. The last-named tells of her association with him in the days when she first accompanied Amy Lyman to meetings as her counselor. "I was always glad to go," she says. "He was always so fair, so wise, and so understanding. I saw the penetrating judgment he had in counseling us." Shortly after she became Relief Society president in 1945 World War II ended, and with building restrictions relaxed, she and her counselors—Marianne C. Sharp and Gertrude Garff

Presiding Bishopric and General Relief Society President Amy Brown Lyman at Relief Society Centennial celebration, 1942.

—agreed that they should "go after a building of their own" as their predecessors had hoped and dreamed for.

Accordingly they met with the First Presidency—George Albert Smith, J. Reuben Clark, Jr., and David O. McKay—and told them that if they charged their hundred thousand Relief Society members a dollar apiece, they could have a fine building. President Clark said, "If you are going to build, build greater than that." After briefly discussing the matter, the Brethren suggested five dollars apiece, with one year to get their money in, and the sisters went to work on this basis. "Bishop Richards had responsibility for the financial matters of the Church and the Building Committee," says Sister Spafford. "And we turned to him, and oh, what a response we got from that great man!" She adds:

> He loved the Relief Society and he loved the women of the Church and he wanted them to have the best, and he was willing to work for it. He went out early in the year to a conference in Idaho Falls, and he phoned me between sessions and said, "Sister Spafford, they've raised their money, and I'm so thrilled."

She recalls how he counseled them on the architect, on the size of the building, and on the location. On the last-named point Elder Richards recounts:

> After the money was all collected, they could not commence construction of their building because the First Presidency [now David O. McKay, Stephen L Richards, and J. Reuben Clark, Jr.] did not tell them where they could build it. Years passed, and the money was depreciating in value and building costs were advancing.
>
> Sister Spafford was in my office one day, and I said to her, "You are never going to build that building for the sisters, are you?"
>
> She asked, "What do you mean, Bishop?"
>
> I said, "Oh, you are going to get credit for raising the money, and your successor will get credit for the building."
>
> She responded, "Well, Bishop, we can't do anything until the First Presidency tells us where we can build it, and my counselor, Marianne Sharp [daughter of President Clark], says her father said, 'Just wait until we tell you where you can put it.' "
>
> I said, "Sister Spafford, Marianne isn't the president of the Relief Society and President Clark isn't the President of the Church. Now, if you will go to President McKay and tell him how embarrassed you are after hurrying the sisters to get their money in, and that the money is depreciating in value, and the cost of building is increasing every day, I believe he will give approval for you to commence construction. And if he asks you where you want to build, tell him that corner [where the building now stands], and if he asks for your second choice, tell him that corner, and if he asks you for a third choice, tell him that same corner. It won't be any harder for them to decide where you can build it today than it will ten years from now."
>
> She went to President McKay, and within ten days she had his approval to go ahead.

As head of the Church's temporal affairs, Bishop LeGrand Richards and his counselors prepared the weekly agenda for the Expenditures Committee meeting with the First Presidency, and Bishop Richards conducted those sessions under assignment from the First Presidency. (Later, members of the Twelve served terms on the committee, and as a member of the Twelve, Elder Richards has so served.) Almost from his youth, the Bishop had known the members of the various First Presidencies under which he served, and he was as outspoken with them as with any other men with whom he associated. On one occasion, with typical frankness he questioned President Clark on a point. "LeGrand, are you questioning my veracity?" the elder of the two asked. "No, sir," the Bishop respectfully answered, "only your memory on the matter," and it passed with no further comment. Mable Chapman, who served as his secretary during his last years as Presiding Bishop, said of him, "He simply has no 'Sunday front.' He treats members, missionaries, branch leaders, General Authorities, and family members with equal kindness and respect." (*Letter*, September 13, 1981.)

In 1942 he was forced by a severe heart attack to temporarily stop all activity—a period he did not like at all. The *Deseret News* reported his illness on May 4, 1942. He had gone to a stake conference in Grace, Idaho, accompanied by a member of the Church Welfare Committee. In the night after his Saturday meetings, intense pain and great difficulty in breathing made it necessary to seek help. He obtained an administration from his host, President M. Ezra Sorensen, and the committeeman who accompanied him. But his condition worsened, and they called in the local doctor and phoned Bishop Richards's family in Salt Lake City. Dr. Gill Richards sent a representative from his office, with oxygen equipment not available in the small town. LeGrand's parents and Ina reached Grace as quickly as they could, and the doctor there told Ina that he would not have given "ten cents for his chances of pulling through that first day."

Bishop Ashton traveled with Elder Harold B. Lee, who had been an apostle for about a year, to visit him the following Sunday afternoon and to give him a special blessing. Elder Lee later spoke of the occasion: "In a brief moment, when my hands were on the head of Brother Richards, I knew that the Lord loved him and that he was going to live. The certainty of that was as sure to me as it is today that he was spared for a great and glorious mission." (*Conference Report*, April 1952, p. 126.)

When it was safe to move him, an ambulance brought

Bishop Richards to the LDS Hospital in Salt Lake. After what seemed to him an interminable convalescence, he met with the First Presidency and his own counselors and said to them, "Well, I found out what hell is!"

"What is it, Bishop?" asked President Clark.

"To see the other man working and not be able to myself." He added, "If there is any truth to the words of the song, 'There's sweet, sweet rest in heaven,' then I'm going to ask to be routed in the other direction."

Bishop Marvin O. Ashton's quick wit could not resist the rejoinder. "Well, Bishop," he said, "you may not have to ask for it."

"Yes, I've thought of that too," replied Brother Richards, who knew he was now comfortably back with the men he loved and in the work which gave him such satisfaction.

From then on he carried his usual work loads, but his associates often saw him walking with a cane. The old hip trouble made him less sure of step, but it did not slow him down.

Illness and death created many changes in Church leadership and personnel during LeGrand Richards's term as Presiding Bishop, and some of these touched him very deeply. Illness and age had weakened President Heber J. Grant, and on May 14, 1945, he died at age eighty-eight after almost twenty-seven years as President of the Church. Only the thirty-year term of President Brigham Young was longer. President Grant had lived to call a total of twelve members to the Quorum of the Twelve Apostles, the first being Melvin J. Ballard (1919) and the last Mark E. Petersen (1944). (*Church News*, April 8, 1944, p. 3.) His passing was keenly felt by Bishop Richards, who had had close personal contact with him since his first mission in Holland—a period of forty years.

On May 21, 1945, George Albert Smith became the eighth President of the Church, and LeGrand's father, George F. Richards, became President of the Quorum of the Twelve on the same day.

The next year, on October 6, 1946, Bishop Marvin O. Ashton addressed the Church as usual at general conference. Elder

Bishop Richards (center) with other General Authorities and government officials at funeral service of President Heber J. Grant.

*Bishops Richards and Wirthlin (seated) with Bishop Thorpe B. Isaacson,
new member of the Presiding Bishopric.*

Richards tells that, that evening, Marvin O. said to his wife,
Rachael, "Rae, I have a cold, and I believe I'll sleep in the other
room so you won't catch it." The next morning, one of the children said, "Unless Daddy soon gets up to take me to school, I'll
be late." Upon entering the room where he had slept, his wife
found that he had passed away. It was a great shock to his family
and his associates.

Part of the tribute paid him by Bishop Richards on October
9, 1946, has already been quoted. He also said: "I'm proud to
have known him. I pray that when my battle is over, I'll be
worthy of his eternal association and companionship. It will be
hard to fill his place." (*Funeral Sermon* [tape], LDS Church
Archives.)

Thorpe B. Isaacson, a capable man who had been serving in
the Yale Ward bishopric, was chosen to fill the vacancy occasioned by Bishop Ashton's death, and he proved an energetic
and able leader in the Presiding Bishopric. He gave up great
financial success to serve the Church in this position.

*Photo taken on Elder George F. Richards's seventy-eighth birthday
shows him with Sister Richards and their thirteen living children
(LeGrand is on back row, right).*

Yet another death was to deeply affect LeGrand Richards
while he was Presiding Bishop. On August 8, 1950, his father,
George F. Richards, died at age eighty-nine. He had served as an
apostle since 1906 and as President of the Quorum for the last
five years. Shortly before he passed away, LeGrand visited him
in his apartment, and his father took him in his arms and, using
his childhood nickname, said, "Grandy, my boy, I love you."
Those words were a great comfort to Bishop Richards. As has
been shown throughout this book, LeGrand's father wielded a
powerful influence for good in his life, as both teacher and
exemplar. A few weeks before his father's death, Bishop Richards
said in a talk at BYU (*Deseret News*, June 23, 1950), "The greatest
evidence of Joseph Smith's leadership were the men who sur-
rounded him. . . ." He could say the same for his father, whose
life from childhood had been lived among the choicest men of
the dispensation—men who had been, and would yet be, increasingly important in shaping the life and ministry of his son
LeGrand Richards.

Of President George F. Richards's family, President Ezra Taft Benson says: "In my early childhood my father always held up as the ideal family that of President Joseph F. Smith; but when President Smith passed away, then he held up the family of George F. Richards. It was Father's ideal for us."

In the year that his father passed away, Bishop Richards's book *A Marvelous Work and a Wonder* (Deseret Book, 1950) was published. That year too the Presiding Bishop's Office moved from 40 North Main Street to the Church Administration Building at 47 East South Temple. Offices and partitions were arranged to give maximum space and utility, and all the various departments and their employees took up the total fourth floor of the building. They were functioning in that location when David O. McKay succeeded George Albert Smith as President of the Church on April 9, 1951.

In addition to the Bishopric's heavy responsibilities of administering the Aaronic Priesthood programs and the temporal affairs of the Church, there were areas of activity which were warmly human, individual, and sometimes personal, and these broke the pace and gave further variety to the work. Some were occasioned by what Bishop Wirthlin described as LeGrand Richards's "open door policy." He said: "It was inaugurated at the beginning of his term, wherein no one who desired audience with him or his counselors should be denied a hearing. Our office doors remained always open, and the widow, the harassed businessman, the youth with his problem, the immigrant, always received a kind word and assistance from Bishop Richards." (Church Section of the *Deseret News*, April 23, 1952, p. 11.) It was about an immigrant that Elder Richards tells this story:

> Old Brother Franz Wiegel from Holland came in one day when I was Presiding Bishop. He'd just been out to attend a meeting in the Holladay area, where his son was ward chorister, and the son's bishop had invited him to come back the next Sunday and be their speaker in sacrament meeting. He was so thrilled with the invitation, he came in to tell me about it. Although he'd been President of Amsterdam Branch, he'd lived many years in his Salt Lake City ward without ever being asked to speak. The morning after he'd preached in Holladay he was waiting for me again when

I came to my office door, and he was all bubbling over with joy for the experience he'd had.

I later spoke at his funeral in LeGrand Ward, and there were five men in attendance who had served as bishops while Brother Wiegel had lived there. I turned to these brethren and said, "You are all great men, but you would have sent this Dutch friend of mine home to his eternal rest a lot happier if just one of you had invited him to talk in your sacrament meeting while he lived here in your ward. It is true he didn't have good use of the English language, but I didn't have good use of the Dutch language when I went to Holland, nor would I ever have done, if they hadn't given me an opportunity to speak." (I spoke to them this way to teach them to recognize people from lands abroad who might come and live in their wards.)

An innovation attributed to Bishop Richards, and one which afforded the General Authorities with some relaxation and enjoyment, was that of having an entertainment and dinner for them on the Tuesday following April conference. He and his counselors hosted the first one. A program titled "The Providing Bishopric Entertains the General Authorities," dated January 8, 1942, is in possession of Mabel Jones Gabbott. A border of line-drawn caricatures is placed across the top—Bishop Ashton chasing a pig, Bishop Richards emptying his pockets of money, and Bishop Wirthlin skinning a cat. Mabel Jones Gabbott wrote the dinner menu in verse. The program itself was one to provide warmth, humor, and merriment with such toasts as "Even the apostles are human," by Amy Brown Lyman; "In the Dust of the Twelve," by Elder Thomas E. McKay; "If our wives would only help us," by President Oscar A. Kirkham; and "Greasing the squeak in the Church," by President David O. McKay. The party was so successful that such entertainments became traditional. Under President Spencer W. Kimball, the number of General Authorities increased dramatically and the nature of their work took on worldwide responsibility and jurisdiction, so the socials are held less frequently now.

Bishop Richards spoke in each of twenty-eight general conferences during his term (1938-1952). His sermons, while continuing to emphasize the importance of the Restoration and the mission of the Prophet Joseph Smith, focused even more upon themes relating to the youth of the Church—faith, chastity, the Word of Wisdom, the payment of tithes and fast offerings, prayer, testimony, following inspired leadership, and achievement through living the gospel. He taught with boldness and enthusiasm and by means of his rich fund of stories and experiences. He always spoke with great clarity.

The Presiding Bishopric years were happy ones for Ina. She was well. She loved her home and the many activities incident to her husband's responsibilities. And she loved him and her children (two of whom were still at home). In a letter from this period she wrote to her husband: "These children of our youthful love have twined themselves into my heart. Oh, may they find the best in life—full strength and beauty, grace of soul and mind; but you, you have first place."

During these years, the last of the children, Nona and Alden, were married in the temple and left. As additional grandchildren came along in the other families, Ina felt an increased joy in life. Her *snoopje* (treat) cupboard and bread bin were always stocked. She taught the little ones in her own special way. If a child bruised himself, she would draw his attention from his hurt with, "Listen, *here* where you bumped the table. Can you hear it cry?" In summer the children came to play in the hollow, rolling down the slopes in old blankets. On the Fourth of July there were fireworks. In winter, granddaughters would dress up in fancy clothes and hats and play theater, with Grandma "Inee" taking part. Also in winter, Ina's girls would come and spend afternoons with their handwork in front of the fireplace over which hung the oil portrait of their grandfather George F. Richards.

On their thirty-fifth wedding anniversary (1944), LeGrand said to Ina, "Mommy, what do you think we'll be doing thirty-five million years from today?" With typical spunk she answered, "Where'd you get such an idea? It makes me tired to think of it."

"Well," he said, "you believe in eternal life. We're told that time is measured only to man, and that with God there is no such a thing as time. It's one eternal round, there's no beginning and there's no end. Now, Mother, if you believe that, you and I ought to be pretty well acquainted with each other thirty-five million years from today."

While this was spoken in fun, such was Bishop Richards's faith, and Ina's, in the eternity for which they were working to prepare themselves.

Chapter 14

A Marvelous Work and a Wonder

1950 -

One day in 1950, while LeGrand Richards was still the Presiding Bishop, a man who was not a member of the Church called on him in his office. The man was well versed in the scriptures and could quote them readily, and he and his host joined in a spirited gospel conversation from which the Bishop reluctantly excused himself to go to an important meeting. Before leaving, Bishop Richards gave the man a copy of *A Marvelous Work and a Wonder*, which had been published earlier that year, and said, "Mark everything you think is wrong in this and bring it back to me." In three days the book was returned to the Bishop's desk while he was absent. The reader had "scribbled round the borders and all through the book." On the flyleaf he had written:

> Up to the time when I had no knowledge of this book, my life was pointless. I could not see myself in proper perspective in relation to God, to Christ, to the Church of God, [or] in regard to those of the sons of God who walk in darkness. By reading, I am enlightened beyond expectation. I begin to become aware of spiritual values which were not apparent before.

Then on the end sheet he wrote, "In this book, I find no flaw. It is an education in itself."

What is it about this book that could draw forth such statements from a stranger? One of its strengths is its doctrinal soundness, which stems from the author's knowledge covering the total spectrum of the scriptures from the Old Testament to the Pearl of Great Price. If anyone will match against the four standard works the scriptural references contained in its pages, he will find that the author has voiced the profound messages of the Restoration with great skill. In its pages we seem to hear the word of the Lord speaking clearly through the ages but sorted out and placed in sequential order so that his purposes, his plans, and his promises to his children in our day can be readily understood. This inspired work reflects the author's lifetime of study, an undertaking pursued not only for his own comprehension but also so that he can make the gospel message intelligible and appealing to others and can lead them to walk in the path he has personally proven by virtuous living and dedicated service.

The spirit of the book is that of the missionary, which Brother Richards later came to appreciate as the same spirit which rested upon John the Baptist when he went forth to proclaim and prepare the way of the Lord. In a revelation given to Joseph Smith in 1830, it is referred to as the spirit of Elias.

> And also with Elias, to whom I have committed the keys of bringing to pass the restoration of all things spoken by the mouth of all the holy prophets since the world began, concerning the last days;
> And also John the son of Zacharias, which Zacharias he (Elias) visited and gave promise that he should have a son, and his name should be John, and he should be filled with the spirit of Elias. (D&C 27:6-7. See also Luke 1:13-17.)

LeGrand Richards's recognition of this special spiritual power had come five decades earlier when, as a boy of fourteen in Tooele, he heard two elders bear their testimonies and tell of traveling without purse or scrip while on their missions in the Eastern States. This same spirit which he had felt as a boy rested mightily upon him in Holland and intensified "almost to the consuming of my flesh," he records. He was often upon his knees thanking the Lord for the great privilege of being a missionary and pleading that he might always be worthy of the precious message which he bore to all who would listen.

The same spirit accompanied him back to the United States, generating a continued sense of commitment. When he found his eternal companion, that prior commitment was explicit in the eternal covenant they made with the Lord.

This summarized development of LeGrand Richards's missionary spirit and skills is reflected in greater detail in preceding chapters. His life continued to follow the "strait" course of obedience, sacrifice, and service in every call that came to him. His steady and constant desire was to share the message of the gospel with as many as would listen. He increased the number of "listeners" when, at the request of his missionaries in the Southern States, he prepared a concise and logical outline to demonstrate the most effective method of presenting the gospel to investigators.[1] This he sent to them under the title "The Message of Mormonism." He also sent them a letter containing additional suggestions for presenting the gospel message. In part it read:

> By us the gospel is to be preached in all the world as a witness to all nations. (See Matthew 24:14; Revelation 14:6-7.)
>
> We are the fishers and hunters the Lord promised to send forth in the last days to fish and hunt Israel "from every mountain, and from every hill, and out of the holes of the rocks." (See Jeremiah 16:16.)
>
> We are sent out two and two as the seventy of old (see Luke 10:1) with this instruction from the Master:
>
> "And into whatsoever house ye enter, first say, Peace be to this house.
>
> "And if the son of peace be there, your peace shall rest upon it; if not, it shall turn to you again.
>
> "And in the same house remain, eating and drinking such things as they give; for the labourer is worthy of his hire. *Go not from house to house.*" (Luke 10:5-7. Italics added by LeGrand Richards.)
>
> In these words and those which follow in this chapter, the Master indicated that those who receive his servants receive him. He seems to want to impress the seventy that when their peace rests upon a house the Lord has done his part of the work, and he then leaves the responsibility to his servants to remain there and deliver the whole message so it can stand as a witness for or against them; and hence the instruction: "*Go not from house to house.*"
>
> If we tell our story we have a right to be heard, regardless of the hundreds of Christian denominations already existent in the land.

---

[1] This was before the days of standard missionary discussions for presentation to investigators.

If we properly tell our story, there is no need for argument, which should remove the fear from the heart of the missionary. Missionaries have usually felt that they were going forth to argue or debate and should be prepared; but if they are prepared to tell our story intelligently and enthusiastically, their hearers will become listeners and questioners.

By explaining a few principles of the gospel we have not delivered our message as a witness against the people any more than a man has built a house by laying the foundation. How can a person judge as to the beauty of the house when the foundation only is laid, or even when part of the sidewalls are built? The same rule applies in the presentation of the gospel—how can a man judge as to its truth before he has heard it?

The outline itself is something of a masterpiece in brevity, logic, and practicality, and it reflects Brother Richards's orderly, building-block approach to inducing an investigator's understanding of the gospel. Beginning with the philosophical basis of Mormonism, it traces the steps of the Restoration via heavenly visitants and delineates the incomparable fruits of the gospel, these together representing the "restitution of all things, which God hath spoken by the mouth of all his holy prophets since the world began." (Acts 3:21.)

It was during the early years as Presiding Bishop that Elder Richards began to receive letters about his outline, "The Message of Mormonism." One from a mission president read:

For some time I have been dreaming over a program of subjects for the missionaries to use in their contacts and follow-ups with investigators, subjects with natural sequence that will make their message more effective and intelligible.

This morning I was cleaning out a drawer and ran across the answer to my dreams—dust-covered and neglected. It was a mimeographed booklet entitled "The Message of Mormonism," by LeGrand Richards. I have read it through, and it embodies just the thing I would like to place in the hands of each missionary.

Would it be agreeable to you if I make copies of it for this purpose? It is excellent and would be effective in stimulating systematic study and regulated presentation. (Preface to *A Marvelous Work and a Wonder*, Deseret Book Company, First Ed., 1950, p. v.)

Not long after this there came another letter from a former

missionary who taught seminary. He had been using the outline
for eight years. It read:

> In all my Church work I have found this the most helpful of
> introductions to the restored gospel. I have often thought that this
> outline, by all means, ought to be circulated in all missions of the
> Church in order that all missionaries might profit by its use, be-
> cause it presents such a clear and comprehensive picture of the
> message we have for the world, and also it presents it in such a
> logical order. . . . I consider it excellent. In fact, the best I have
> seen, and I am writing this with the hope that it will get more, yes,
> much more publicity. . . . (*A Marvelous Work and a Wonder*,
> Preface.)

Locked into the most demanding assignment of his life, and
by the very nature of that calling prevented from doing full-time
missionary work, Bishop Richards pondered the requests and
letters. One day the thought occurred to him, "Why don't I
develop these outline subjects the way I would present them if I
were going into a home one night a week for six months?" Since
"The Message of Mormonism" had proven valuable to many,
how much more valuable to the missionary work might a book
be which could have much wider distribution!

Now he began to write industriously as he traveled by train
or stayed overnight in hotels. It was shortly after Mable S.
Chapman became his secretary in August of 1943 that he began
bringing her "sheaves of handwritten papers, partly in ink and
partly in pencil. That was when one must carry a bottle of ink to
fill a pen," she says. "The pages were written as he traveled to
and from his conference assignments, no doubt using his knees
as a table. With the movement of the train, there were sometimes additional humps in the writing, though he was an excellent penman." (*Letter*, September 13, 1981.)

Of his project, Brother Richards says: "I wrote it in
longhand. On my assignment to Portland I don't think I looked
out of the window once going up or coming back. Then I went
down to Arizona and attended the Mesa conference. My next
conference was over in Inglewood, so I stayed the whole week
rather than come home for one day in Salt Lake. I sat in the

motel writing until my eyes were so tired that I was sick to my stomach."

Bishop Richards had a conference scheduled for Farmington, New Mexico, at the time when the manuscript was well advanced, and he said to Lee A. Palmer, secretary to the Aaronic Priesthood program, "How would you like to go with me and let me read to you as you drive us down and back?" This was agreeable to Brother Palmer. When the reading was complete, the Bishop asked his friend, "Does that sound to you like it's worth publishing?" The other man answered, "If I could have had that information before going on my mission, it would have saved me half of my mission time." Together, they then decided to work toward its publication.

"Lee had some literary ability," says Elder Richards, "so he went over it. He deleted some of my material. I have a tendency to repeat; and not only that, but I can fill a whole page with one sentence, so he broke it down—shortened sentences, paragraphed it, put headings in, made it read easier." Mable Chapman comments, "Bishop Richards was anxious to have the manuscript published as a missionary tool, so the approval of the Church Reading Committee was obtained."

As the material went through the reading and editing steps, three *Improvement Era* staff gave their assistance—Doyle L. Green, managing editor; Marba C. Josephson, associate managing editor; and Elizabeth J. Moffitt, manuscript editor. (Bishop Richards gave them grateful acknowledgment at the beginning of his book.) Lee Palmer followed through with Deseret News Press on the printing, and the first edition appeared in 1950, the year LeGrand's father, President George F. Richards, passed away. Unfortunately, his father did not have the pleasure of seeing the completed work, although he was well aware of its preparation and had made some suggestions for a title along with those possibilities indicated by President George Albert Smith. "President Smith didn't like us using the words *Mormon* and *Mormonism*, which of course my outline title had done," Brother Richards explains. "So the President's and my father's suggestions were considered." None of them seemed just right to the author. He waited. As he was reading the scriptures one day, he was forcibly impressed with these words of Isaiah:

> Wherefore the Lord said, Forasmuch as this people draw near me with their mouth, and with their lips do honour me, but have removed their heart far from me, and their fear toward me is taught by the precept of men:
>
> Therefore, behold, I will proceed to do a marvellous work among this people, even a marvellous work and a wonder: for the wisdom of their wise men shall perish, and the understanding of their prudent men shall be hid. (Isaiah 29:13-14.)

These were the words which had so impressed him during the last months of his mission in the South that they served as the text for his April 1938 general conference talk. Now he could hardly wait to tell Brother Palmer about his "discovery."

At the office the next day, he said, "Lee, I think I've found a name for that book."

"What is it?" his friend asked.

"The words of Isaiah, 'a marvellous work and a wonder.' "

"That's it!" Brother Palmer enthusiastically agreed. So it was decided.

It was an arresting title, and it would often pique the curiosity of the potential reader. One man in England reported that he had been in a public library and had seen a copy of *A Marvelous Work and a Wonder* on the shelves. "The title intrigued me," he said, "so I borrowed the book, read it, looked up the missionaries, and applied for baptism." He later became a bishop and visited Elder Richards at general conference time.

Over the years few changes have been made in the text of the book, and those made were designed mostly to update the scientific references or the statistical detail as the Church expanded worldwide. In thirty-one years and twenty-three printings (1950-1981), *A Marvelous Work and a Wonder* sold more copies than any other Church book save the Book of Mormon—the publisher reports one and a half to two million copies printed in the United States, and to this number must be added fifty thousand copies printed in Europe. It has been translated into eighteen languages, including French, Italian, Spanish, Portuguese, Korean, Samoan, Dutch, and Thai. Elder Richards has never accepted a penny of royalty on the book.

As sales manager of Deseret News Press at the time, Elder Thomas S. Monson saw the work from the printer's viewpoint—he "had the opportunity of printing that book," having seen it in manuscript form "written just as LeGrand Richards speaks." Says he:

> I've watched the book go through printing after printing. I've watched as it's gone from modest runs on letterpress printing to high-speed rotary printing, to offset printing, and finally to the point where it is mass-produced like no other LDS book except the Book of Mormon. It is a missionary in print.
>
> We wore out nickel and chromium-surfaced electrotype plates of LeGrand's book because it had to be reprinted so many times on such long runs. It is a phenomenon!

In the LDS Church insert of the October 1980 *Readers Digest*, the book was offered free by the Church Publicity Department to anyone who sent in a coupon or called on a toll-free number. By this means the offer went into 18,700,000 homes and businesses in the United States and 1,225,000 in Germany. Through that offer, as of June 1981 there had been 9,871 requests for copies. One forwarded to Elder Richards by the Church Publicity Department reads: "I think it is a remarkable book. I've never read anything like it! If it is at all possible, please send me another copy. Send more literature. I would like to congratulate the author of the book very much." This reader's recognition of its compelling power is quite typical of the responses received.

Many others who have been spiritually touched and/or converted have told of its effect upon them, and their stories come from all over the world, from people of all ages, and from those in all walks of life. Scarcely a day goes by but what letters or people come to Elder Richards's office to tell him about his book and to thank him for writing it. A mere sampling of the stories can be included here.

A mission president from West Australia wrote: "A young man, while residing in Kalgoorlie, had a brief encounter with the

Mormon elders. He became curious about the gospel and ordered your book. He said after receiving it, 'That night I read it through and gained my testimony.' As soon as he was able to get leave from his work, he journeyed to Perth and was baptized."

From the Norwegian Mission came this story: "On Tuesday, August 22, a good looking athlete, twenty-five years of age, walked into the mission office and asked to be baptized. He had read your book. He knew it was true and had prayed about it and had his knowledge confirmed. I have not seen such faith and humility before. He should become a great leader for the Church in Norway."

A note came from Millbrae, California: "This is to inform you of a testimony I heard at the California Merced Stake conference last Sunday. A black from Ghana asked to speak in an investigators' meeting we held after the conference. He said he had searched for the true Church for a long time and in his searching came across your book. He was so impressed that it told the truth that he looked up the Church. He was there to present himself for baptism."

A newspaper reporter in Chile read a copy of the book and wrote a two-column article about it which was published. It said that *A Marvelous Work and a Wonder* was the most wonderful book he had ever read. The mission president sent Elder Richards a copy of the article with an English translation. The reporter applied for baptism.

Elder Richards attended a stake conference in New Orleans where a Scottish convert with a beautiful voice sang. After the meeting Brother Richards visited with her. She said her greatest sorrow was the fact that she couldn't get her husband interested in the Church.

"Why don't you get the missionaries to help you?" he asked.

"He won't talk with them," she replied.

He asked if her husband did much reading. She answered, "Quite a bit."

"Well," he responded, "when I get home I will send you a copy of the missionary book I have written, then you get him to read it."

A few years later Elder Richards attended that stake for another conference. The husband, now an elder, was there with the book in his hand, and with him were his neighbor and his neighbor's wife, whom he had brought into the Church by the use of that book.

Once when Elder Richards filled a stake conference assignment at Price, Utah, the next morning a sister visited him in his office who had traveled from that town for that purpose. She was in tears. Her bishop had just released her as president of the Primary and asked her to serve in the Relief Society. Since she did not know much about that organization, she had not learned to love it. Wiping the tears from her eyes, she said, "It wouldn't be so bad, but my husband is not a member of the Church and I have to teach the children all alone."

Elder Richards asked, "Why don't you convert him?" She assured him that she had tried.

"What of the missionaries?" he asked.

"I have tried that too," was her response.

"Does he read?" Elder Richards queried.

"Yes," she replied.

"Then I will autograph one of these missionary books, and you get him to read it as a compliment to me, and then you write and tell me what he has to say."

In a few weeks he received her letter. Her husband had read the book but didn't say much about it. Then he read the Book of Mormon. Then he read *A Marvelous Work and a Wonder* again. After that he said, "Now I am ready to join the Church."

After he was baptized he became active in missionary work, and when he had been a member for a year his wife again wrote that they were going to the Manti Temple to be sealed. It wasn't long before this man was called to be the stake mission president, a position in which he served with distinction.

An eighty-four-year-old man in Springfield, Missouri, who had recently been baptized wrote that *A Marvelous Work and a Wonder* had done more for his conversion than any other factor.

A fourteen-year-old girl wrote: "I am a recent convert to the

Church. I am now in process of reading your book. You can't imagine the way the Spirit has touched my heart while I have read it. . . . Since this year's school has started I have given the Golden Questions to 225 people. I am getting pretty good results. I would love to go on a one-and-a-half-year mission for the Church when I am older and am going to try my hardest to achieve that goal.

A doctor in Ashland, Kentucky, wrote: "A copy of your book was given to us as a Christmas gift by an LDS physician and his wife with whom we became acquainted while I was serving an internship in Phoenix, Arizona. I will soon be ordained an elder. We have received our temple recommends and will be sealed for time and eternity on March 12 in Salt Lake City. We would like it very much, if possible, if you would perform the ceremony." He did.

An FBI agent and his family moved into a Mormon community in Wyoming, and his wife said to her Mormon neighbor: "We know you are Mormons and we don't know much about the Mormons, and should we ever say anything that is offensive to you, you will know that it is because we don't know better." The Mormon neighbor said, "Would you be willing to read one book that will tell you what we believe?" She said she would, and after reading *A Marvelous Work and a Wonder* she and her husband and family joined the Church. They have since served in the mission field, as also has their daughter, and they have visited Elder Richards in his office to thank him for writing the book.

President N. Eldon Tanner wrote a memo to Elder Richards saying: "A short time ago, I sent to a man in prison a copy of your book. I asked the man to tell me what he thought of it and how it affected his life. This was his response: 'For you, sir, to truthfully believe and accept my interpretation, and evaluate what one book has done to my soul and [my] belief of the prophecies fulfilled from its contents, I would need to write you a book myself. I express endless admiration and confidence for the truths revealed.' "

Others of Elder Richards's associates have expressed their appreciation of the book. Elder Richard L. Evans wrote: "I am constantly hearing appreciative, wonderful comments of you and your work, and of the influence that your great book is having in the Church and out of it. I have taken pride and satisfaction in sending *A Marvelous Work and a Wonder* to some of my critical but honest friends who are not members of the Church."

From Bishop Victor L. Brown he received the following: "... I am grateful for your great missionary leadership. I hear comments constantly on the tremendous effect your book has not only upon investigators but upon members. This is certainly a monument to your great efforts."

And Elder Sterling W. Sill, with typical enthusiasm, wrote: "If someone were going to try to select an apostle Paul for this dispensation, it would be LeGrand Richards. The apostle Paul wrote the largest segment of the New Testament, but of all [the contemporary Church books except the scriptures themselves], I am sure that your book stands unchallenged at the top of the list. So far as I know, it has been responsible for more converts than all others put together."

Mission presidents also are impressed with the book's remarkable converting power. One of these wrote:

> Many times since returning from presiding over the Southern Australian Mission, we have expressed to you our appreciation for the great help your book was to us in bringing souls into the kingdom in the great country of Australia.
>
> We can truly say that we know of no single book other than the Book of Mormon that reached and interested more people and caused them to become converted to the gospel of Jesus Christ.
>
> The book is so straightforward, so true and so convincing, we felt that if we could get an investigator to read it, he was well on the road to conversion. It is a wonderful help to the missionary also, for his own understanding and development, whether used at home or in the mission field.

Elder Richards considers *A Marvelous Work and a Wonder* to be his most significant contribution to the building of the Lord's kingdom in our day. "I think there are thousands of men and women in the world who have been good enough to be members of the Church all the time," he said, "but no one has stopped long enough to fit the truths together so they can understand. This my book is doing." (*Blue Book*, p. 36.)

Surely the patriarch George Bowles was prophetic in his blessing to the then President LeGrand Richards of Hollywood Stake when the latter had just been called to preside over the Southern States Mission. The patriarch said: "I . . . bless you, for in the past thou hast desired to have the voice of an angel to declare unto mankind the restoration of the gospel of Jesus Christ. That gift is yours and shall be henceforth a fullness thereof." (Hollywood Stake Tabernacle, December 16, 1933.)

That powerful converting "voice" is nowhere more evident than in *A Marvelous Work and a Wonder*.

Apostle: Early Ministry

1952-1959

*I*t was shortly after noon on Sunday, April 6, 1952. The morning session of the 122nd Annual General Conference had just concluded. With no premonition or forewarning, Bishop Richards received word from Henry D. Moyle, counselor to President David O. McKay, that the President wished to see him at his office. When he arrived there, President McKay told him he had been chosen to fill the vacancy in the Quorum of the Twelve occasioned by the death of Elder Joseph F. Merrill on February 3. Recounting the experience, Elder Richards said, "I wept and the President wept, and we hugged each other, and then we went over to the afternoon meeting."

When President J. Reuben Clark, Jr., read the names of the Twelve and Elder LeGrand Richards's was among them, an audible ripple of approval arose from the audience. At the conclusion of the sustaining vote, President McKay said, "Elder Richards, will you take your place here in the Council," and immediately after that he called upon the new apostle to speak. At the podium, where he had stood many times before, Elder Richards said: "Only the men on this stand can know what has gone through my mind and heart since President McKay called me to his office following the morning meeting. . . . My soul is subdued." (*Conference Report*, April 1952, pp. 111-12.)

Elder Richards was sixty-six years old—seasoned, tried, and virtuous; virtuous in the larger, knightly sense of the word, which adds to chastity all the qualities of moral excellence— faith in the cause; valor; courtesy; compassion; justice; and loyalty. These had come from a lifelong love of the truth and an unswerving determination to follow it at any cost. He was a man

purged of "woodenness and earthiness," "a vessel unto honour
. . . and meet for the master's use, and prepared unto every good
work." (2 Timothy 2:20-22.)

President McKay acknowledged many of these qualities when
he spoke at an event to honor the former Presiding Bishop
shortly after the conference. Said he: "Devotion and duty char-
acterize his life. . . . Fealty and brotherliness together describe his
loyalty to the cause and to his friends. He would gladly give his
life for the truth, even as Christ made the supreme sacrifice. His
loyalty extends to those less worthy—he always stands by his
friends and helps them in their need." (Church Section of the
Deseret News, April 23, 1952, p. 11.)

One leader, however, expressed a note of sadness at his call.
General President of the Relief Society, Belle S. Spafford, remembers leaving the conference saying, "What am I going to do without my Bishop?" She says:

> I just couldn't keep my feelings down, and I said, "I don't under-
> stand why they would move a man from one position to another
> when he is so needed, so competent, and so valuable where he has
> been serving." I felt bereft and as if I couldn't function without his
> wise and valuable counsel, so I went to see him. I told him, "I feel
> so lost that it is hard to accept my disappointment. May I occa-
> sionally come to you anyway?"
>
> Then he taught me a great lesson in Church government
> which I have never forgotten. He said, "Now, Sister Spafford, you
> have a new Bishop and he will be your advisor, and you wouldn't
> want me to step into his role, now, would you?"

Elder Richards had already moved on to other good works,
as had the new Presiding Bishop, Joseph L. Wirthlin, and so
must she.

Before his new call came, Elder Richards had already participated in the concluding event of a project which had received
his care and close attention. The Primary Children's Hospital
had been dedicated the previous month. As Presiding Bishop he
had not only located and purchased the site but had arranged all
the business for its construction.

The year before, while still in that same position, Brother
Richards had accompanied President McKay on his first out-of-

state trip after the latter became President of the Church. They traveled to Gridley, California, to dedicate the new ward and stake building there, and LeGrand Richards was called upon to speak in three of the meetings. (*Church News*, April 25, 1951, p. 2.) It was such trips as this (added to his wide travel experience as Presiding Bishop) which helped him to pace right into the regular tight routine which is standard for members of the Quorum of the Twelve—travel assignments, council meetings, conferences, interviews, preaching, committee work, correspondence, and so on.

Now, as he went to work in new assignments, Elder Richards was often in the news. He and his family were frequently photographed. The May 1952 issue of the *Improvement Era* carried his picture on its cover, with a biographical sketch and family picture inside.

Elder Richards and Ina were at the railway station along with many other General Authorities who traveled to Omaha, Nebraska, for the dedication of the Mormon Pioneer Memorial Bridge, named to honor the early Church members who crossed the Missouri River near Florence, Nebraska, in 1846.

In June 1952 Elder Richards, along with Lowell S. Bennion and Alfred M. Durham, was given an honorary M-Man Award for his "inspiring influence among the youth of the Church." The other two men were cited, respectively, for "inspired counseling" and writing of the song "Carry On."

At the October conference that first year of his ministry, Elder Richards's talk still reflected his interest in and devotion to the youth of the Church. He counseled them to enter the "strait gate"; refrain from profanity; live the Word of Wisdom; and be chaste. He now spoke to them not as Presiding Bishop but as a special witness for the Lord. Between conference sessions he allowed a candid shot by the Church photographer of himself with Belle S. Spafford, General President of the Relief Society, and Emma Rae McKay, wife of President McKay.

The next year was filled with hard work and with many assignments from the Brethren. One of the latter was a tour to the South Pacific, where he dedicated three chapels and inspected four others then under construction. He and his traveling com-

Elder LeGrand Richards and family, at the time he became an apostle.

General Authorities and wives at Salt Lake City railway station as they leave for dedication of Mormon Pioneer Memorial Bridge at Omaha, Nebraska.

panion, Evon W. Huntsman, returned from the trip late in December, 1953. On December 13, while they were gone, Elder Matthew Cowley passed away. The following year Elder Richards was appointed by Utah's Governor J. Bracken Lee to succeed Elder Cowley as a member of the Board of Trustees of Utah State Agricultural College. Considerable disharmony had arisen between the board and the school faculty, and Elder Richards's appointment had a great leavening, stabilizing effect upon both groups. His amiable personality, his gracious manner of dealing with people, and his philosophy of letting differences mellow and narrow before acting upon a matter ("better united on a poor policy than divided on a good one") resulted in his appointment as chairman of the Board of Trustees, after which business proceeded "without a riffle." He combined congeniality with strong leadership based on well-defined aims, orderly procedure, and close attention to needs and priorities. As one associate said, "He is either hot or cold, never lukewarm. We always know where he stands, yet he never offends."

A letter to Elder Richards from R. H. Walker, a dean and director at the college, reflects the feeling there for Elder Richards. In part he wrote:

> The statements you made at the Advisory Committee meetings were most effective, and helped to clinch the message we were trying to put over better than anyone from the College could do. It helped to give a sense of dignity, sincerity, and honesty that could not be given by anyone else. . . .
>
> All of the time you have served as a member of the Board of Trustees your influence has been felt in great measure, not only by the members of the Board but also by the faculty and the students. It has contributed in great measure toward harmonious working relationships . . . [which] mean more to the effectiveness of the faculty and students at the College than money or physical facilities. (*Letter*, November 1, 1956.)

While Elder Richards served as chairman of the board, he lent his support in changing the name of the college to Utah State University, which was a more representative designation than the one by which it had been known since its establishment as a land-grant university in 1888. The name change was offi-

Elder and Sister Richards in Hawaii.

Bishop Richards and Daryl Chase, respectively chairman of the Board of Trustees and president of Utah State University.

cially approved during the first half of 1957, and when commencement exercises were held and graduating students received their diplomas, these bore the new name of Utah State University. Elder Richards's term of office on the board expired on July 1, 1957.

Three years before that, the *Church News* carried an article announcing the publication of Elder Richards's second missionary book, *Israel, Do You Know?* (October 16, 1954, p. 12.) Without preplanning, this served to mark and make a special contribution to the nationwide Jewish Tercentenary. This was the year when national attention was being centered on American Jewish people who had just begun an eight-month-long celebration to commemorate the arrival of the first permanent Jewish settlement in New Amsterdam (New York) three hundred years earlier, in September 1654.

In the preface to the book Elder Richards expressed his "sincere love for the descendants of Judah; an unswerving faith in their destiny as a chosen people of noble birthright; an unbounded admiration for the manner in which they have maintained their racial identity through two thousand years of trial and abuse." The book had been written out of "a deep-rooted desire to bring them hope and the feeling of good will and fellowship wherever they are throughout the world."

That desire had come to him early in his Church service. When he returned from presiding over the Netherlands Mission in 1916, he spoke privately with his father, George F., saying, "I don't know what the Church has in mind for the Jewish people, but if it ever starts the missionary work with them, I would like to have a hand in that." He thought that if he could take the Bible and the Book of Mormon to them he could convince any of them that "we have the truth." Ina of course was well aware of his desire to so serve, so on the day when President Grant called their home and tried to locate Brother Richards to tell him he was being called as Presiding Bishop, Ina told LeGrand, "I thought surely that was your call to Jerusalem."

Bishop Richards had sorrowed over the brutal treatment of the Jews during World War II and had rejoiced when Israel became a nation in 1948. Then, after *A Marvelous Work and a Wonder* had proved to be so helpful in missionary work, he thought again of his desire to address Israel in like manner. "I will never get to go to the Jews now that I am the Presiding Bishop," he told himself, "so why don't I write our message to them the way I would like to tell it." So it was that he began the book when *A Marvelous Work and a Wonder* had reached a fairly wide market. He wrote it in much the same way as the previous book—as he traveled, an hour here and two hours there, in spare moments as the work of his ministry would allow. Lee A. Palmer again assisted him in preparing the manuscript for publication.

Early in the preparation of the book, Rose Marie Reid, a Canadian Mormon who achieved great success as a designer and manufacturer of clothing, visited Elder Richards in Los Angeles. She was enthusiastic about doing missionary work among the Jewish people with whom she associated in her business. She said to Elder Richards, "I have many Jewish friends who are interested in Mormonism and I don't want to make mistakes while teaching them." To her inquiries about books or lesson outlines that might be used, he told her of the book *Israel, Do You Know?* which he was writing. After it was published he sent her a copy.

In the meantime she wrote some introductory materials keyed to the special needs she had in teaching her Jewish friends, including "do's and don'ts" for others who wished to work with their Jewish acquaintances. Introducing her lesson material, she wrote: "Teaching the gospel to the Jewish people requires a completely different approach from teaching anyone else. . . . The very first thing to do is to read *Israel, Do You Know?* by Elder LeGrand Richards. It is a presentation of the gospel never before given, but which every member of the church should know. Encourage others to read it so they will not undo, in ignorance, their work with Jewish investigators." ("Plan for Teaching the Gospel to Jewish People," LGR office file.)

Sister Reid's plan for teaching was tailored to her particular needs and her way of presenting the gospel to the Jewish people, so the Missionary Department of the Church did not adopt it for general use; but she was diligent and sincere, and she succeeded in bringing some of her Jewish friends into the Church.

With the publication of *Israel, Do You Know?* in 1954, letters began to come to Elder Richards which gave evidence that it would do what he had hoped. One multimillionaire in New York read the book with profound interest. The chief heart specialist in San Francisco read it three times and expected to take it to the most learned among the Jewish people in that city. A Jewish friend in Salt Lake was given a copy and purchased three dozen more to give his Jewish friends in New York. A rabbi in Chicago read it and, while he was not prepared to say he could accept it, the book set him thinking. He wanted to take it to New York and discuss it with a Jewish friend.

Letters came also from members of the Church whose understanding and appreciation grew through reading the book. One of these came from a friend in California who wrote: "I find myself with a keen urge to mail copies of this message to the Jews and all Israel, to my many minister friends, as well as to my Jewish acquaintances in Palestine. I already have copies on their way to Israel with letters of further explanation. . . ." From another member of the Church came this comment, "It is indeed heartening to know that one of the Lord's apostles in our day has set forth our call to Judah in such clear and ringing tones. If some way can now be found to get the Jewish people to actually read and ponder the message you have so well set before them, it surely will hasten the time when they at long last will rejoice with us in the precious gospel of Jesus. . . ." And from Elder Spencer W. Kimball came this note: "I took your book with me this weekend and read it. My, it is wonderful, wonderful!" (Letters in LGR files.)

With this encouragement, Elder Richards's desire to teach the Jewish people grew. When he was taking a conference assignment in Los Angeles on one occasion he said to Elder Joseph Fielding Smith, then President of the Quorum of the Twelve, "Would it be all right with you if I set up a little missionary work with the Jewish people down in California?" President Smith answered, "You may do whatever you wish." Thereafter, as he took his regularly scheduled assignments, Elder Richards began the work in various cities. "We didn't make any great progress with conversions," he said, "but we tried to get some of the missionaries trained to tell our story in a manner acceptable to the Jewish people." Los Angeles became the center of this activity under the supervision of Stake President John M. Russen, with the help of J. Leland Anderson and Leo J. Muir.

In a brief report of that period, Elder Richards writes about his work with the Jewish people. In it he tells of the Lord's promise to the Jews:

> And it shall come to pass in that day, that the Lord shall set his hand again the second time to recover the remnant of his people, which shall be left. . . .
> And he shall set up an ensign for the nations, and shall assemble the outcasts of Israel, and gather together the dispersed of Judah from the four corners of the earth.
> The envy also of Ephraim shall depart, and the adversaries of Judah shall be cut off: Ephraim shall not envy Judah, and Judah shall not vex Ephraim. (Isaiah 11:11-13.)

Elder Richards then suggests that "we of Ephraim should lead out in establishing this friendly relationship, for we are to take the everlasting gospel to the Jewish people, including the Book of Mormon, which was preserved for 'the convincing of the Jew and Gentile that Jesus is the Christ, the Eternal God, manifesting himself unto all nations.' " (See title page to the Book of Mormon.) He continues by saying that it will be through our doing this and their being restored to the church and fold of God that they "shall be sanctified in holiness before the Lord to dwell in his presence day and night forever and ever."

He concludes his report by saying, "We feel their sanctification as we listen to the testimonies of some of these wonderful people of the house of Judah who have joined the Church, and we feel to say with the apostle Paul:

> For ye are all the children of God by faith in Christ Jesus.
> For as many of you as have been baptized into Christ have put on Christ.
> There is neither Jew nor Greek, there is neither bond nor free, there is neither male nor female: for ye are all one in Christ Jesus.

And if ye be Christ's, then are ye Abraham's seed, and heirs according to the promise. (Galatians 3:26-29.)

Two testimonies of Jewish converts follow: The first is that of an industrial designer and artist whose grandfathers were both rabbis. After relating how he studied the gospel and the words of the missionaries, he states:

> The study completed, the words of the missionaries impressive, but not by any means totally convincing, there was only one place left for a very confused heart to turn for counsel—the ultimate source of all wisdom—God himself. I asked him the questions that were destroying my peace of mind and troubling me so greatly, and requested a sure and infallible means of recognizing the answer. No vision was obtained, no glorified beings were seen, no heavenly voices were heard. Deep down in the recesses of my mind a feeling that this man Jesus was, as he claimed, the Son of God and the Christ of the world was made manifest in a sure and positive manner.
>
> This humble testimony I can leave with you. Since becoming a member of The Church of Jesus Christ of Latter-day Saints I have been happier than ever before. The knowledge that it is possible to possess my family through all eternity, easily compensates for all earthly riches or scorn by relative or friend.

Another testimony comes from a certified public accountant and business counselor whose activities are nationwide.

> With all my mind and energy I believe this gospel to be true. In January of 1958, the only thing I knew about Mormonism was a word called polygamy. That month I met an individual who introduced me to the subject of Mormonism. It was the first time I ever discussed religion with anyone that was not dogmatic, loud, or smug. It was reassuring to find someone who did not make a mystery of the Bible or religion and could logically discuss the subject. The usual cliches were missing, the vile language when you disagreed or asked questions was gone, and the abrupt ending of a discussion due to differences of opinion was certainly not evident. Hence, for the first time in my life, a discussion of religion did not seem distasteful and I was interested enough to want to know more about the subject.
>
> How does one go about this? The logical thing was to do some reading. I asked for some literature and began to read. The more I read, the more questions I asked. Strangely enough, I got answers without evasiveness. The answers made sense. My desire to

read the Mormon literature became quite intense and I no longer was interested in reading anything else but this and the tax literature necessary for my work. I decided that if it were the truth, I did not want to miss it, and if it were not true, I could trust my own mind to determine that. . . .

As accounts of these conversions came to his attention, and as *Israel, Do You Know?* reached an ever wider audience, Elder Richards was full of gratitude for the Lord's blessing to these people and for his part in helping the work go forward.

At the 1956 October general conference he was prompted by the Spirit to speak concerning the work of the Lord among the Jews in the latter days. He concluded with these words:

> It is my privilege to be personally acquainted with quite a few converted Jews of prominence, and I find in their hearts the same love of God, the same love of the truth, the same testimony of the divinity of the work that you and I have. . . . I have burning in my soul a testimony that if we will be kind to them, the Lord will richly reward us for every kindness we show unto these, our brethren of the house of Israel. (*Conference Report*, October 1956, p. 26.)

Three years later, in March of 1959, the Brethren recommended that organized missionary work among the Jewish people be temporarily discontinued. While it was personally disappointing to him, Elder Richards did not question but accepted the decision and instructed those who were working in the program to lay it aside.

Elder Richards's personal interest and effort with Jewish people continued. *Israel, Do You Know?* sold forty thousand copies during the next twenty years. (As with *A Marvelous Work and a Wonder*, he accepted no royalties from it.) The interest generated by the reading of his Israel book brought many Jewish people to the Church offices, and they were sent to Elder Richards, who was delighted to visit with them. As he explained the relationship between Israel and Judah to them, his teaching skills increased, and this prepared him for later blessings and opportunities with Jewish people.

He continued to fill all regular assignments incident to the work of the ministry, as well as many special calls. One of the latter was his further service as chairman of the Church Old Folks Central Committee, from which President McKay declined to release him, and it was in this connection that he had the pleasure of honoring Ruth May Fox on the occasion of her hundredth birthday. (*Church News*, November 14, 1953, p. 9.) She had performed great service in helping and inspiring the youth of the Church, first as a counselor in the Young Women's Mutual Improvement Association (1905-1929), then as its General President (1929-1937). It was she who had volunteered to help Ina with her children when LeGrand was deathly ill with the flu during the epidemic of 1918-1919.

Through all the early years of his apostolic ministry, Elder Richards worked with unremitting, consuming energy. His father, George F. Richards, was no longer there to worry over him, so his long-time friend J. Reuben Clark, Jr. took upon himself the fatherly role. He wrote: "I have enjoyed my association with LeGrand very, very much—an association I would like to help him preserve by remembering that once he had a very serious trouble which sometimes returns if due care is not taken. Please be careful of yourself, LeGrand, and remember that you are a 'heart-scarred' veteran." (Letter, December 28, 1957, *Blue Book*, p. 16c.)

President Clark also spoke of LeGrand's great contributions in missionary service. "May the Lord continue to bless you as he has so abundantly done in the past in your work in the cause of the Lord. For you, Brother LeGrand, have had a great achievement, bringing the message of the gospel to the hearts of the honest that they might enjoy blessings by embracing and living it." (Letter, September 2, 1958, *Blue Book*, p. 16g.)

It was May 19, 1959, when LeGrand and Ina celebrated their golden wedding. He was seventy-three and she would be the same on September 14 that year. On that occasion he gave the sage advice to inquirers, "Don't ever argue and you'll have a happy home." And as they looked back over fifty years, the trials, joys, losses, and gains were distilled and summarized in Ina's brief statement, "Nobody could have a better, sweeter life than we've had."

Chapter 16

Apostle:
The Middle Years

1959-1975

*L*eGrand Richards's bride of fifty years, Ina Ashton Richards, was by nature a home-loving person. Although her health during the most recent years had much improved, it was still far from robust; and her energy was never great. Consequently travel was a strenuous activity to her, and she rarely accompanied her husband on his many Church assignments, preferring instead the quiet routine of caring for her home and of having children and grandchildren come in and out. When on one of his many trips Elder Richards had expressed his concern that she was too much alone, she had written, "No, LeGrand, I really don't get lonely any more. The Lord makes it up to me in a very special way and I love him as I have never done before." In another letter, she wrote, "Even though you have always been very busy, and away much of the time, we have felt great security in your love and faith. You have been better to me than I have ever deserved."

But despite her preference for the home life, during their golden wedding year (1959) Ina consented to accompany her husband on the most extensive trip of their lives—a mission tour of three Scandinavian countries plus Finland and the Netherlands. They left Salt Lake on June 20 and sailed from New York in the *Oslofjord* of the Norwegian Line, landing in Copenhagen, Denmark, on July 1, where they were met by President and Sister Holger P. Petersen. Together they all met the plane which brought Ezra Taft Benson, apostle and U.S. Secretary of Agriculture, to speak at the Rebild-fest on the Fourth of July, the American holiday celebrated there. He was also met by the

United States Ambassador, Val Petersen, and many high Danish officials, who had arranged for a state reception.

The plane was taxied up near the terminal and a red carpet was rolled out along which the dignitaries stood in positions dictated by protocol. It was at this point that President Petersen saw demonstrated an example of brotherly love between the Authorities that he has never forgotten. Secretary Benson came off the plane and greeted the first two or three officials, then he caught sight of Elder Richards. He left his distinguished hosts, walked over to greet and embrace his fellow apostle, and returned to the welcoming line as if nothing had happened.

When the appointed day arrived, approximately thirty thousand people came to hear Secretary Benson's forceful talk on the value of freedom and the right of man to choose his course in life. Elders Benson and Richards and Ambassador Petersen later spoke to four hundred Saints in the Copenhagen Branch. The remaining nine days of the Richardses' stay in Denmark were spent with President and Sister Petersen touring the mission districts, holding conferences, missionary interviews and testimony meetings, baptismal services, and leadership sessions, and conferring with the mission president on mission matters.

From July 13-23 they similarly toured the Swedish Mission with President and Sister Harry T. Oscarson. Again they heard the testimonies of the missionaries, and Elder Richards interviewed each one. He checked into building and legal matters with the president and inspected and approved a choice building site just outside of Stockholm. He also recommended the sale of the mission headquarters, which was located in a factory area, and the building of a new mission home and chapel in a more favorable location.

The next week he and Ina spent in Norway with President and Sister Ray Engebretsen. Again the rapid pace of the mission tour schedule, the business matters, and building considerations filled the days. The Richardses were particularly impressed with the energetic efforts of the missionaries in that land. In the course of their travel, partly by air, they had opportunity to view the breathtaking scenery—mountains, valleys, fjords, and coastline—during a spell of perfect weather.

By August 1 they were in Finland. The rigors of the trip were telling on Ina—the interminable meetings, the travel, the varied accommodations and food, and the hours and hours of talks and sermons were noticeably tiring her. Wife-like, she suggested to her husband that he vary his talks with a few literary quotes (which she often carried with her in a little notebook). He said, "Now, Mommy, you can't preach my sermons for me. My mission is to tell the message of the Restoration, and I can't use up the people's time with pretty pieces." (Interestingly, however, he had already memorized many of her "pretty pieces" and had often pleased her by quoting them at firesides, at family gatherings, and in his homey talks to the countless couples he married in the temple.)

A most rewarding part of their journey came near the end, for after forty-three years away they returned to Holland for a twelve-day visit. One of Elder Richards's former Holland missionaries, Rulon J. Sperry, was now the mission president. (He had pleased his longtime friend by sending him the first copy of A Marvelous Work and a Wonder in Dutch. It had arrived just before the Richardses left on the trip.) Now, with President and Sister Sperry, they saw the old places and noted the many changes. The mission headquarters were now at The Hague, but the party went back to the old home at Crooswijkschesingel 7b, and Ina sat on the steps in front, reminiscing, and wondered if they shouldn't ring the bell and go inside.

As her ears and tongue became accustomed to the strange yet familiar sounds of the Dutch language, Ina was able to speak briefly in the meetings without the aid of an interpreter. Elder Richards, however, was immediately back in his element and preached with ever greater ease to the countless Dutch Saints and strangers in both meetings and informal conversation. While there, he dedicated chapels in Zeist, Holland, and in Antwerp, Belgium, from the latter of which, during World War I, the refugees had fled when the German howitzers shelled the city. Belgium was now again part of the Netherlands Mission.

When they had completed their tour, had visited the graves of Elders Welker and Gold in Groningen, and had said good-bye to their hosts, Brother and Sister Richards reluctantly left the beloved little country of their earlier mission experience, with its waterways, windmills, and flower fields, and especially the Saints they found so wonderful. They then traveled to Hamburg, Germany, to attend the European Mission Presidents' Seminar to be held there.

Elder and Sister Marion G. Romney had been touring the missions of continental Europe simultaneously with the Richardses' northern tour, at the conclusion of which the two couples met for the seminar. The meetings were held in the new district (now stake) center, which was dedicated by the visiting General Authorities as part of the business of the seminar. As senior apostle (1951), Elder Romney presided in the joint sessions. Elder Richards conducted and spoke in many of them.

October conference found the travelers home again, and when Elder Richards spoke at the Tabernacle he was filled with the spirit of missionary work. He told of the five hundred missionaries he had interviewed and of listening to their testimonies. He paid tribute to their parents, who in many cases were struggling to keep their young people in the field. One missionary had asked Elder Richards, "Couldn't I stay here for another six months?" to which the apostle replied, "No, you had better go home. You have your military work to get behind you, and your schooling. Then you ought to get married and raise your boys as your father raised his and send them on missions so they will do the rest of your missionary work for you."

A family in Finland had impressed him. They had long saved to go to the temple in Switzerland and were very thrilled about it. The mother said, "Brother Richards, we have been members of the Church for only six years, and we figure we are only six years old. We did not know how to live, and what to live for, until we found the Church." (*Conference Report*, October 1959, p. 34.)

The trip which Elder Richards and Ina took in 1959 was only one in a long list of those he has taken during his ministry, lifting his voice in testimony. In addition to the European countries mentioned, he has toured missions and attended conferences in Australia, New Zealand, South America, South Africa, the Central American countries, Mexico, Tonga, Samoa, Hawaii, Japan, Canada, and in all of the United States. And he has attended area conferences which have taken many of the General Authorities to people who could never hope to attend general conferences in Salt Lake City.

Illustrative of these was the one in Munich, Germany (August 24-26, 1973), when he and many of his associates accompanied President Harold B. Lee to meet with "the largest group of Latter-day Saints ever assembled on continental Europe." Some fourteen thousand members from all over Europe came to hear the counsel and messages of the leaders and to listen to the Tabernacle Choir and to their own superb singing groups. Elder Richards had a twenty-minute speaking assignment for the conference, "ten minutes of which," he regretted to say, "were used up by an interpreter."

Whether abroad or at home, his preaching was and is distinctive. One characteristic is his use of the parenthetical insert which allows him to "breathe" during his rapid-fire delivery. By this means he also takes his listeners into his confidence and thereby disarms them. Two examples are typical: He will say, "I drove up to a gas station in Florida. To a man sitting by one of the pumps, I said, 'Are there any Mormons around here?' (I knew there were, but I wanted to hear what he would say.) He replied, 'There is a whole colony of them living out here a few miles.' " Or he may remark, "Then I said to this man (I always like to challenge a person, because then it gives him something to look for), 'Would you be willing to let me come into your home and tell you the story of Mormonism?' "

Another of his preaching abilities is that of calculating the length of a sermon. Elder Richard L. Evans wrote, "You were masterful Sunday morning on television, speaking . . . without note or script, and finishing on the precise second. It was a remarkable performance." (Memo to LeGrand Richards, April 19, 1968, *Blue Book*, p. 19f.) Elder Richards's eyesight does not now permit him to see the clock clearly, so in a recent general

LeGrand Richards speaks.

"I finished on time!"

conference he handed President Benson his cane and asked him to tap Elder Richards's heel one minute before he was supposed to finish. He closed on time.

Presidents of the Church who have conducted when he spoke in general conference have variously remarked: "We have just listened to a tornado" (Joseph Fielding Smith). "We have just heard from 'a marvelous work and a wonder' " (Harold B. Lee). "Is there anyone who doesn't know Brother LeGrand Richards who has just spoken? Is there anyone who does not know the great missionary he has been?" (Spencer W. Kimball).

Others of his brethren comment on his preaching as follows:

> He has traveled the world, lifting his quick-paced voice like a clarion in proclaiming the gospel which he so much loves. (Thomas S. Monson.)

> He lifts his voice as a trump. He believes in speaking with a loud voice and can quote scriptures to demonstrate that this is the way it should be done. He takes every request to speak — at firesides, seminars, institutes, whatever. Some would sidestep, but he likes to do it, is talented in it, and does it endlessly. (Bruce R. McConkie.)

> He meets the needs of the Saints that want to hear the gospel preached, and he does it with such a sense of conviction and sincerity and enthusiasm that those who hear him know whereof he speaks, and invariably he touches the hearts of his congregation. His capacity for remembering scripture, stories, and the experiences he has had is remarkable. His power of recall is, I think, an absolute miracle. (Gordon B. Hinckley.)

With typical self-deprecation, Elder Richards expresses his own view of his preaching: "What is a good meal for a sparrow may not be a good one for an elephant. While I might please the common people, when you get up to the elite and the educated, they may not enjoy listening to me because I'm just simple."

The stories and experiences to which President Hinckley referred are elements which give vitality and appeal to Elder Richards's sermons, and they endear him to his audiences, whether vast or intimate. In order to preserve them as a collection, Marvin W. Wallin, manager of Bookcraft, asked him to allow their publication, and Elder Richards reluctantly agreed.

Accordingly, he jotted down from memory a list of a hundred and thirty incidents, stories, and experiences, and from these he dictated the actual "illustrations" just as if he were telling them to a friend or an audience. As a result, the editors say, "they are told in crisp, clear language, and applied with telling insight." They were transcribed, organized, and published in 1961 under the title of *Just to Illustrate*. Many letters received by the author attest to the delightful hours of reading they afford.

Yet another book was to appear which would broaden the base of enjoyment in Elder Richards's sermons. In October 1971 he had delivered his seventy-fifth general conference talk—more such talks than any other living man except President Joseph Fielding Smith. (Only his second heart attack and the subsequent hospitalization at Cedar City in March 1964 had kept Elder Richards from a conference session, and that was the only one he had missed since his first conference address, given while he was yet president of the Southern States Mission.) So popular had his sermons become that many had asked when someone was going to publish a book of them. It was his son G. LaMont Richards who, recognizing their value and popular appeal, responded to the many requests. Drawing from sermons given in the Salt Lake Tabernacle, at the stake conferences, at temple dedications, at funeral services, and at campus devotionals, he organized them under subject headings and prepared a biographical introduction. To the satisfaction of Elder Richards's many admirers, Deseret Book Company published the compilation, *LeGrand Richards Speaks*, in 1972.

Since that time many of Elder Richards's sermons have been recorded and made available on cassette tapes through leading bookstores. By this means his talks have been enjoyed over and over again and his spirit made manifest through the voice quality and style of delivery which are uniquely and enthusiastically his own.

Another characteristic, often demonstrated before and after his sermons, further endears Elder Richards to the people—his availability, his personal touch, through which he shows his love, his warmth, and his sincerity. He readily admits that Presi-

*With First Presidency and other General Authorities after
close of general conference session.*

dent David O. McKay was his exemplar in this. Years ago he
attended the wedding reception of the President's daughter in
her parents' home. As the then Presiding Bishop Richards and
Ina came within speaking distance of the McKays, he said, "Well,
President, I guess you'll be happy when this handshaking is
over?" "Happy nothing," President McKay answered, "I'm
having the time of my life!" Again in Gridley, California, when
Bishop Richards accompanied President McKay to dedicate a
ward and stake center, the leaders there, thinking to spare the
President, tried to hold back the crowds who pressed to reach
him. "Let the people come," the President said, and he stood and
shook hands until all who desired to had had the opportunity.
He was a man for the people and he taught Bishop Richards a
great lesson, the importance of which he has never forgotten.

Elder Richards often says, "Long after they've forgotten what
we say, the people will remember that a General Authority
shook hands with them." To illustrate, he tells this story: "I
dedicated a chapel in Lethbridge, Canada, and ten years later a
man met me here in Salt Lake and said, 'Elder Richards, don't

you remember me? Just as you left that building [in Lethbridge], we shook hands together.' "

It is not only adults who remember, but children as well. A woman wrote to him in 1975:

> When I was about seven or eight years old, I attended a stake conference with my parents in Panguitch, Utah. Elder LeGrand Richards was the visiting Authority, and he told story after story of faith-promoting experiences. I listened with such intent that I felt he was talking directly to me. When conference was over, Elder Richards came down into the audience and shook hands with all who remained, including everyone on the row where I was sitting, except that he passed me by, as I was short and sandwiched in between my parents. I was so hurt to think the warmth and love I felt in his message wasn't meant for children. As these thoughts went through my mind, Elder Richards paused and came back to me. He took my hand, kissed it, and said, "We musn't forget a little lady." I don't remember any of his talk now, but I do remember the conviction I felt at the time that he was an Apostle of the Lord. (*Letter*, LGR office files.)

In yet a different way his handshake conveys his warmth and sincerity in putting forth his own missionary effort. Elder Bruce R. McConkie tells a story that to him was "the most dramatic illustration of missionary zeal and what we ought to do" of anything he had ever witnessed:

> I was seated on the rear of a plane in Denver. I had come in from the Texas area, had gotten on and seated myself at the rear. We had a few minutes before take-off and Brother LeGrand Richards got on. He'd come in from some other area. He started at the front and walked the full length of the plane shaking hands with everyone aboard—people he'd never seen before—and he asked each one if he was a Mormon. He came clear down to me at the back of the plane, greeted me, and shook my hand. He then turned around and walked up to his seat in the front, raised his hand in typical fashion, and said, "There are seventeen of us on board tonight. Isn't it wonderful to belong to the Church?" and sat down. The plane was full of non-Mormons, some had never heard of the Mormons, but that is exactly what he did. I got up and went to sit by him, thinking to myself, "That would never have occurred to me to do," yet all over the plane people smiled, laughed, were pleased. He hadn't offended. He hadn't hurt any-

one's feelings and he'd left a good impression and feeling for the Church.

Another thing that has endeared Elder Richards to the people and has given memorable guidance and inspiration to countless couples entering the temple, often for their first visits there, has been the thousands of marriages he has performed. Elder Thomas S. Monson remembers that before the underground tunnel connecting the Church parking lot with the temple entrance was constructed, "Elder Richards would walk out of the front door of the Church Administration Building on many a snowy day, and with his cane, make his way west on South Temple, then north on Main Street to the little east gate, so that he might not disappoint some couple waiting expectantly for him to marry them. He never thought of the inconvenience to which he was put, only of his responsibility to respond to the commitment that he had made to perform that service." In recent years the Brethren have discouraged people from asking the General Authorities to perform marriages, because of their immense work loads and in many cases their advanced years, yet Elder Richards still finds a way to do it for family members, children and grandchildren of his missionaries, Dutch friends, and other acquaintances of a lifetime.

In 1969 Elder Richards was given a generous gift by two friends—a trip to Israel. This was the realization of a lifelong dream. He went in company with Daniel H. Ludlow, who thoughtfully kept a daily diary of the trip and presented it to Elder Richards as a memento of their experience. It shows the days packed with sights and sounds as they traveled the ancient paths back into sacred history. Unfortunately the trip was cut short, for while he was gone Elder Richards's son-in-law died, and he returned home to help comfort his daughter Mercedes and to attend Grant Iverson's funeral. The December 1970 *Instructor* (center insert) carries an article by LeGrand Richards titled, "In the Land of the Nativity." In it he expressed his feelings about the many places associated with the birth, ministry, trial, and crucifixion of the Lord Jesus Christ. "As we toured the country," he wrote, "in my mind I tried to follow him and imagine I was present with him in many of the important experiences of his life."

As interesting as Elder Richards felt the Holy Land was, the two things that stood out most forcibly were his meeting with some of the Jewish people and the burning desire he had to tell them of the relationship of Judah to Israel and of future events which would eventually see them walking together as children of our Heavenly Father. He had little opportunity to share that message in Israel. At home, however, he did so whenever Jewish visitors were referred to his office. He still does. He welcomes them with a hearty handshake and his twinkling smile, discusses with them matters pertaining to the developing land of Israel, and then invariably challenges them with the question, "What would you say if I were to tell you that you are not an Israelite?"

"What do you mean, Mr. Richards?" they quickly respond.

"Well, where does the name Israel come from?"

Then they must admit that it was the name the unidentified visitor gave to Jacob when he wrestled with him.

"And how many sons did Jacob have?" he continues.

"Twelve," is the ready answer.

Then he reminds his visitor that after a few generations the twelve tribes were divided into two kingdoms—that of Judah and that of Israel. "To which do you belong?" he boldly asks.

"Judah," they say.

"Well, I belong to the kingdom of Israel."

Throughout the interview, Elder Richards has kept the lead and is satisfied. He can now tell the story of Joseph who, through his sons Ephraim and Manasseh, and because of Reuben's transgression, received a double portion. He can point out the prophecies concerning the land of Joseph (America) and their fulfillment, and he can explain about the stick of Judah (the Bible) and the stick of Joseph (the Book of Mormon).

Brother Richards then expresses his gratitude for the stick of Judah which, initially, their people preserved for us, and says that we are now ready to return the compliment and present them with the stick of Joseph. He challenges his visitor to hasten the day when "Judah shall walk with the house of Israel"

(Jeremiah 3:18), by investigating and by reading the Book of Mormon. He also offers a copy of his *Israel, Do You Know?* with an invitation to criticize anything in the book with which the visitor does not agree.

So challenged and instructed, one government official from Israel indicated that if Mr. Richards would come to his land, he would invite all his friends into his home and give the entire evening for his visitor to tell the things he had heard that day. Another man—a doctor from Israel—was brought to see Elder Richards by a couple from California who after their visit wrote:

> Gratefully we acknowledge the wonderful half-hour we spent in your presence with our guest Dr. _____ of Israel. He expressed great respect and admiration for you and the things he listened to. The twinkle in your eye caught his fancy and won his heart. Several times during the day, he remarked that nothing he had seen in America impressed him half so much as the things he saw and heard that one day in Salt Lake City. (Excerpted from "My Experiences with Visitors from Israel," by LeGrand Richards [xerox pp. 1-8], office copy.)

Another Jewish visitor who found his way to Elder Richards was a young convert to the Church from New York, who had been rejected (buried) by his family because of his conversion. Upon hearing his story, Elder Richards offered to be family to him. The young man was in Salt Lake to receive his training before entering the mission field, so for the duration of his mission Elder Richards wrote to him, encouraged him to hold fast to the faith and keep up his good work, for, he said, "The more you give away, the more you have left to give." Then in a postscript, he told of baptisms among Jewish brethren—a prominent rabbi in Tempe, Arizona, and "a bright, intelligent man in California," adding, "so you see, we are getting a foothold with our Jewish friends." On the other hand, the missionary wrote of his struggles, disappointments, and successes, and often signed his letters, "Your Utah missionary, the roaring, testifying lion of Judah." (*Letters*, August 21 and 29, 1975, office files.)

By the time these letters were written, Elder Richards had seen the reward of his patient waiting and quiet efforts as he looked for the work with the Jewish people to go forward again. It came about early in the administration of President Spencer W. Kimball.

Within a four-year period, the Church saw three changes in its First Presidency. President McKay died January 18, 1970. His successor, Joseph Fielding Smith, served from January 23, 1970, until his death on July 2, 1972. He was followed by Harold B. Lee, who became President on July 7, 1972, and served for only a year and a half before he died suddenly December 26, 1973. On December 30, 1973, Spencer W. Kimball became the twelfth President of the Church.

Elder Richards had known President Kimball for many years, and later he told of their early association:

> I visited him in Arizona when he was stake president and I was Presiding Bishop. I said to him one evening after our meetings, "Spencer, I don't know what the Brethren have in store for you, but I expect to see them move you up." It wasn't long before he was called into the Quorum of the Twelve. He hasn't forgotten that and I haven't. I've loved him ever since. He's about as Christ-like a man as I've ever known. He's like my Daddy." (Ninetieth Birthday [tape transcript], February 6, 1976.)

President Kimball indeed remembered the incident. He spoke in the October 1979 general conference of the time when he and Bishop Richards went down to Miami, Arizona, and after their meetings talked most of the evening. "I don't know whether he [Elder Richards] will remember that or not," he said, "but it was very impressive to me." (From "Give Me This Mountain," *Ensign*, November 1979, p. 76.)

Of Spencer W. Kimball's Presidency, Elder Richards says: "I'm one who believes that the fundamentals of the Church will never change; but we will learn how to do our work finer and better than it's ever been done before. President Kimball has done so many new things. You can't hold him down. He's an original."

One of the things he did not long after he became President was to call Elder Richards to his office and ask him to review what had been done to carry the gospel to the Jewish people.

Brother Richards experienced a great thrill as he told of his sincere earlier efforts. "He took my book, *Israel, Do You Know?* so he could reread and discuss it. I told him a little about the different cities where we'd set up the work and what had been said to me when I had asked what program we were going to have for teaching the Jewish people, but was told to discontinue it. President Kimball was interested and wanted the work to go forward, so I gave him all the information I had."

The President was very attentive and thanked him for his report. Then, with typical energy and directness, he reactivated the program. It was April 3, 1975, when President Kimball spoke at the Regional Representatives Seminar, saying, "We are neither Greek nor Italian, nor Mexican, nor Jew. We are all Latter-day Saints—brethren and sisters—just fellowmen with the same overpowering responsibility." He then told of his long-time concern for the Jews and said that he "hadn't quite understood why the work had been discontinued." He continued:

> This does not mean a proposed mission to Jerusalem. It means that we go to New York, Philadelphia, Chicago, and the other cities and spread the gospel to the Jews as we do to the Lamanites, as we do to the Gentiles, and give them an opportunity to hear the gospel . . . and that day, I think, cannot come until we, the witnesses of Jesus Christ, get busy and present the message to them.
>
> I remember a period of time when some special effort was given by Elder LeGrand Richards and others of his associates to the convincing of the Jews that Jesus is the Christ. I believe some progress was made, but the work was discontinued. I quote from Elder Richards: "When all the facts are known and fully understood, the descendants of Judah will realize that Joseph fed his father, Jacob, and his eleven brothers and their families from the granaries of Egypt during the period of famine that saved their lives. That gift is not to be compared with what the descendants of Joseph have to offer the descendants of Judah at this time." [LeGrand Richards, *Tract*, "The Mormons and the Jewish People," p. 6.] (*Report of Regional Representatives Seminar Proceedings*, pp. 5, 21-22.)

On November 20 of the same year a Jewish Mission Task Committee (JMTC) was organized by the Missionary Committee of the Church. Jewish converts Philip A. Rennert, Rod Zeidner, and Harry L. Glick were called to make a thorough study of all pertinent source materials, the first of which was Elder Richards's *Israel, Do You Know?* They then conducted an extensive survey by means of a questionnaire to be used with Jewish converts and Jewish nonmembers. From these interviews they developed a status report, a summation of mission plans for Jewish people, and the resulting training material for missionaries and mission presidents, investigator discussions, and related flip-charts. These they reported to President Kimball in May 1976.

Another report went to the President on July 12 expressing the feelings of the JMTC members. "Since the day of our assignment," it read, "we have been impressed with the urgency of the Lord's missionary program to his people. With his continued help it will be completely operational in a very short while." Soon after that, the work commenced in cities containing major Jewish populations.

Aside from missionary effort, from which he is never far removed, some other areas in which Elder Richards functions as a member of the Council of the Twelve are those of special administrative assignments (for example, he has served as Director of Mid-American, U.S.A., Missions); various boards (with his associates in the Quorum, he has served on the Board of Trustees of Brigham Young University); and committee work.

Committee work done by the General Authorities is "routine" in the sense that it follows a regular meeting schedule for review, study, and deliberation, and deals with ongoing matters of Church administration, but the results of such work affect the whole Church. One area of Elder Richards's jurisdiction is that of boundary changes—the dividing of wards and branches and the creation of new stakes of Zion Churchwide— over which committee he serves as chairman. He is also chairman of the committee to approve changes of counselors in stake presidencies, bishops of wards, and all temple workers worldwide.

Because of his vast and lengthy Church experience, Elder LeGrand Richards brings to the committees on which he serves a wisdom, a spirituality, and a practical direction which is invaluable to the total Church as touching the matters within the committees' concerns. On each of these committees, two or three other General Authorities have variously served with him. One of them, Elder Bruce R. McConkie, gives valuable insights into the nature and character of his chairman as he observes him in council:

> When Elder Richards has a meeting, he thinks the prayer should appertain to the business that is coming before the committee. We all know what is expected of us in that situation. His full attention is given to us, and invariably, after the prayer is over, he will make some comment on it, showing that he was centering his interest upon what was being said. In fact, in all matters that come before the committee he is attentive. As the secretary sits and reads the material under consideration, sometimes for an hour or more, you must center your faculties or you'd be off in the "ethereal blue," but Brother Richards is very attentive. He'll catch every point. He does not let anything get by him. He is always in command.
>
> He does not repeat himself. He doesn't, in conversation, say something and then, not realizing he's said it, say it again, which is a characteristic of age. He is simply not subject to that.
>
> He doesn't waver. He speaks his mind freely. He is conservative in the financial sense of the word. He is courageous; he is unhesitant; he is admirable.

Important to Elder Richards is the efficient work done by his personal secretary, Margaret Bury, who is also secretary to the Boundary Change Committee. She has been with Elder Richards for seventeen years and affirms that in no word or action has he ever disappointed her. Having had secretarial training himself, he knows what her job involves and he is quick to praise work well done. He has the ability to make those around him feel relaxed and comfortable while doing their work, to feel a sense of personal worth, and to have freedom to use their initiative. She feels herself to be a happy, contributing part in the complexities of his busy office—an office in which important matters are resolved and one through which many people and letters pass.

For his part, he appreciates her pleasant telephone manner, her loyalty and good judgment, her quiet efficiency, and her cheerful disposition. It would, in fact, be difficult to imagine anyone working with him daily who is gloomy or negative. For himself, he says, "I try to see the bright side of life instead of the dark. Like the girl sings in the musical *South Pacific*, 'I'm only a cock-eyed optimist.'" ("Elder Richards Notes Eighty Years," *Church News*, February 5, 1966, p. 3.)

Further illustrating his bent for optimism is a story he told while still serving as Presiding Bishop:

> A young lady phoned me for an appointment, and when she came to the office she sat there and cried for a little while, and then she said, "I guess I'm jittery."
>
> "Well," I said, "that's all right." Then when she had composed herself, she said, "Bishop, what is there for the young people today? We have war. They are taking all the boys; it looks like another great war is ahead of us. What do we young people have to live for?"
>
> I looked at her for a few minutes and said, "Have you ever thought of the other side of the story?"
>
> She said, "What side?"
>
> "Well," I said, "you remember the story of the two buckets that went down in the well; as the one came up, it said, 'This is surely a cold and dreary world. No matter how many times I come up full, I always have to go down empty.' Then the other bucket laughed and said, 'With me it is different. No matter how many times I go down empty, I always come up full.'"
>
> I said, "Have you ever stopped to realize that of the millions of our Father's children, you are one of the most favored? You are privileged to live in the Dispensation of the Fulness of Times that the prophets of old have looked forward to, when there is more revealed truth upon the earth than there had ever been in any other dispensation of the world's history, and where we enjoy blessings and comforts of life that kings did not enjoy a few years ago. Have you ever stopped to think of that side of the story?" And before she left, she decided that probably it wasn't as cold and dreary a world after all as it might be.
>
> I said, "You just go on, and live right, and don't lose your courage, and don't think that life isn't worth while and isn't worth living. Whether you are permitted to live a long life or a short one isn't going to be the thing that is going to determine your success or failure; it's how you live. . . ." (*Conference Report*, April 1951, pp. 39-40.)

In the lesson he taught this young woman, Elder Richards was only reflecting his own life and experience, for he has lived

*Presidents Spencer W. Kimball and N. Eldon Tanner with
Elder Richards at Brigham Young University on occasion of
his receiving honorary doctorate.*

to merit unexpected, unsought, and sometimes overwhelming
blessings, honors, and awards. Although he is never certain that
he deserves them, he feels joy and gratitude because of them.

As examples, for his efforts with the youth, particularly in
connection with the Aaronic Priesthood as it related to Scouting, he was awarded the Silver Antelope by the National Council of the Boy Scouts of America at Pasadena, California. (*Church
News*, November 15, 1958, p. 3.) In 1964 he received the Silver
Beaver for "distinguished service to boyhood," this at the hands
of President N. Eldon Tanner, himself a former high official in
Canada's Scouting program. (*Church News*, February 15, 1964, p.
3.)

Because as a young man he had longed for a more extensive
education, the recognition by three universities meant a lot to
him. On June 6, 1964, he was awarded an Honorary Doctor of
Humanities degree from Utah State University where he so successfully served as Chairman of the Board of Trustees; Brigham
Young University awarded him an Honorary Doctor of Christian
Service degree on April 17, 1974; and on June 2, 1977, the Col-

lege of Southern Utah at Cedar City awarded him an Honorary Doctor of Letters degree.

In spite of his high position, recognitions, and honors, Elder Richards continued to retain his down-to-earth, human approach. At the suggestion of his son LaMont, he purchased a lovely home at 1291 Wasatch Drive in October of 1960. It was a pretty white rambler with grey-blue shutters and a fenced-in backyard where the grandchildren could play while the grown-ups visited. Always "a farmer at heart," Elder Richards enjoyed working in the soil. His daughter Mercedes retains a vivid picture of her father "down on one knee planting tulip bulbs."

Whether it was a "borrowed Dutch know-how" or a "green-thumb" carry-over from boyhood is not certain, but neighbors say that his tulips stood straighter and showier than theirs and bursting with such vitality that no one could match them. Someone accused him of "praying over them." One neighbor tells that when he was a campus bishop a student ward member came to his door for home teaching. He rang the front door bell excitedly, saying when it was opened, "Bishop, do you know what I just saw?"

The bishop couldn't imagine.

"Well, Elder LeGrand Richards is over there kneeling by that tulip patch," the student said incredulously.

"Of course," his bishop answered matter-of-factly. "Why don't you go over and visit with him. He'd love it."

The young man did so, and his former bishop says that even now that he serves as a stake president he has never forgotten the impact of his visit.

When they were in their eighties, it became more difficult for LeGrand and Ina to care for garden and home. The time came when, for his safety's sake but nevertheless to his chagrin, President Benson forbade Elder Richards to drive his car any longer (he still chafes over that, saying when people must drive him, "They've made a beggar of me"). Finally he sold the Wasatch Drive home and moved into the Bonneville Towers Apartment on South Temple. There his daughter Mercedes lived, and as Ina's health worsened she was near at hand to give loving assistance to her mother when Brother Richards was away.

With all my heart and soul, I bear you my witness of the divinity of this work, that God the Eternal Father has decreed its destiny. It is built on the foundation of apostles and prophets, with Christ our Lord as the chief cornerstone, and he is guiding his Church today, and will continue to do so until he comes in the clouds of heaven as the holy prophets have declared, and I leave you that witness in the name of the Lord Jesus Christ, Amen.

LeGrand Richards

8-25-72

President and Sister Benson also lived there, and as neighbors they observed Elder Richards's devotion to his wife. Elder Benson also remembers that his friend would come in from a conference saying to Ina, "Aren't the Saints wonderful?" and she would answer good-naturedly, "Indeed they are, and they surely spoil you."

To the Richardses, their family has always been of the utmost importance, and out of love for them (as well as in obedience to the prophet, Spencer W. Kimball, who charged each Church member to write his personal history), Elder Richards wrote a biographical sketch of his life, including special letters, important family data, and his testimony, then placed them in a genealogical binder. This is the *Blue Book* referenced in this book. He did the typing himself and he has each year added a page of highlights to update the story. He began the account with his large and distinctive signature and the statement: "There should be a desire in the heart of every man, however humble, to leave some vestige, as he passes, to attest to future time the fact that he has been on earth and acted something there." (Author not identified.)

He wrote his testimony (shown on preceding page) in longhand, its carefully formed letters showing no trace of shaky unevenness. This still characterizes his penmanship at ninety-six.

Apostle: Past Ninety

1976-

*F*ew leaders in this century have preached the gospel with the
fervor and far-reaching effects of this apostle of the people. . . .
At ninety, he continues to sparkle like a mountain spring with
wit and wisdom and hard work in building the kingdom of God
around the globe." Elder Thomas S. Monson said this to a large
assembly of General Authorities and the members of LeGrand
Richards's immediate family who were gathered to honor him on
his ninetieth birthday, February 6, 1976.

Following that introduction by the chairman, Elder Ezra
Taft Benson, President of the Council of the Twelve, addressed
the group. In part he said: "Sitting beside me is one of the noble
and great ones shown to Father Abraham. There is no better
example of our religion in action than that of our faithful and
honored guest—Elder, Bishop, President, Brother LeGrand
Richards. . . . We love you and honor you, and hand you this
little volume of the scriptures [signed by all of the Brethren]. I
imagine that you have worn out one or two copies."

Accepting the gift, Elder Richards asked, "Who have you
been talking about, Ezra?" Then turning to family and associates
he said, "I don't deserve this, but it's very nice and I appreciate
it. I love my family with all my heart. I love the Lord in like
manner and the privilege of bearing his name honorably throughout the world in this calling. I love you Brethren—and I love the
women as much as the Lord permits." He touched Ina's shoulder
and smiled. He closed with the words: "No matter what happens,
I can only expect a short time to tarry with you. The words of
Moroni as he closed his writings express my feelings at this
time." He then quoted from them: "And now I bid [you] all,

farewell. I soon go to rest in the paradise of God." (Moroni 10:34.)

President N. Eldon Tanner responded by telling of his question to Brother Richards when he entered the door on that occasion, "Have you lived all your life in the United States?" and of LeGrand's answer, "Not yet!" which seemed to refute his sober, Moroni-like farewell of a few moments before.

President Tanner then told of once asking Elder Richards which book he liked best beyond the scriptures, and of the ready answer: "*Life of the Prophet Joseph Smith* by George Q. Cannon, which I read as a boy. It made me wish that I could have lived in his day and helped him through all the hardships and trials that he had to endure." "I think," said President Tanner, "that he's done that with every President of the Church under whom he's served, and with every associate he's had. He's tried to help them carry their responsibilities in addition to his own and to make their loads lighter."

All the guests stood to honor Ina Ashton Richards, small and frail beside her husband, and she thanked "whoever thoughtfully gave the lovely corsage" she was wearing. The birthday event came to a close with Elder S. Dilworth Young's words of benediction for LeGrand and Ina: "Be kind to them in their remaining years, enlarge them, keep them. May we have them with us as long as they would care to stay." The Brethren, including Elder Richards, then left for their respective offices to pick up their important work where they had left it.

Always the missionary and anxious to share the gospel with an ever-widening number of people, Elder Richards had recently sent to all ministers in the Salt Lake area the following letter:

Dear Reverend _____ :

> Under separate cover I am taking the liberty of sending you a copy of the book I have written called *A Marvelous Work and a Wonder*. Since you are living here at the headquarters of The Church of Jesus Christ of Latter-day Saints, it would please me very much if you would take time to read this book carefully. . . .
>
> This will enable you to give correct answers to inquirers that come to you from time to time regarding our Church. . . .

Ninety years young.

Elder and Sister Richards study the scriptures.

In the same spirit of friendliness, he had many opportunities to talk with and share his book with churchmen as they visited in his office. One of these invited him to speak to his congregation for their Lent service on the subject of "My philosophy of life." This gave him much pleasure, as did the fact that so many of his audience came up to shake his hand afterwards. Part of his effectiveness, of course, was his unusual command of the scriptures which he loves deeply, having studied, taught, and lived them for nearly a century. In spite of impaired vision he remains an ardent student, reviewing all of the standard works each year.

That same April, at general conference, he spoke to his own people about the value of the scriptures:

> If we didn't have the holy scripture, what would we know about our Father in heaven and his great love that gave us his Only Begotten Son? What would we know about his Son and his great atoning sacrifice, and the gospel that he has given us, the pattern of life to live by, and the answers to where we came from, why we are here, and where we are going? Without a knowledge of these things, we would be like a ship upon the ocean without a rudder or sail, or anything to guide it. We might keep afloat, but we would never come into port. (*Conference Report*, April 1976, p. 12.)

On May 4 that year, Elder Richards received the first of a new fifty-thousand-copy reprint of *A Marvelous Work and a Wonder*, always a thrill as he contemplated the missionary thrust this represented. He also found satisfaction as he was able to touch an ever-increasing number of young missionaries through regular speaking assignments to the Missionary Training Center on BYU campus, and more recently by means of direct telephone hookups to mission conferences in the field. For the latter he preaches to gatherings of missionaries and their presidents while sitting at his office desk. In response to one of these sessions, President Donald B. Jessee of the Oregon Portland Mission wrote: "The highlight of these conferences was your enthusiastic message. . . . The reception was excellent and all in attendance could hear as if you were standing at the pulpit. . . . This work will accelerate because of your words." (*Letter*, February 26, 1981.)

On July 1, 1976, Elder Richards entered the hospital and Dr. Russell Nelson operated on his ulcerated foot "to make sure the blood was reaching it," so he spent his country's great Bicentennial Birthday sitting at home with his "foot on a stool." A bit dejectedly he reported that he "didn't get back to the office until the fourth of August." (*Blue Book*, p. 9.)

That December he contributed a generous sum to be used for the establishment of a park honoring Orson Hyde upon the

Mount of Olives in Jerusalem, as willing a gift as he ever made in his life. By this time the preliminary negotiations going forward in Jerusalem between Elder Howard W. Hunter and the Jerusalem Foundation (of which Jerusalem Mayor Teddy Kollek was president) were bearing fruit. The foundation is a charitable organization, one of whose functions is the beautification of the ancient city. It was the dream of the mayor and his group to develop a greenbelt around the city as a national park. Through initial contacts with Church leaders, President Harold B. Lee and Elder Ezra Taft Benson, and more recently with President N. Eldon Tanner and Howard W. Hunter, the Church had developed a good rapport with Jerusalem leaders and had become a likely candidate for "one of the largest and most prestigious sites on the Mount of Olives." It so happened, however, that this site was part of a larger parcel of land owned by an Italian corporation—the Institut Luigi Gedda, headed by a doctor in Rome—upon which that corporation planned to build a genetics institute. Through various talks and negotiations, an agreement was reached that the Institut would grant to the Municipality of Jerusalem a nine-hundred-and-ninety-nine-year lease for the five-and-a-quarter-acre site in exchange for other property considerations, and the Orson Hyde Foundation, a corporation organized for that purpose, was given the opportunity to develop the Mount of Olives site in return for a million dollars. The money would be used for grading, paths, walks, planting, water, amphitheater, etc. The Orson Hyde Foundation's contract was not with the city of Jerusalem but with the Jerusalem Foundation, with Mayor Teddy Kollek as its president and spokesman. Upon completion of the garden, the Municipality of Jerusalem would assume the responsibility for the park's perpetual maintenance and care. These arrangements agreed, only the task of raising the million dollars remained.

All of these developments Elder Richards followed with keen interest, but it looked as if he might not live to see the fulfillment of the project. On February 4, 1977, he became very ill and was taken to the LDS Hospital. His son-in-law Harold R. Boyer administered to him, and the family wondered whether this was to be his last illness. On his ninety-first birthday, February 6, he received visits from "all members of the Quorum of the Twelve except one who was out of town on assignment," the "highlight" of his total hospital stay. (*Blue Book*, 1977 Summary.)

In spite of his serious illness, and in his absence, he was elected president of the Orson Hyde Foundation. He wrote that on March 1, 1977, "through President Tanner, Elder Hunter, and the Hyde family, I was elected president with the responsibility of raising a million dollars. I am pleased with this assignment and am enjoying it very much." (*Blue Book*, 1977 Summary.)

He worked hard to accomplish the goal. On September 7, 1977, he met with the officers of the foundation and outlined a campaign for collecting the funds. A beautiful booklet was prepared which included colored photos of the grounds for the proposed park, a map of it in relation to the city of Jerusalem, and architectural renderings of the projected memorial. A picture of Orson Hyde and his October 1841 dedicatory prayer offered on the Mount of Olives were included, as was a picture of Elder Richards and his brief letter of invitation to "good people everywhere [to] join us and share the joy of doing something positive to beautify the Mount of Olives."

Money in large and small amounts began to come in, along with pre-prepared contribution cards which served as a record of donor names. These names would eventually be inscribed on a scroll, protected by a time capsule container, and placed in the stone wall of the grotto within the park. Elder Richards commented, "It is wonderful to see how our friends are responding to our invitation to join us in this venture." In October the *Church News* (October 29, 1977) printed a special issue on Jerusalem and the park and made a general invitation to Church members who would like to participate in the fund-raising for the project.

That same October, Elder Richards had delivered a stirring general conference address and had given the devotional talk to an estimated fifteen thousand BYU students assembled at the Marriott Center to hear him. His days were crowded and his calendar full, and in between meetings, assignments, and com-

mittee work a steady flow of people came to his office or wrote
for counsel and encouragement. Both were given in his typical
commonsense, optimistic approach. To a child, he said, "Sustain
and respect your father in his position. Give him love, understanding, and some appreciation for his efforts." A granddaughter was told:

> Just keep living in the clouds. You remember that little song
> in *South Pacific*, "If you don't have a dream, how're you going to
> have a dream come true?" Dream of the wonderful things that you
> want to accomplish in life and the kind of people you want to be
> associated with forever, and then keep yourself sweet and clean so
> that when you are married in one of our Heavenly Father's holy
> temples, there will be no skeletons in the closet that you will have
> to worry about. (LGR files.)

To the woman whose husband had been accidently killed,
leaving her with three small children, he wrote, "Don't try to
live your whole future at once. Take it one day at a time and the
Lord will bless and sustain you." To another who was worried
about evil spirits, he wrote:

> I don't think you should hesitate to go to the temple. I think
> you ought to try and live a normal life and quit worrying about
> your condition and about evil spirits. . . . Worry is one of the
> devil's best tools, and I think the fact that you are worrying about
> evil spirits opens the door for them to annoy you. Just don't think
> of such things. Think natural thoughts and happy thoughts. Sing
> happy songs to yourself and quote happy poetry to yourself, and
> don't think negative thoughts. (LeGrand Richards files.)

To single women longing for a husband and children, he
said:

> If you do not have opportunity to marry a good man in this
> life, the Lord has made ample provision for you during his thou-
> sand year Millennial reign, when the righteous dead will be called
> forth on the morning of the first resurrection. There will be mil-
> lions of good men who have died without marriage, including
> multitudes of war casualties, or like my own wonderful son Le-
> Grand, who died as a result of an accident. We will all be young
> again and there will be thousands of temples (as the prophets have
> said) where marriages for eternity will be performed. The Lord has
> told us "His purposes fail not, neither are there any who can stay

his hand. From eternity to eternity he is the same, and his years never fail." (D&C 76:3-4.) So he will not provide these blessings for some and withhold them from others. Now, if you live for it and work for it, you will have opportunity to marry one of the Lord's choice sons, and don't you forget it.

To the newest apostle, feeling the weight of his call, he said, "Don't worry too much about things you can't change. Focus on what you've got to do that you can do something about, because the kingdom is complex and you can't always fix what you might want to fix. Remember, it's the Lord's Church. Let him worry about it! He is able to take care of things even though you might not be able to."

While Elder Richards's life continued to be full, rich, and vast in area and influence, his wife's sphere of activity diminished. Ina's health was failing. She had sustained through spinal deterioration the crushing of three vertebrae, about which she cheerfully and incongruously said, "Wasn't I lucky not to have broken them?" The pain often kept her in bed. A granddaughter, who came most mornings to help, would arrive in time to find Elder Richards dressed for the office and reading the scriptures as he waited for his ride. (Ina always wanted to be wakened for his good-bye if she'd been sleeping.) She treasures the experience she had with her grandmother, noting her patience; her femininity, as she always "kept a white handkerchief in her hand"; her courtesy and concern for anyone caring for her; and her optimistic, "I *am* getting better, aren't I?" As her son Alden often said, "She is a little bundle of sweetness." And her life revolved around LeGrand. His homecomings were the highlight of her day, his presence her strength and her comfort. In the early afternoon she would call his office for a brief chat and to inquire when he expected to be home. The waiting was long.

One time when she was especially ill and her daughter Nona sat with her, she turned her face to the wall and was very still. It appeared that she would die. Nona phoned her father and he came home. As Nona stepped back to leave a chair free for him, he sat close to Ina, took her hand, and pleaded with her, "You can't leave me. I need you. I've told the Lord I can't live without

Shortly before Sister Richards passed away—still sweethearts.

you." His strength then literally flowed into her and she rallied. They clung to each other and expressed their love in such tender terms that Nona bowed her head and left the room. Later she said, "I saw such pure love, I felt that I was in the hallowed halls of heaven and that if I raised my eyes I would see the angels."

Although still very weak, Ina occasionally improved a little. On December 19, 1977, she and Elder Richards attended their family Christmas party, held in the cultural hall of Nona's ward, their family having far outgrown any home. (These yearly Christmas parties are among the grandchildren's fondest memories.) On December 29, LeGrand and Ina hosted a Christmas dinner at the Lion House for his brothers and sisters and their companions. There were twenty-three present.

The next day at about 8:00 A.M. Ina fell and broke her hip while attempting to help her husband in the kitchen. She was taken to the LDS Hospital and x-rayed. Upon hearing of the imminent operation necessary, she said, "I'm just glad that it's me and not Daddy." When he had seen that her medical needs were attended to, Elder Richards went to his office to take care of his responsibilities, then returned to see Ina safely out of the anesthetic in the evening. The next day he worked a full schedule. About 5:00 P.M., before he could reach her, Ina passed away. Her daughters Marian and Mercedes were with her. Alden had just left to get his father. Marian said at the time:

> If women could have the spirit of service to others that Mother had, not extolling their own virtues or wishing to compete, they would find joy in their roles. She was perfectly willing to be Father's companion and his support and to do anything she could to help him. One of the last things we heard her say was, "I never stood in Daddy's way, did I?" She lived and died true to her partnership agreement.

Norinne came from California for the funeral, carrying with her a white hyacinth—a favorite flower of her mother's. President Marion G. Romney spoke feelingly of her kindness and her great qualities. Ina's son LaMont enumerated the rich dividends her faithfulness had paid to them all. In his private farewell to Ina, Elder Richards was heard by one of his sisters to say, "Good-bye, Mommy, I'll be seeing you in a few days." Whether days, months, or years, it would be but a brief moment of the eternity in which they lived. To his children, he said, "I'm grateful I'll have her forever. She is as good as any of the angels she will meet on the other side, so she'll be able to feel at home with them."

The days of the new year, 1978, were filled with assignments and responsibilities, and as he traveled, his mind often turned to

Ina. He knew she was there waiting for him, but he had a question. He expressed it to Elder M. Russell Ballard as they flew to Atlanta, Georgia, for a conference. "I'm not afraid of dying," he said. "The only thing that worries me is, will I be able to find Mommy when I get over there?"

Brother Ballard says he knew Brother Richards had asked that question of other associates, who had reassured him he'd find her with no difficulty, but his own answer—"Brother Richards, in your case that might be difficult"—really got his attention. He sat right up and said, "What do you mean?"

Elder Ballard replied, "Well, with all of the thousands of people that you've converted to the Church through your personal ministry, plus those your book *A Marvelous Work and a Wonder* has converted, you'll probably have a hard time finding "Mommy" in the crowd that will be there to greet you."

"Now, you don't mean that," Elder Richards responded in his modest way.

It was while at the same Atlanta conference that Brother Ballard made some observations of Elder Richards which he later recalled in an interview:

> His spiritual insight is unequaled. He let me and the Regional Representative participate heavily in the interviewing, but he was very, very attuned to everything that was happening spiritually. When the moment came to make the decision [on who to call as stake president], there was no question. He and the Lord had already chosen. He is a great spiritual motivator. He just has that gift.

It is this attunement—the light within, the steady affirmation that the veil is thin and the Lord is near—that is the dearest of all the gifts Elder Richards possesses. He has lived for it. He treasures it. In his great sermon, "The Gift of the Holy Ghost" (*Ensign*, November 1979), he said: "To me, the gift of the Holy Ghost is as important to man as sunshine and water are to the plants. You take them away, and the plants would die. You take the Holy Ghost out of the Church, and it would not be any different than any other Church." He continued with the promise given to the faithful priesthood bearer: "The Holy Ghost shall be thy constant companion, and thy scepter an unchanging scepter of righteousness and truth; and thy dominion shall be an everlasting dominion, and without compulsory means it shall flow unto thee forever and ever." (D&C 121:46.) A granddaughter recalls hearing him say to a group of young people who visited him, "I would rather have my priesthood than all the money, marbles, or peanuts in the world."

Following Ina's passing, two manifestations were given to Elder Richards which indicate his ever-increasing attunement to the Spirit—even to the seeing of things not visible to the eyes of those who are closest to him. In the first, he felt Ina's influence in a matter which was of great importance to the family. For years the Ashton family had been trying to find a record of the father of Henry P. Lindsay, Ina's great-grandfather. He was from North Carolina, where the vital records were largely destroyed during the Civil War. Elder Richards's daughters had spent much time and effort trying to establish the name and record. Three of them—Nona, Marian, and Mercedes—had made a trip to North Carolina for that purpose, but without success.

When he was ill in the hospital, Brother Richards and Nona were watching television one day when a group of eight people appeared on the screen. One said, "We are going to the funeral of James Lindsay, father of Henry P. Lindsay," after which the picture disappeared. Elder Richards said, "Nona, please call Alden at KSL and have them rerun that picture so we can make a record." Nona had not seen the picture. Nor, apparently, had anyone except Elder Richards, for when Nona phoned Alden there was no picture to rerun. (*Blue Book*, p. 3.) On the strength of what Brother Richards had so plainly seen and heard, the temple work was done for this ancestor.

The second experience occurred in the Salt Lake Temple on May 4, 1978, at a meeting of the General Authorities. It is told in part by Elder Boyd K. Packer, upon whom it had a profound effect. Testimonies had been borne, Elder Richards first and then each taking his turn. Later, Brother Richards asked to speak. Elder Packer quotes him: "Brethren, I have something to tell you. A little while ago, I saw a man seated above the organ there and he looked just like that." (He gestured toward President Wilford Woodruff's portrait which hangs in the room.) He then added, "I saw him just as clearly as I see any of you Brethren."

Of the experience, Elder Richards said: "He was dressed in a white suit and was seated in an armchair. I thought at the time that the reason I was privileged to see him was probably that I was the only one there who had ever seen President Woodruff while he was upon the earth. I had heard him dedicate the Salt Lake Temple and I had heard him give his last sermon in the Salt Lake Tabernacle before he died. I thought it wonderful that the Lord could project, without mechanical means, the likeness of a man long since dead." As Elder Packer says of Brother Richards, "He links us back. Here is a man who rubbed shoulders with those who stood with the Prophet Joseph Smith."

In June of 1978 Elder Richards went into the hospital for a hernia operation. He had the operation on a Monday, recuperated Tuesday at the hospital, returned to his apartment Wednesday, and was back at his office on Thursday. "The operation was successful," he said. "I had no pain." Perhaps by this time he was becoming inured to pain. Elder Packer, one of those whom Elder Richards designates as his "guardian angel," facetiously asked him one day as he lent his arm to his associate and they walked to their meeting in the temple together, "Who is going to help you over when I die of old age?" They chuckled together, then Brother Packer, feeling the pressure of weight upon his arm, solicitously inquired, "Are you in constant pain?" "No more than I can stand," was the cheerful answer. "Which means," the younger apostle surmised, "that he is in pain all the time. He simply lives above it." In spite of pain or discomfort, Brother Richards exercises his leg and foot many times each night to keep it as limber and usable as he can.

On his ninety-third birthday, February 6, 1979, Elder Richards was asked to offer the opening prayer at the Utah House of Representatives, where his son LaMont was serving. On February 23, his father's birthday, he was taken to the hospital, where he remained in critical condition for nearly a month. In the March 2 temple meeting of the First Presidency and the Twelve,

President Kimball asked if any of the Brethren had heard how Brother Richards was. One said that he had talked with the doctor that morning and had been informed that it was only a matter of hours. Elder Richards's obituary had been written. His daughter Mercedes and her husband, serving a mission in Malaysia, were notified. Some of the Brethren had canceled their conference assignments so they could attend the funeral. Then a remarkable thing happened which Elder Thomas S. Monson relates:

> One of the most circumspect and quiet members of the Twelve, Elder Howard W. Hunter, asked to speak. Recognized, he said, "Brethren, LeGrand Richards is going to be back. He is not going to die at this time. He is going to be out of the hospital and functioning effectively." He then turned to the empty chair next to him, normally occupied by Elder Richards, and said, "And he is going to be sitting right here in this chair participating in the discussions of this council!" It was as prophetic a statement as I've ever heard in my life.

At the hospital, however, there was no indication that the doctor's prognosis would not be correct or that the life forces would again flow back into the quiet figure that lay suffering and unconscious. His daughter Marian kept vigil in turn with the other family members and watched once as his forehead wrinkled as if an actual struggle of will were in process. Elders Packer and Maxwell had earlier entered the room to give Brother Richards a blessing and, when they had gone, she noted a few of the words Brother Packer has spoken. "Ina is close from the other side," he said. "If you still have work to do here, you can do it, and you can communicate with the Savior upon your desire."

Not long after that, a granddaughter and her husband were taking their turn watching at his side when they heard Brother Richards making strange, low sounds. Alarmed that her grandfather was dying, she was about to call for medical help, but her husband restrained her, saying, "Listen, he's singing." Bending near, they could make out the words: "Oh, bless me now, my Savior, I come to Thee."

On two occasions he tried to get up with all the hospital

paraphernalia attached and was intensely disturbed that he was forcibly returned to his bed. The first occasion was at not being allowed to attend the funeral of President Marion G. Romney's wife; the second, that he was kept from joining his Brethren for the rededication of the Logan Temple.

Finally the day came when he roused up in bed, looked at the IV tube attached to his wrist, and said, "Who did this without my permission?" Marian, who sat by his bed, laughed with a sense of deep relief. It was the turning point. Although yet a very sick man, he would now begin to mend. LaMont tells of his father saying, "Get me out of this bed or I'll never get out again." LaMont got medical help to remove the attached tubes so he could get his father up for a brief time.

The patient was deeply appreciative of every family member who stayed with him or came to visit, as he was for the visits and blessings of the Brethren. He did all in his power to hasten the healing process for himself. He sat or stood when allowed and "practiced getting well." At every opportunity that presented itself, he preached the gospel. According to one family member who was visiting him, a fellow patient in hospital gown and green carpet slippers brought a nonmember Greek doctor to see him and stayed to listen while Elder Richards expounded the gospel plan to him (in a weaker voice than usual). He greeted a group of young people who wondered if they might look in on him, and he gave them both his smiles and his counsel.

Most days his secretary visited for an hour or two, keeping him informed of office business and the progress of the Orson Hyde Foundation fund-gathering, letting him know how greatly he was needed back at his work. Others encouraged him toward what then seemed an impossible goal—his actual attendance at the dedication of the Memorial Park in Jerusalem, now set for the coming October 24. Finally, on March 20, 1979, he went home with his daughter Nona and her husband, J. Glenn Dyer. Later he wrote: "Nona and Glenn are taking such good care of me, I will likely remain here the rest of my life." (*Blue Book*, recap for 1979, p. 1.) Until his illness he had lived alone in the apartment, missing his companion very much but glad he had outlived her, "because," said he, "I figured (having taken care of all our business affairs) I could get along better alone than she could without me." But it had been a lonely time, and he felt at home and grateful to Nona and Glenn.

At the April conference following Brother Richards's release from the hospital, President Spencer W. Kimball announced in the first session that all General Authorities except Elder Richards were present. A stir of disbelief went through the audience as they took in the situation. Elder Richards had come in and taken his place on the stand, sitting in full view of the congregation, a blanket over his knees, oxygen tube in his nose, and a broad though wan smile on his face. President Kimball turned, saw his beloved associate, and delightedly corrected his previous announcement.

The following week in the meeting of the Twelve, Elder Richards said, "I read in the minutes where you'd received word of my imminent demise, but I fooled you, didn't I?" That day his associates witnessed the literal fulfillment of Elder Hunter's prophetic utterance of the month before.

As Elder Richards meets weekly with the Council, its members observe him as a man unique among them. Elder Neal A. Maxwell, newest member of the Quorum, speaks of this uniqueness with the Latin phrase *sui generis* (forming a kind by itself). He then comments upon some of his unique qualities:

> He has an innocence concerning the sins of the world and their many aberrations. They are difficulties to be dealt with, but are not part of the focus of his life. He is unspotted. His single-mindedness in serving the Lord is an emancipating thing, for it frees him in so many ways. He is uncluttered by any ego considerations.
>
> Elder Richards has a disposition not to be too bound by precedent or handbook but to do what is most redemptive in the lives of people, trusting them and giving them a chance. His instincts are to do what makes the most sense and not fret and stew. He is a pragmatist in terms of problems being solved.
>
> He will say what he wants to say—emphatically and boldly, but sweetly; he does not require a lot of "air time" in the councils of the Church in order to feel good. He can be in a meeting and feel it has been successful even though he didn't give a long speech

Elders Mark E. Petersen and Bruce R. McConkie visit with Elder Richards when, following his near-fatal 1979 illness, he puts in surprise attendance at general conference with blanket and oxygen supply.

in the middle of it. Because he doesn't comment excessively, people tend to listen more when he does.

(Elder Packer smiles as he comments upon the latter characteristic. "Brother Richards will say, 'Well, I've had my day, you "boys" can do the talking. I take my case to the people.'")

With the others, Elder Maxwell also recognizes the historic vantage point from which Elder Richards functions. "He has a sweep of history which no one else in the councils has."[1] Elder McConkie further comments upon Brother Richards's wide experience and stabilizing influence: "He is an old 'war horse' who has been through it all and whose judgments have been good in the past and continue to be good in the present."

President Gordon B. Hinckley adds his view on the same subject:

> His unswerving devotion to what I would call true principles, not only of the gospel but of Church government, has been, to me, a great thing. He has been an anchor, holding for consistency in doctrinal teaching and in the operation of the Church in its many programs. I think that has been a most significant thing that has come out of his long life of experience in the Church. He's seen it all from then until now. He's been an active participant for almost a century. That coupled with his reading of Church history and his capacity to remember what he reads (and his powers of retention are tremendous), has given him a background that very few men have. No one among the General Authorities has lived as long as he nor been exposed to the breadth of experiences that he has.

Elder Packer picks up the same theme on a slightly different note. He refers to the *venerable* Brother Richards who, "when we approach and wrestle with a problem, has seen some version of it

---

[1] Our comprehension of his "sweep" of Church history alone is aided by a few comparative statistics. It is estimated that when LeGrand Richards was born [1886] there were about 200,000 members. There were 30 stakes, 12 missions, and approximately 550 missionaries. When he left on his first mission to Holland [1905] these figures had risen to 322,779 members, 55 stakes, 22 missions, and approximately 1,700 missionaries. In December 1980, there were 4,638,000 members, 1,218 stakes, 188 missions, and 29,953 missionaries. (Figures from the Historical and Missionary Departments of the Church and from *Ensign*, May 1981.)

three or four times before. It will have been enacted on a different stage and the actors have been changed, but the script is the
same as far as the problem is concerned. When you have been
through it in 1918, 1937, and 1969, you just aren't afraid of it.
You have both perspective and perception to see what is right
and the absolute courage to do what is right."

President Hinckley pinpoints another area in which Elder
Richards has performed a unique service:

> His great concern for those who were born elsewhere and came
> here as immigrants and didn't speak the English language nor
> understand it with ease has been a major contribution. He has
> worked and talked with persuasion to his Brethren to see that
> these people were provided with opportunity to teach, to serve as
> officers in the Church where they could grow and develop and feel
> the great enthusiasm that comes with service in the Church.

Building upon President Hinckley's statement, Elder Packer
recalls that Brother Richards will say in council, " 'I think we
should give the people what they want' (meaning, of course,
what they need). We are talking now about the oppressed people,
the minority groups. He is large-souled in their behalf." Also
toward the erring, wayward ones he is great-hearted. Elder
Monson speaks of a case wherein a missionary had done something foolish and embarrassed the Church. "We might tend to
quickly find fault," he said, "to wonder what had possessed the
young man to do such a thing, to judge a bit harshly, but
Brother Richards will say, 'Yes, Brethren, if we could put a forty-
year-old head on the missionary's nineteen-year-old shoulders,
then we might judge him so.' "

President Tanner seemed to speak for all of the Brethren
when he recently said, "LeGrand, you are an example to us all,"
to which the latter quickly replied, "Only in age, President, only
in age."

Miraculously, considering his recent serious illness and his
advanced age, Elder Richards was able to again carry on his official duties between April and October general conferences in
1979—meetings, committee work, groundbreaking (Jordan River
Temple), area conference in Atlanta, Georgia, mission presidents'

seminar, and the final gathering of the funds to bring the total to over a million dollars for the Orson Hyde Memorial. The only concession he asked for was that during the time he needed oxygen on a regular basis at night, his conference assignments be within a day's travel time; but (according to President Benson) he was unhappy if he didn't receive a stake conference assignment every week.

Miraculous also was the fact that on October 21 he and ten members of his family left for the dedication of the park in the Holy Land. Elaine Cannon, General President of the Young Women of the Church and a close friend of the family, said to Elder Richards in greeting as they boarded the plane, "I think you're fabulous to go and buy a new suit and a beautiful new foulard tie for the trip." He smiled and answered, "I bought *two* suits. I have a lot of work yet to do." It is this forward-looking attitude of his which Sister Cannon greatly admires in him— "the take-charge-of-yourself approach. Now get on with your life and don't look back. If you've had a heart attack, move forward. If you've got a bad leg, keep walking. If you have to have oxygen, buy a new suit. I think," she concludes, "he's simply marvelous."

As soon as the party arrived in Jerusalem, he wanted to go directly to the Memorial Gardens to determine that all was in order before he turned the remaining $225,000 to Mayor Kollek. He found President Tanner and Elder Hunter already there. The garden was beautifully planted, and all was in readiness. The next day he attended the meeting held in the Jerusalem Council Chambers with Presidents Kimball and Tanner, Elder Hunter and Mayor Kollek, and others. One of the Brethren said to the mayor, "Now we still owe $225,000," to which Mayor Kollek replied, "I trust you." Elder Richards then gave him the check paying the balance of the million dollars in full.

On Saturday, the Jewish *Shabbot* or Sabbath, Elder Richards and his party held a testimony meeting in the grotto area of the park. There were about a hundred persons present. They sang "Come, Come Ye Saints" and "God Be With You," after which Elder Richards wished "to get on with the meeting." One of those who bore testimony was Wilford C. Edling, Brother Richards's former friend from Hollywood Stake, whom he embraced in greeting. A family member heard Brother Edling say, "Until the time comes when the Savior kisses me, this will be the high-light of my existence." Participants commented on the beautiful spirit present, which lingered as the family group returned to their hotel.

On Sunday, October 24, 1979, the American visitors and Church leaders along with their Jerusalem hosts and guests as-sembled at the park for the dedication services. Formalities were attended to and talks were given, among which was a ten-minute address by Elder Richards. It was a long-awaited opportunity— to speak to Jewish people in their own land—and he made the most of it. In part he said:

> When Israel first became a nation, one of your great leaders, Dr. Chaim Weizmann, said that it was a mystical force that had brought your people back to the promised land. It is that same mystical force that made it possible for me, as president of the Orson Hyde Foundation, to collect a million dollars for the devel-opment of this park. As much as it is worth to the community here, what we have to offer you would be worth far more than the million dollars.

He then told them of the stick of Judah, the stick of Joseph, and the land of Joseph. He explained about the new covenant with the house of Israel and the house of Judah spoken of by Jeremiah (3:14-15, 18), which covenant "we have," and of Jeremiah's words that the "house of Judah shall walk with the house of Israel." He then gave invitation for the house of Judah to come and partake of the blessings promised wherein "there shall henceforth be no more two kingdoms, but one kingdom, and one God shall rule over them all." (See Ezekiel 37:22-23.) He then concluded, "I can't think of anything about which Fathers Abraham, Isaac, and Jacob would be more thrilled than to know that these two branches of their posterity had come together and were walking together as the prophet said they should."

In that talk, Elder Richards again boldly and fearlessly bore witness to a people not yet ready to receive the word, but they heard his witness along with the prophet's and others'—a witness which at least made a deep impression upon some. Israel Lippel, former Assistant to the Chief Rabbi of Israel and Director-General of the Ministry of Religious Affairs, now Chairman of the Jerusalem Institute for Interreligious Relations and Research, wrote "Apostle LeGrand Richards" on August 4, 1981:

> Dear Honorable Friend,
>   . . . I shall never forget your presence at the dedication of the Orson Hyde Garden, which was an unforgettable event at the Mount of Olives in Jerusalem about two-and-a-half years ago. Furthermore, as I recall, you were the only one who made the speech straight out of the heart and not from a speech sheet.

After the dedication, a little luncheon was held for about a hundred invited guests. Seeing Elder Richards standing and holding a plate in his hand, Mayor Kollek rustled up a little table so his guest could sit down. Elder Richards thanked him for the courtesy and then said, "Mayor, I want to tell you something."

"What's that?" asked the mayor.

Looking Mayor Kollek directly in the eye, the apostle said, "Ten years ago I was here in Jerusalem, and one day I went into three synagogues, and hanging up on the wall in one of them was a large armchair. I asked the rabbi what it was there for (I knew, but I wanted him to tell me, which he did). He said that it was so that if Elijah comes, 'we can lower the chair and let him sit in it.' Now, Mayor, I want to tell you something, and what I tell you is the truth. Elijah has already been. On the third day of April 1836 he appeared to Joseph Smith and Oliver Cowdery in the Kirtland Temple."

The mayor said, "I guess I'd better tell them to take that chair down."

Through these and other encounters in Israel, Elder Richards and Mayor Kollek have continued a dialogue by correspondence. The latter sent to "Mr. Richards" an album of fine photographs pertaining to the dedication. Also, his contacts in Israel have opened a new dialogue of discussion between various Jewish educators and our Church representatives there through the Jerusalem Institute of which Israel Lippel is chairman. According

Speaking at Orson Hyde Memorial Park dedication, 1980.

*On ninety-fourth birthday, 1980, he holds his ninety-ninth
and hundredth great-grandchild, Elizabeth Boyer, left, and
Eliza Jane Boyer.*

to Professor Dov Noy of the Hebrew University of Jerusalem, who wrote Elder Richards on August 30, 1981, more than twenty people had gathered for a "very, very friendly discussion of religion." Rex Skidmore represented the Church in the meeting, and all twenty signed a page to include in the letter for Brother Richards.

It was on the Christmas Eve following the Jerusalem trip (1979) that Elder Richards's granddaughter Carla Welling received a tape from her missionary son, Richard, in Holland, wherein he expressed the hope of his mission president, John Lindberg, that "Grandpa might come to our missionary conference in May." Upon hearing of this informal request to once again visit the little country he loves, Elder Richards considered it, and the conference assignment was given him along with an additional conference visit to England. Inasmuch as the Netherlands conference coincided with the time of Richard's release, it was decided that his parents, Carla and Duane Welling, would accompany Elder Richards.

Immediately he began to review his Dutch scriptures. On May 1, 1980, the group left for Holland. On the plane, Brother Richards was his usual outgoing, hand-shaking, mission-oriented self, but some of the time he sat with eyes closed, having explained, "Now, I'm not asleep but just practicing my Dutch, so if any refreshments come by, tell me, because I don't want to miss anything good." He enjoys food, is a hearty eater, and has the Richardses' sweet tooth.

His language review, overlaid upon his ever-ready linguistic skill, gave him complete freedom in speaking when the party arrived in Holland. Meetings and visits were a joy to him and a delight to his audiences and friends, particularly to the older members who drank in the rich and sonorous tones of the beautiful High Dutch of the scriptures that he spoke so well. Many tears of joy where shed for both the sound and the spirit of his preaching.

In Utrecht Richard was called upon to speak, his great-grandfather following him. When the young elder finished and offered his Dutch scriptures, Elder Richards touched his own

At missionary graves in Groningen, Holland, 1980.

With missionary great-grandson Richard Welling in Holland, 1980.

forehead saying, "No, Richard, I have it all up here." Not only did the hectic pace take them from one meeting to the next, but while in that land they visited the old mission home in Rotterdam where Carla's mother, Mercedes, had lived as a child. There the two Dutch missionaries, Elder Richards and his greatgrandson, had their picture taken.

He wished to again visit the missionary graves in Groningen, although Richard doubted they could find the place. It was a cold day, but when they arrived at the cemetery they were met by a sight to warm the heart. A small cluster of Dutch Saints had gathered. The memorial marker was scrubbed, the wrought iron fence freshly painted, and an exquisite spray of fresh flowers lay against the stone shaft with a gold ribbon upon which the words "Greater love hath no man. . . ." were inscribed. Elder Richards wept openly in memory of his friends and in gratitude for the precious Saints who had cared for the graves so tenderly.

After Richard Welling's release and the conference in England, the party returned to Salt Lake. The next morning, Carla thoughtfully waited until about nine o'clock before calling to inquire how her grandfather had fared. Nona reported that he had been at his office for two hours. No, he had experienced no jet lag from the long trip.

Between his decision to make the trip to Holland and the actual trip, Elder Richards had been given a wonderful ninety-fourth birthday party by his family members. The event was held in the Relief Society Building and to it came President Kimball, his counselors, General Authorities and their companions, members of the Richardses' extended family, friends acquired during his long life, and many state and city officials, including Utah's Governor Scott F. Matheson and his wife. When Sister Belle S. Spafford, under whose direction the building had been erected, greeted him, he said, "I hope you don't mind my party being held in your building, because I already sent you a letter thanking you for the privilege." Touched by his thoughtfulness, she answered, "I consider this to be as much your building as mine."

Elder Richards's grace, humor, optimism, and unique physical, mental, and spiritual powers have made him something of a legend in his lifetime. Everywhere people have their own Richards stories which are repeated to their children and friends, so that he becomes ever more widely known and loved. Many letters come to his office which have the flavor of legend. One man writes that he is sure Brother Richards will pass the century mark. A woman thinks he is "one of the Three Nephites." Another, in her thirties, proposes marriage. A former secretary applies to work for him "during the Millennium." Another is certain he will "be translated."

His Brethren of the Twelve affirm that "his powers have not diminished, if anything they have grown sharper." They show him special deference, not as an elderly man but as a beloved associate, a valiant co-builder of the kingdom, a "missionary prince" whose greatest contribution, according to one, is "his testimony and his voicing of it." Says President Gordon B. Hinckley:

> No one who listens to LeGrand Richards has any doubt that he knows that God lives, that Jesus is the Christ, that Joseph Smith was and is a prophet, and that the Church is true; and I think there is no more significant contribution that any man can make than to serve as a witness of the Lord with power and conviction and sincerity, and LeGrand Richards does that in a marvelous way.

For his own part, Brother Richards says, "Whether I work on this side of the veil or that doesn't matter so long as I can preach the gospel. If the Lord wants me over there, he knows what to do, but he hasn't found a place where he can use me yet."

By Father's Day, June 20, 1982, Elder Richards will have outlived all other General Authorities of the Church in this dispensation up to that time. With youthful optimism he feels certain he will make that date and beyond. His son LaMont speaks of his youthful outlook in words from General Douglas McArthur: "Nobody grows old by merely living a number of years. People grow old only by deserting their ideals. . . . In the central place of every heart, there is a recording chamber; so long as it receives messages of beauty, hope, cheer, and courage, so long are you young." (General Douglas McArthur, Los Angeles, January 16, 1955.) LaMont adds, "And Father is young."

Death holds no terror for him, although he would like to go as his brothers Joel and Oliver went—in an instant. He does not look to the next life as "sweet, sweet rest"—he would be miserable in that state. Rather, he sees and anticipates that life in the stimulating terms of a comment by Richter which many years ago Elder Richards recorded in a journal:

> The ambitious man rejoices in the thought of time and space without limit in which to strive and improve forever. Ambition and hope are always young. The youth of the soul is everlasting, and eternity is youth—a glorious thing to the man who believes his soul and his life will endure forever.

Sources Consulted

Primary Source Material

The primary source material for this book consists largely of Elder LeGrand Richards's personal holdings and of selected items from his office files. Most originated with him; a few are about him, were under his direction, or are in his or the author's possession and not otherwise available. They follow in alphabetical order under the name of the originator or owner. Within items, LeGrand Richards's name is abbreviated to "LGR."

Ludlow, Daniel H. *Israel Diary*. Prepared for LGR as the two traveled in the Holy Land together (July 2-12, 1969).

Reid, Rose Marie. *Plan for Teaching the Gospel to the Jewish People*. Pamphlet. LGR office files.

Richards, Ina Jane Ashton. *Note Book*. Collection of poems, notes, and quotations.

———. Patriarchal Blessing. 1908.

Richards, LeGrand, *Album*. Pictures from the Netherlands and Southern States mission presidencies.

———. *Bibles*. Dutch (1903); signed and dated by LGR (June 29, 1905), with many subject notations in Dutch and English. English; inscribed and dated by Ina Ashton Richards (February 6, 1923), with twenty-three pages of subject notations by LGR.

———. *Black Book*. Writings of LGR while he was president of the Netherlands Mission.

———. Blessings. 1894, 1905, 1933, 1938.

———. *Blue Book*. Letters, family data, testimony, personal history, and yearly up-dates on that history from 1973 (when it was prepared) until 1981.

———. *Green Book*. Collection of poems, quotations, and sayings from LGR's first mission to Holland. 1905-1908.

————. Hollywood MIA Stake News. 1933. LGR office files.

————. *Journals*. (LGR kept journals only during his four missions and his tenures as bishop of Glendale Ward and as president of Hollywood Stake in California.) Vols. I-III cover his first mission to Holland, with a summary up to his marriage on May 19, 1909. Vols. IV-VI cover his Netherlands Mission presidency (1913-1916), with a summary up to his call as bishop of Sugar House Ward. Vol. VII records his short-term mission to the Eastern States, with a summary up to and including five months of his Hollywood Stake presidency (1926-1931). Vol. VIII contains entries for the remainder of the California period up to his departure for the Southern States Mission (1931-1933). There follows a two-year gap indicating one or two missing volumes; to fill in this period (1934-1936) the official *Record of LeGrand Richards, President of the Southern States Mission*, an almost daily record of mission progress and business, was used. Vols. IX-X cover the remaining part of the Southern States Mission presidency (1936-1937) and the family's return trip home to Salt Lake City.

————. Letters. There are 178 letters to his wife, children, father and mother, brother, and a few friends, and theirs to him. They cover the period from 1910 to 1943. Four are undated.

————. *A Marvelous Work and a Wonder*. Typewritten manuscript.

————. Picture Collection, including those photographs owned by LGR and those lent by family members. Others were supplied by the Church Photography Department and the *Deseret News*.

————. Printed Programs. "Prepare Ye the Way," Aaronic Priesthood pageant under direction of the Presiding Bishopric (1941); LGR office files. "The Providing Bishopric Entertains the General Authorities" (1942), courtesy of Mabel Jones Gabbott; LGR office files.

————. Sermons. Principally from *Conference Reports*, LDS Church Archives. As Southern States Mission president, LGR spoke at each general conference (1933-1937). As Pre-

siding Bishop of the Church, he spoke at each general conference (1938-1951). After he became an apostle (1952) he
preached in every general conference except one when he
was confined in the hospital with a heart attack. Other sermons reviewed were BYU Devotional Addresses, BYU Press
collection, and *LeGrand Richards on Cassette*, Covenant Re-
cordings (1979).

————. Tract. "The Mormons and the Jewish People."

Tate, Lucile C. Interviews. Question and discussion sheets were
prepared by LCT and formed the basis for nearly a hundred
interviews with Elder LeGrand Richards, other General Authorities, family members, and LGR acquaintances which, in
effect, covered the entire expanse of his long life. Wherever
material is quoted in the text without source reference, it is
taken from these interviews.

West, R. B. *Diary*. (Richard B. West was secretary to the Netherlands Mission under President LeGrand Richards.) Courtesy
of his son Hugh S. West.

Woodbury, Orin F. *Memoirs*. Copy in possession of author.

LDS Church Archives Materials

"Evaluation of the Jewish Proselyting Program." 1975. Missionary Department.

Journal History of the Church. 1938-1982.

Netherlands Mission Historical Record. 1905-1908, 1913-1916.

Presiding Bishopric Files. "Progress of the Church." 1939, 1943.

————. Subject Files. 1938-1952.

Richards, George F. *Diaries*.

————. *Personal Record Book*.

Richards, George F., Jr. *Diaries*.

————. Oral History Program. Interview by William Hartley.
1973.

Richards, LeGrand. Oral History Program. "Presiding Bishopric
Years." Interview by William Hartley. 1974.

Reid, Rose Marie. Oral History Program. Interview by William
Hartley. 1973.

Sugar House Ward *Minutes.* 1919-1926.

Tate,.George F., ed. "Nanny Longstroth Richards." In *Stephen Longstroth and His Fathers.* 1979.

Tooele Ward *Records.* Book 7716A.

University Ward *Historical Record.*

Books

Allen, James B., and Leonard, Glen M. *The Story of the Latter-day Saints.* Salt Lake City: Deseret Book Company, 1976.

Cannon, George Q. *Life of the Prophet Joseph Smith.* Salt Lake City: George Q. Cannon & Sons, 1888.

Hymns. Salt Lake City: The Church of Jesus Christ of Latter-day Saints, 1948.

Jenson, Andrew. *Encyclopedic History of The Church of Jesus Christ of Latter-day Saints.* Salt Lake City: Deseret News Publishing Company, 1941.

Jordan, William George. *The Power of Truth.* Salt Lake City: Stevens and Wallis, 1943.

Kelsch, Louis A. *A Practical Reference.* Chicago: Northern States Mission. The Church of Jesus Christ of Latter-day Saints, 1897.

Nibley, Preston. *Inspirational Talks for Youth.* Salt Lake City: Deseret Book Company, 1941.

———. *Faith Promoting Stories.* Salt Lake City: Deseret Book Company, 1943.

Pratt, Parley P. *A Voice of Warning.* Various ed. beginning 1837.

Richards, G. LaMont. *LeGrand Richards Speaks.* Salt Lake City: Deseret Book Company, 1972.

Richards, LeGrand. *Israel, Do You Know?* Salt Lake City: Deseret Book Company, 1954.

———. *Just to Illustrate.* Salt Lake City: Bookcraft, 1961.

———. *A Marvelous Work and a Wonder.* Salt Lake City: Deseret Book Company, 1950.

Robinson, [Alice] Minerva Richards Tate, *et al. Life of George F. Richards.* Provo: J. Grant Stevenson, 1965.

West, Franklin L. *Life of Franklin D. Richards.* Salt Lake City: Deseret News Press, 1924.

Periodicals

Church News and Church Section of the *Deseret News*. 1937-1982.
Deseret News. 1933-1982.
Ensign. As referenced.
Instructor. 1962-1970.
Juvenile Instructor. As referenced.
Liahona. As referenced.

Index